I0812441

IMAGES
of America

CRESCENT CITY AND DEL NORTE COUNTY

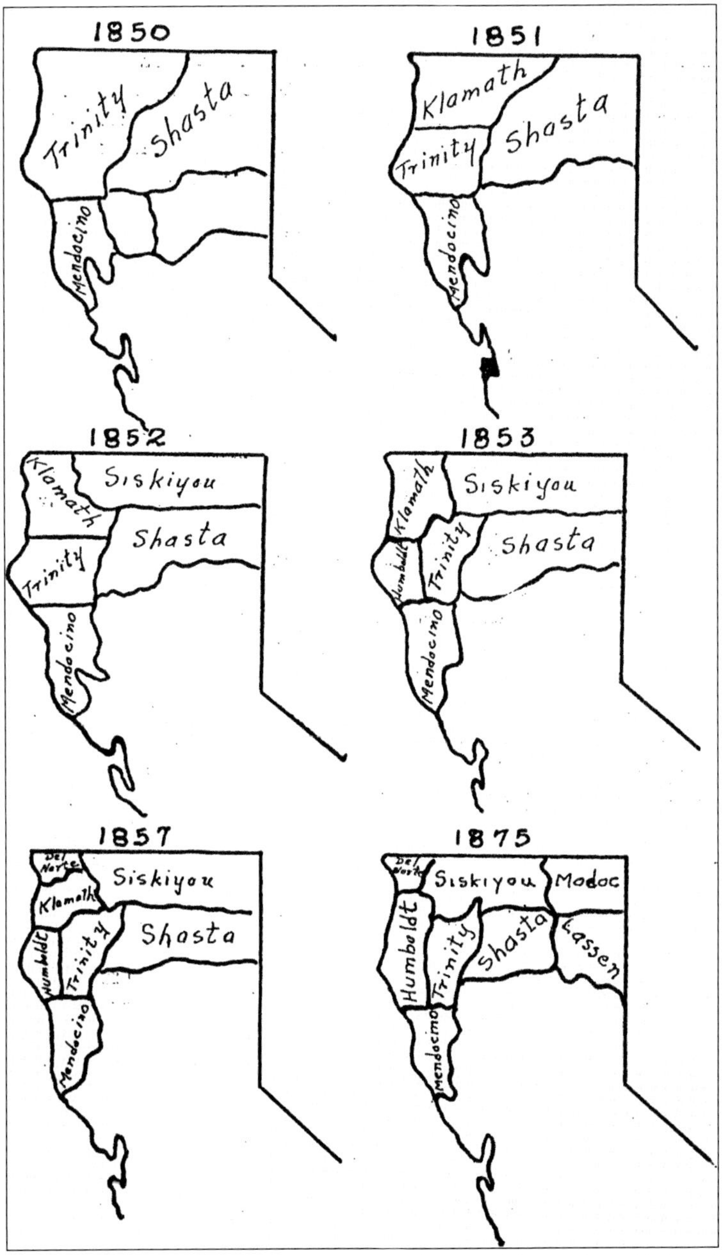

These maps show the evolution of the counties of Northern California from 1850, when California became a state, to 1875, when Klamath became the only county in the state that completely disappeared and ceased to be a political entity.

ON THE COVER: The second quarry site for rock to construct the Crescent City breakwater was Preston Island, just offshore. The minimum size of boulders needed was 20 tons, and Preston Island was completely quarried to provide that rock. A rail line was constructed from the quarry operation to the breakwater site, with the track running along the bluff overlooking the Pebble Beach area. Part of the route later became Pebble Beach Drive.

IMAGES
of America

CRESCENT CITY AND DEL NORTE COUNTY

Del Norte County Historical Society

ARCADIA
PUBLISHING

ISBN 978-0-7385-3075-8

Published by Arcadia Publishing
Charleston, South Carolina

Printed in the United States of America

Library of Congress Catalog Card Number: 2005932499

For all general information contact Arcadia Publishing at:
Telephone 843-853-2070
Fax 843-853-0044
E-mail sales@arcadiapublishing.com
For customer service and orders:
Toll-Free 1-888-313-2665

Visit us on the Internet at www.arcadiapublishing.com

Contents

ACKNOWLEDGMENTS

I would like to thank the board of directors of the Del Norte County Historical Society for all of their help and support in producing this book. Special thanks go to Sandy Nuss and Phyllis Tedsen for all of their contributions and time spent aiding in the selection of photographs for this book and for their vast knowledge of the history of Del Norte County. Also special thanks to Sean Smith for his work in preparing the photographs. Finally, the museum staff and board of directors wish to thank the people of Del Norte County for their continuing support of the Del Norte County Museum.

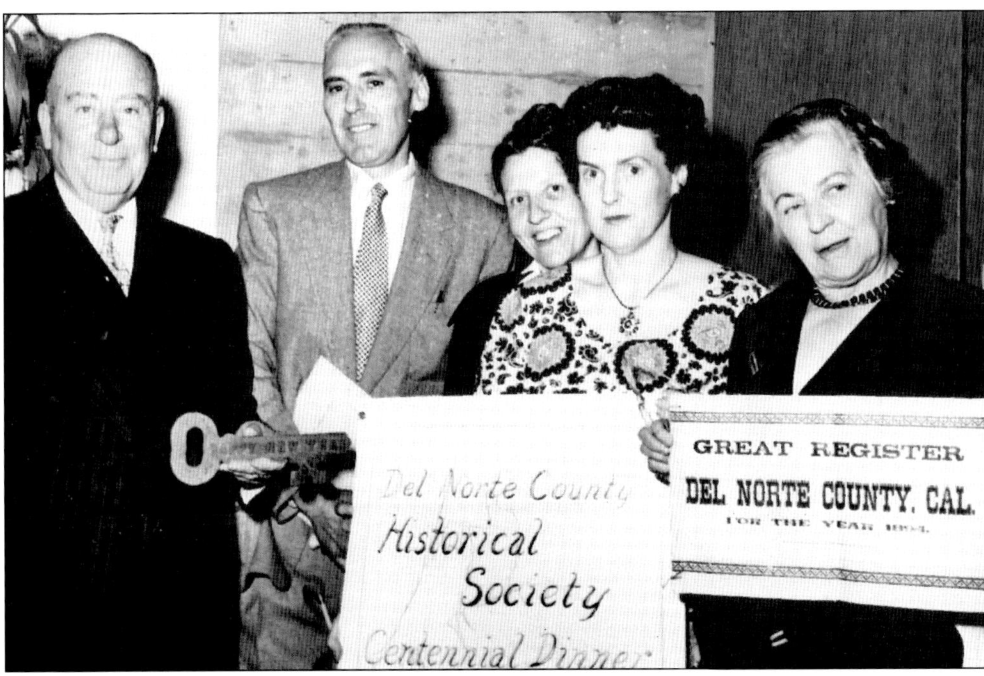

The Del Norte County Historical Society was formed in 1952, and it hosted a centennial dinner on the 100th birthday of Crescent City's founding in 1954. Pictured, from left to right, are Chester Endert, Allen Lehman, Ester Ruth Smith, Carol McClendon, and Margaret Duffy. Smith wrote extensively on the history of Del Norte County, while Lehman was considered one of the most knowledgeable historians of Del Norte County.

INTRODUCTION

The 1848 discovery of gold in the Trinity Mountains drew hordes of prospectors to Northern California. By 1850, when California gained statehood, mining communities were springing up along the rivers and streams. The Klamath River and its tributaries proved to be fairly rich in gold, but there was little access and the main route was from the ocean. Exploration of the coast began in an attempt to find good harbors to develop.

Meanwhile, Klamath City was settled a short distance from the mouth of the river in April 1850 where the channel was adequate to allow larger ships to enter the river. By the end of the summer, 20 houses had been built. By January 1851, Klamath City was booming and 20 to 30 more houses and businesses were under construction. Unfortunately, the winter rains of December and January caused an additional sandbar to form across the mouth of the river, access was cut off, and the town was abandoned.

In 1850, an expedition was organized by Maj. J. F. Wendell to explore the area to the north of Klamath River. A group of trappers reported finding a good bay that could be developed into a harbor, and once located Wendell felt it had great promise. In February 1853, the land along this harbor was surveyed into town lots. The new community, named Crescent City after the shape of its harbor, was incorporated in April 1854, and by June there were nearly 300 homes and businesses with between 800 and 1,000 inhabitants. Crescent City became a starting point for miners heading for the interior gold fields and was a major shipper of supplies and merchandise for the inland miners and mining communities as well as a port for ships from San Francisco.

In 1854, local merchants pushed for development of roads considered vital for continued growth of the area. On June 10, 1854, the Crescent City and Yreka Plank Road and Turnpike Company was formed to build a road from Crescent City to the Illinois Valley. An engineer was hired to survey a route, which was completed in October. However, several San Francisco business houses failed in early 1855 and liquid assets in Crescent City disappeared, so the project was abandoned. Then gold was discovered on Elk Creek, which caused a healthy improvement in local business. By December 1856, the defunct Plank Road and Turnpike Company was revived and construction went ahead. The road was completed in May 1858.

The earliest farming activity was in the fertile Smith River Valley. Most of the land rose rapidly into the mountains, so farmland was limited mainly to the Smith River and the Elk Valleys. By the summer of 1854, there were nearly 75 farms, mostly dairies, located in various parts of the county. Smith River Corners was becoming a major community, and its dairy farms produced top-quality butter that was in great demand in San Francisco.

As settlers poured into the area, the Tolowa Indians were forced off their land by settlers who claimed it for themselves. The Native Americans lost access to food sources, and state laws were passed that took away all of their rights. When they resisted, the Tolowa were slaughtered and their villages were burned. Ultimately they were forced onto a series of reservations, and when those lands became desirable for settlement, the Tolowa were relocated to other areas. Many of them were virtual slaves.

In 1857, Horace Gasquet purchased 320 acres of land along the Middle Fork of the Smith River, the mouth of the North Fork, and the flat on the south side. It was here, on the road to Oregon that had become a popular stopping place, where he developed Gasquet Village. He constructed several buildings to lodge guests, including a store, saloon, dance hall, butcher shop, and winery. It became a renowned and popular summer resort.

The railroad between Redding, California, and Roseburg, Oregon, was completed in 1865. Crescent City was no longer the hub supplier of goods to miners and mining towns, as it was easier to ship by rail. Obviously this had a profoundly negative effect on Crescent City's economy.

Jacob Wenger Sr. organized a stock company to establish the first commercial sawmill in Del Norte County in 1869, and the Wenger Mill was constructed on the southern shore of Lake Earl. The vast timber resources of the area had been virtually untouched, but this was the beginning of the county's great timber era.

In 1886, John Bomhoff obtained permission from the Indian agent on the Klamath River to build a cannery. This was the beginning of the salmon industry and the development of the town of Requa, California. Requa was also the site of the only ferry crossing on the Klamath on the coast.

In 1926, the Douglas Memorial Bridge was completed over the Klamath River and thus the town of Klamath was born. Highway 101 bypassed Requa and the end of commercial fishing on the Klamath in 1933 meant the end it as a commercial center while the town of Klamath grew and flourished.

Over the years, Crescent City and Del Norte County witnessed many disasters—from shipwrecks, to floods, to tsunamis. In March 1964, a tsunami struck Crescent City and destroyed most of its downtown. Then, in December of the same year, torrential rains and melting snow pack pushed the Klamath River to 55.2 feet, the highest level ever recorded. The entire town of Klamath was washed away, along with the Douglas Memorial Bridge.

The pioneer spirit of the people of Crescent City and Del Norte County still survives, and the citizens came together to overcome the tragedy of the tsunamis and the floods. Much of what had been destroyed in 1964 has been rebuilt. Crescent City earned the nickname of Come Back Town, U.S.A.

This book offers a glimpse of the pioneer spirit present during the development and growth of Crescent City and Del Norte County, despite the numerous setbacks encountered over the years. The images within cover the period from 1854 to 1986 and show how the locals lived, worked, played, and overcame hardship and tragedy.

One

CRESCENT CITY
THE EARLY YEARS

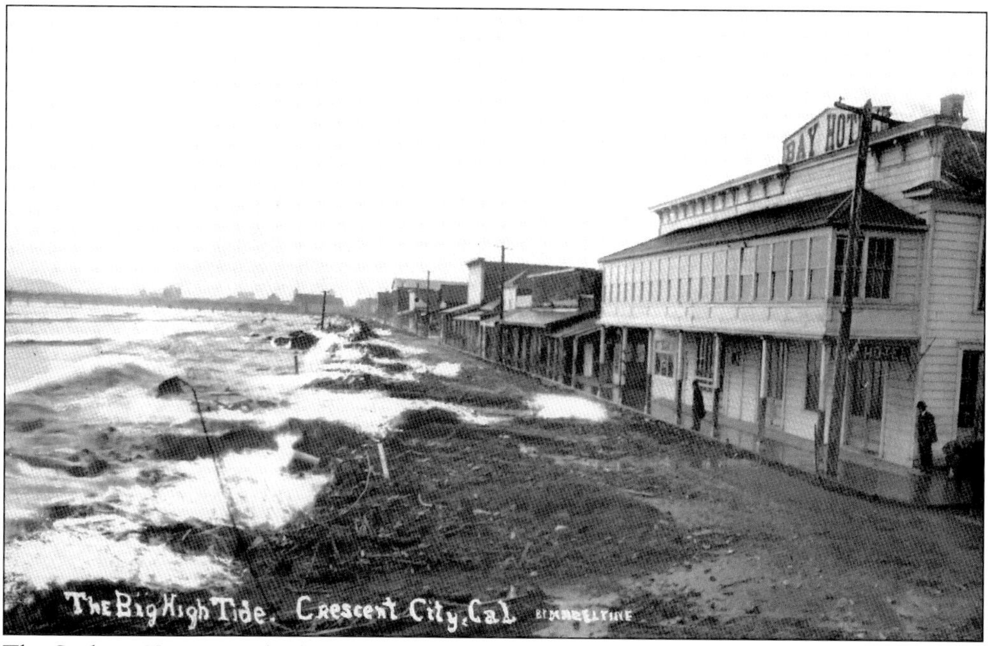

The Cushing House was the first hotel in Crescent City. Built in 1853 on Front Street, it was sold the next year and became the Crescent City Hotel. The next owner, Gotlieb Meyer, changed the name to the City Hotel. Francis Burtschell purchased the property in 1857 and changed the name yet again, this time to Bay Hotel. Front Street was right along the beach, and during winter storms, waves washed driftwood and debris right up to the buildings.

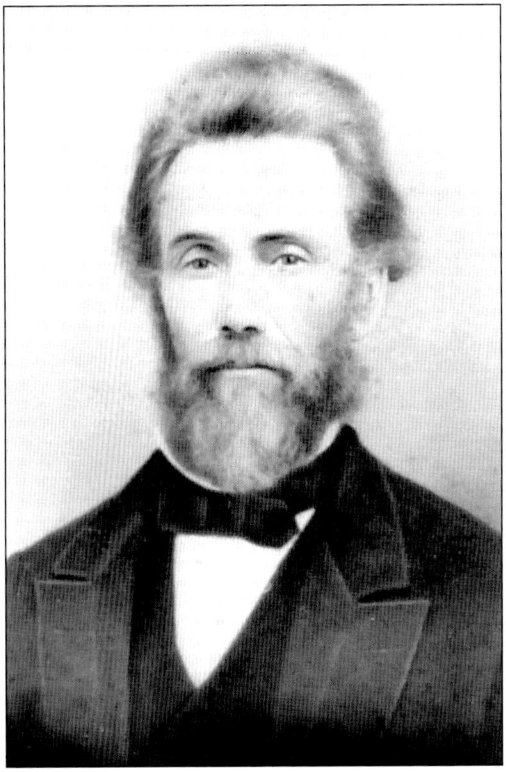

Dr. Edgar Mason moved to Crescent City in 1853 and was the first doctor and surgeon in Crescent City. He was elected the first district court judge in 1859, a position he held until his death in 1871. He was responsible for donating land for the Masonic lodge, property for the first grammar school built in the city, as well as the space for the city park called Citizens Plaza.

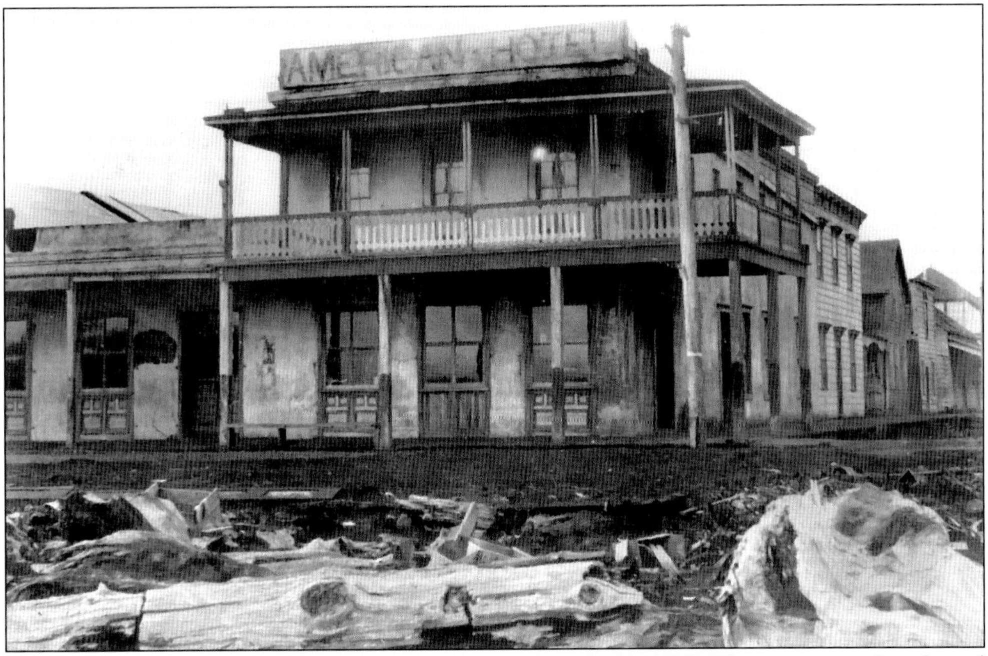

Nicholas McNamara arrived in Crescent City on March 12, 1853. There were no hotels and everyone was camping out, so Nicholas decided to build a hotel at Front and J Streets called the American Hotel. Built in 1853, the hotel was one of the first in Crescent City. Several years later, it burned. McNamara replaced it with a brick structure.

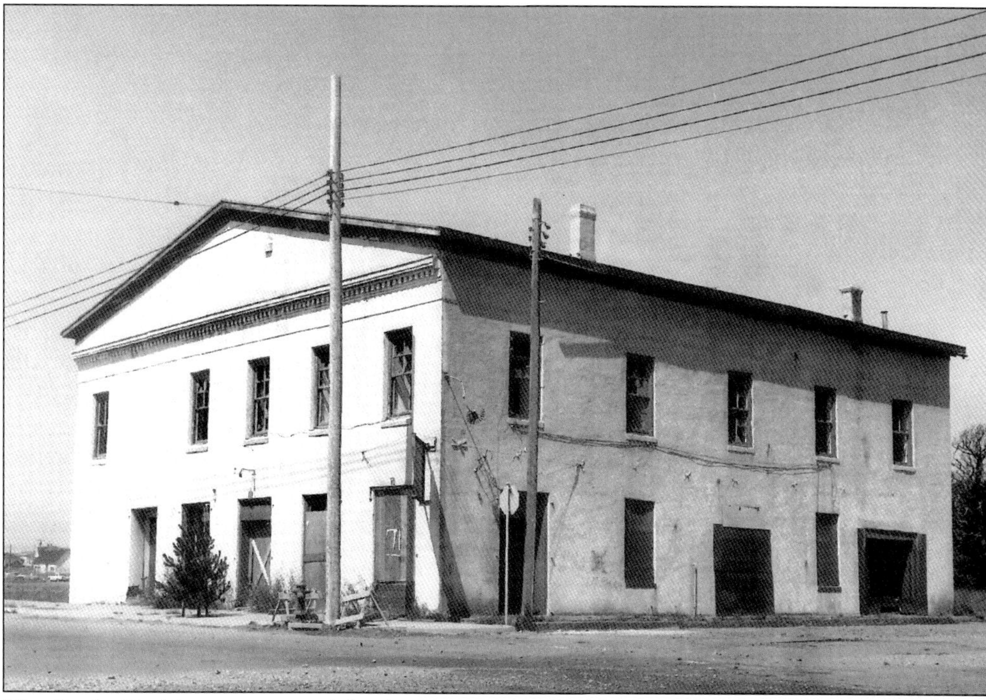

The Darby Building was one of the first permanent buildings in Crescent City, constructed in 1854 on the corner of Front and F Streets. It was a two-story structure built of red brick, which was manufactured on the Walton Ranch. The first floor housed the Wells Fargo Express office and the Saville Saloon. The second floor contained a dance hall and a theater with a seating capacity of 200.

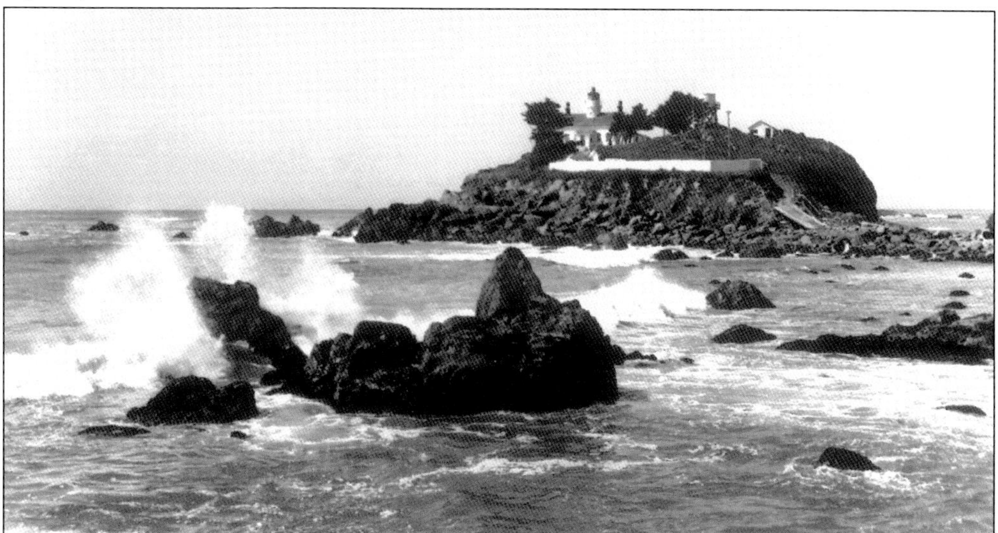

The entrance to the Crescent City harbor was very rocky and considered dangerous, and a light station was needed. In 1855, Congress authorized $15,000 for the construction of the Crescent City light station, which began in the spring of 1856. It was constructed of stone and masonry, with 20-inch-thick walls. The first light was ignited on December 10, 1856. Still standing today, the light station is now called the Battery Point Lighthouse.

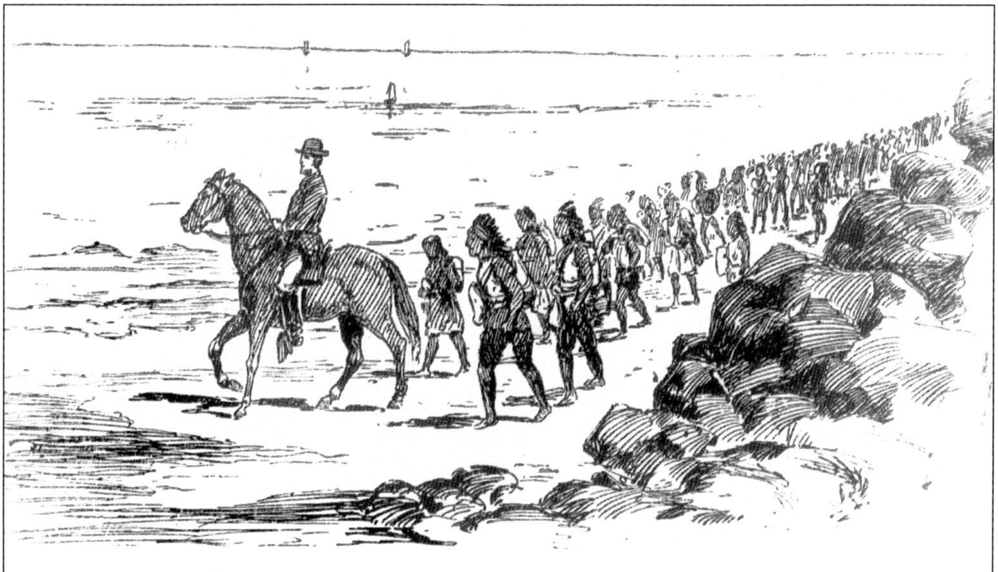

MAJOR BRADFORD CONDUCTING INDIANS TO A PLACE OF SAFETY.

Maj. Ward Bradford arrived in Crescent City in 1853 and bought land in Smith River Valley, where there was a Native American village. In 1857, war broke out in the Oregon Territory and a group of roughnecks threatened to kill all of the Indian males on his land. Bradford obtained permission from Crescent City and moved all the Indians to the lighthouse island, where they remained until the end of hostilities.

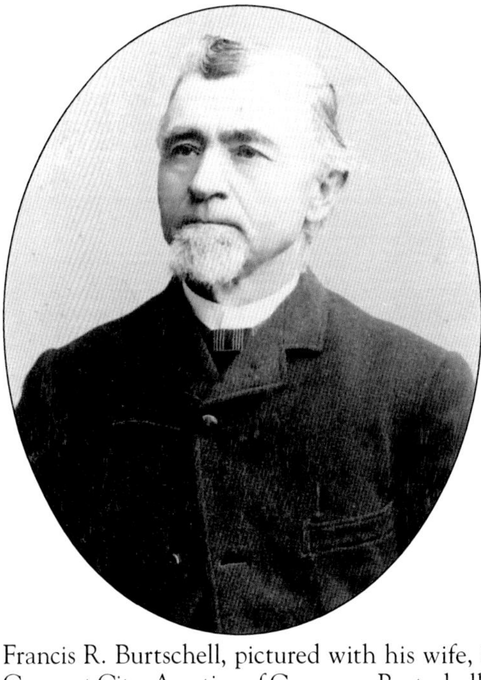

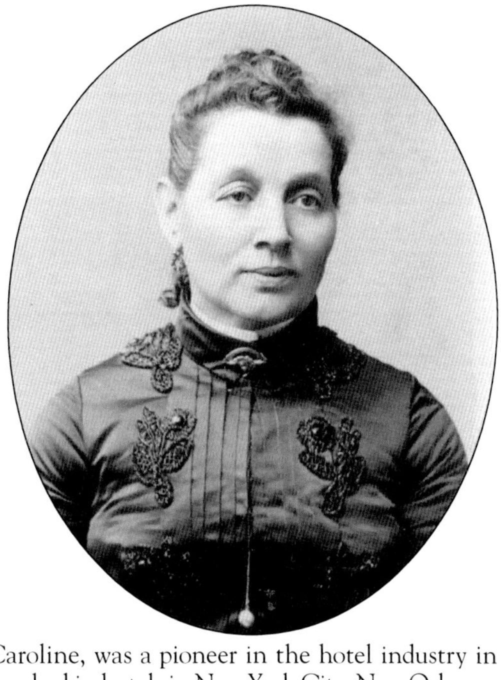

Francis R. Burtschell, pictured with his wife, Caroline, was a pioneer in the hotel industry in Crescent City. A native of Germany, Burtschell worked in hotels in New York City, New Orleans, Philadelphia, and San Francisco before arriving in Crescent City in April 1856. After living at the Crescent City Hotel for four months, he bought it and took over its operations. He also ran a livery stable in the city.

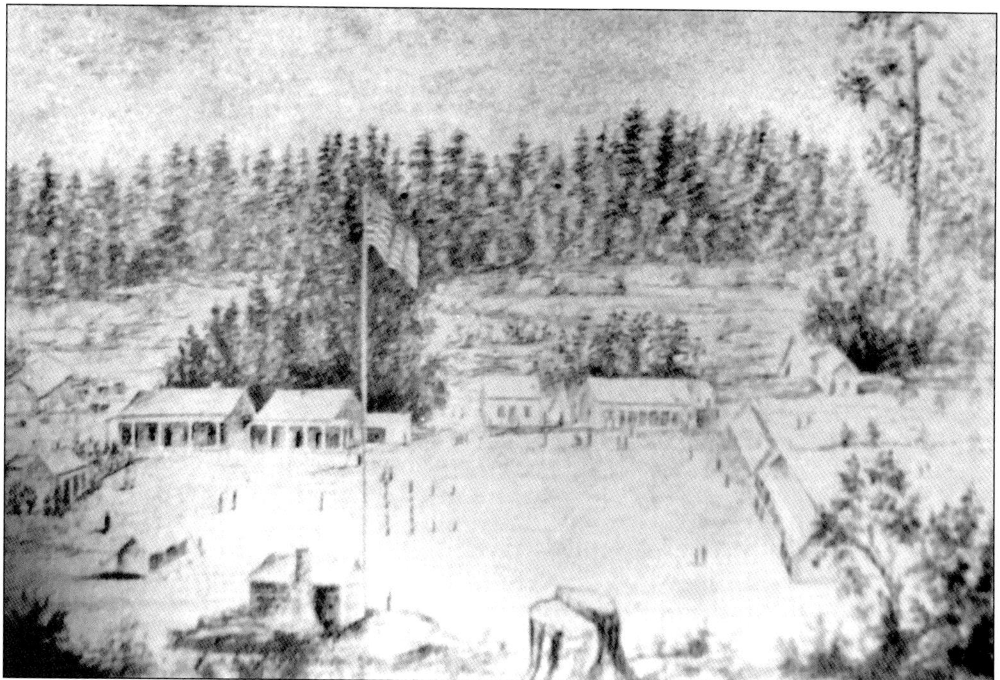

The 1860 and 1861, floods of the Klamath River destroyed Fort Ter Waw. In 1862, the Smith River Indian Reservation was established and Camp Lincoln was built. The Smith River Reservation was terminated in 1868 and all the Native Americans were relocated to the Hoopa Valley and Round Valley reservations. With the reservation gone, Camp Lincoln was no longer needed and it was ordered closed in July 1869.

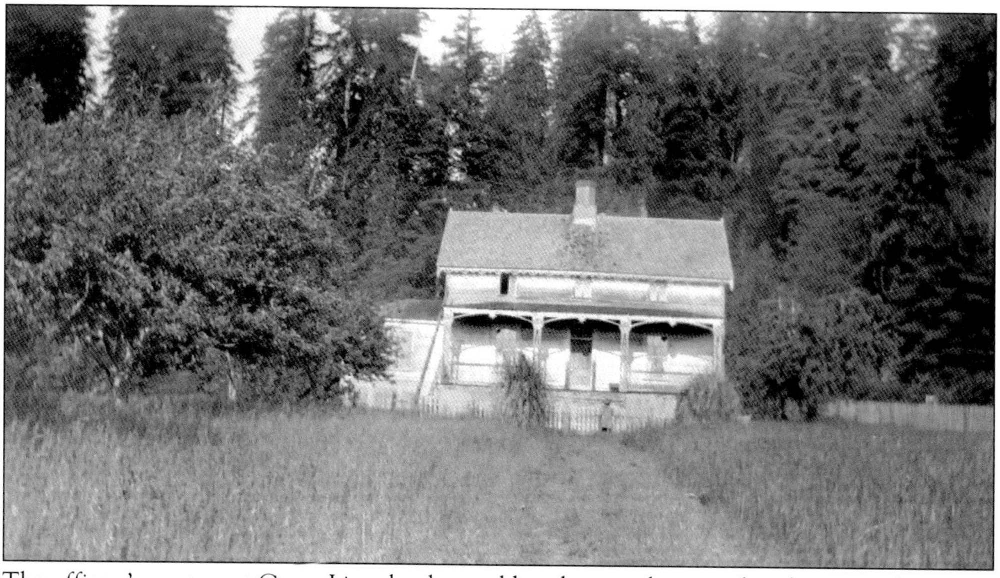

The officers' quarters at Camp Lincoln changed hands several times after the camp closed and is the only structure still standing. Now owned by the State of California as part of the Jedediah Smith Redwoods State Park, it is used as a park residence.

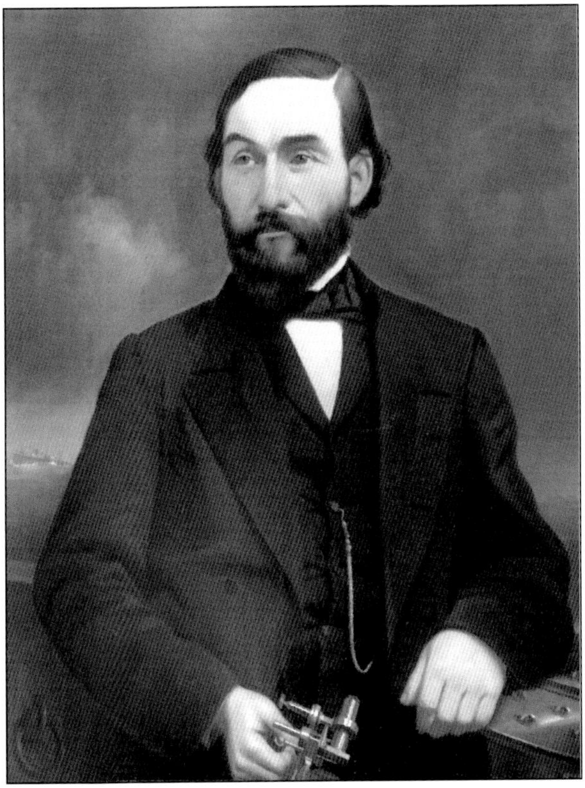

Capt. Samuel De Wolf was commander of the *Brother Jonathan* on July 28, 1865, when the ship sailed out from San Francisco harbor. He complained to a company official that the ship was overloaded and he was concerned about safety. He was reportedly told that the ship would sail on schedule with or without him.

The *Brother Jonathan* sailed from San Francisco with a heavy load and approximately 232 passengers and crew. On July 30, just north of Crescent City, they ran in to heavy seas and high winds and De Wolf decided to head back to Crescent City harbor until the storm passed. The ship hit a submerged rock and became stuck. With a tremendous cracking sound, a portion of the keel floated to the surface and the ship was doomed. Only 19 people survived. Captain De Wolf went down with the ship.

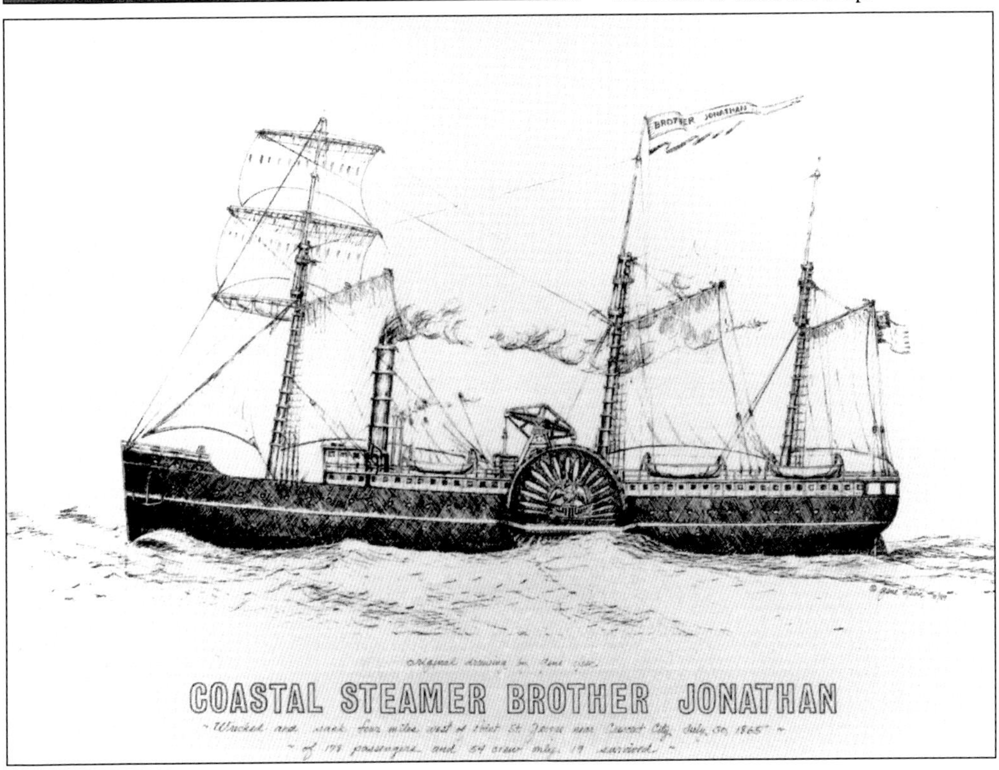

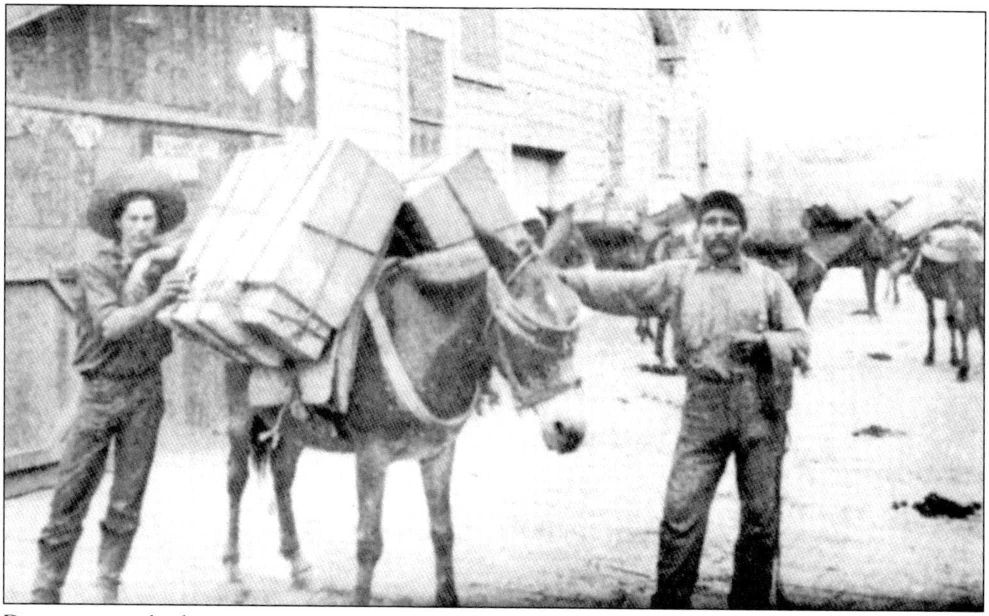

During its early days, Crescent City was a hub of commerce for supplies and materials for the interior mining communities. There were no roads, just trails, and everything had to be sent by pack-mule trains. Sometimes these pack trains consisted of as many as 200 mules.

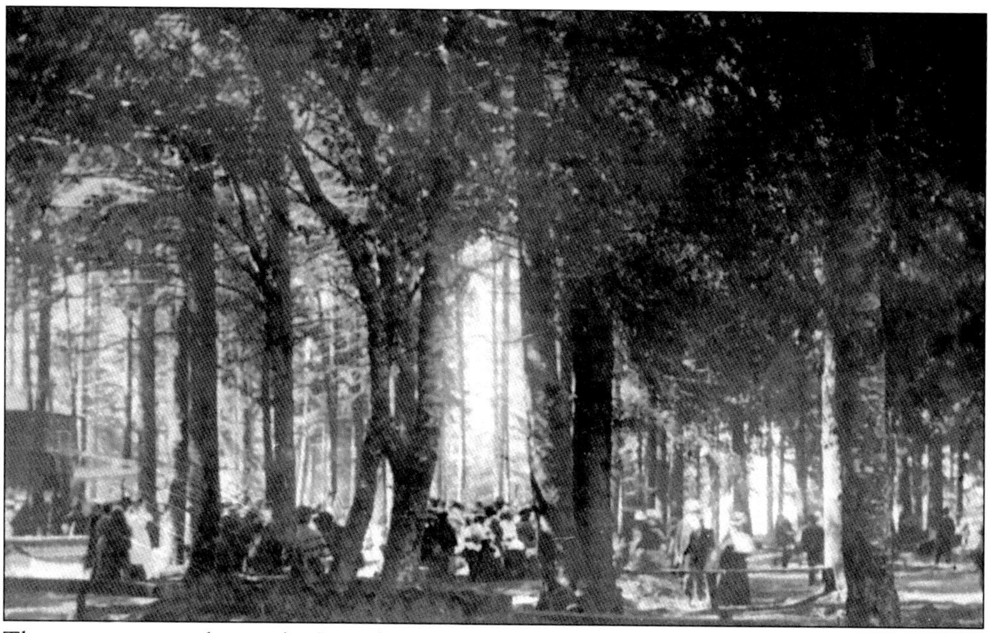

The greatest contribution by Dr. Edgar Mason was a four-city-block area that was designated Citizens Plaza. It was a wooded park and used for many civic functions including picnics and political rallies. It was also the center of activity for Fourth of July celebrations for years.

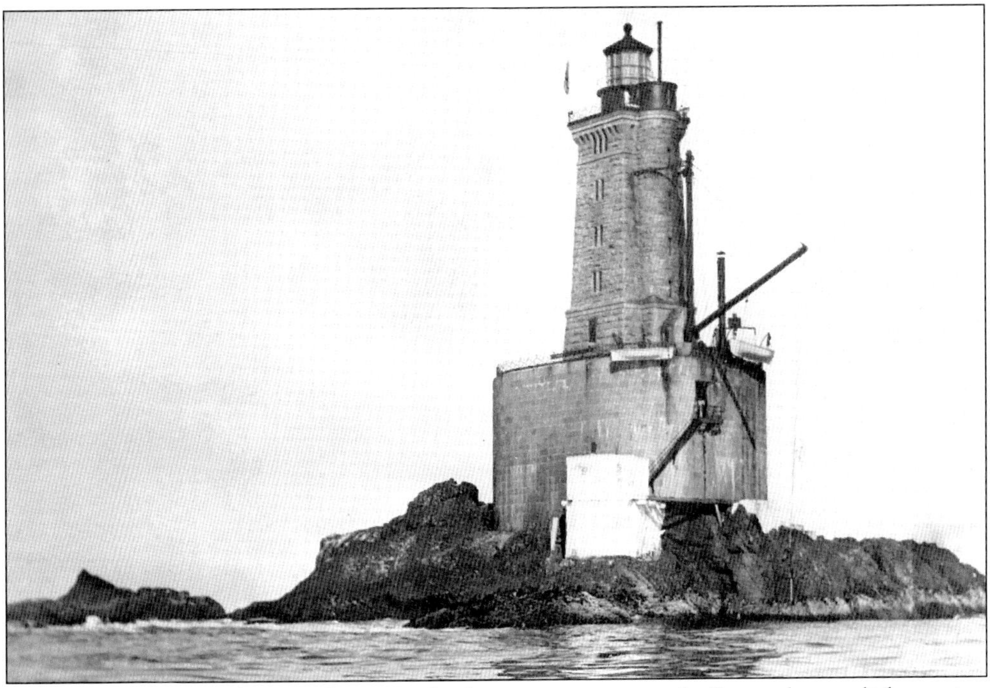

As a result of the *Brother Jonathan* tragedy, there was a concerted effort to have a light station constructed on the St. George reef. In January 1867 Pres. Andrew Johnson reserved all of the rocky islets off Point St. George for a light station.

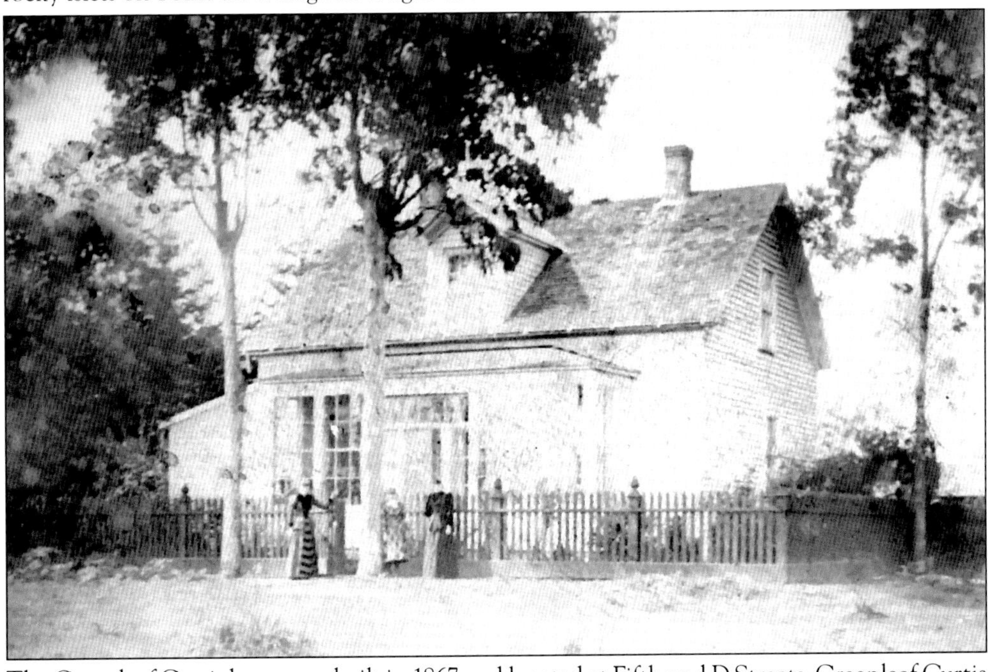

The Greenleaf Curtis home was built in 1867 and located at Fifth and D Streets. Greenleaf Curtis was a solider at Camp Lincoln, and after mustering out of the army, he returned to Crescent City, where he was involved in mining. Later he became the foreman of the Hobbs, Wall and Company sawmill.

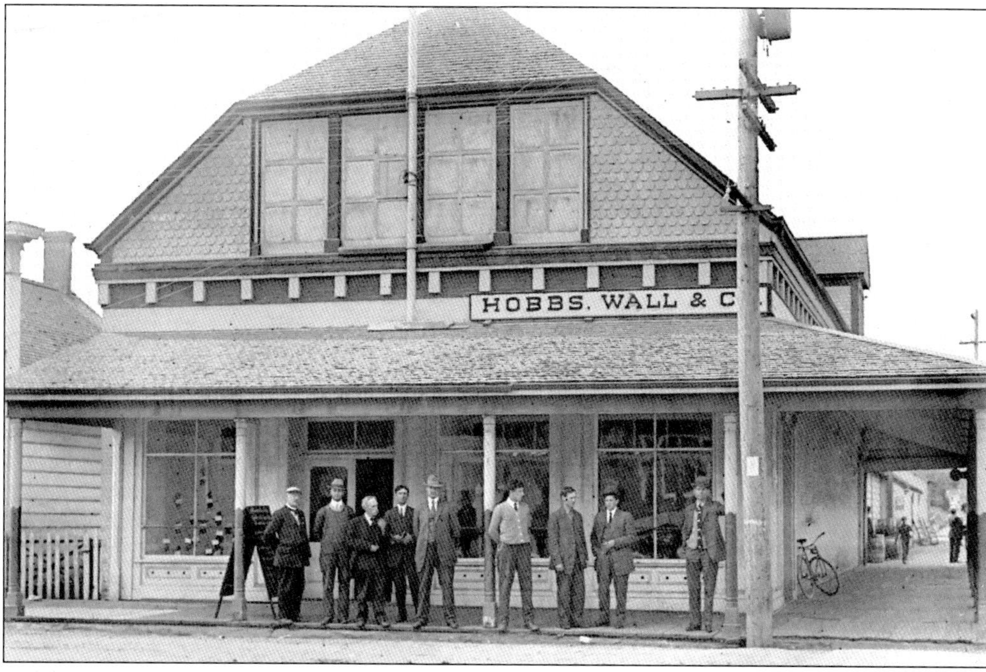

Caleb Hobbs and David Pomeroy of the San Francisco firm of Hobbs, Gilmore and Company established the Hobbs, Gilmore sawmill and box factory in Crescent City in 1871. Their store opened in 1873 and was located on Second and J Streets. It carried staples, coveralls, and groceries and later added dry goods. The store served Crescent City and supplied all of the lumber camps and camp stores operated by Hobbs, Gilmore.

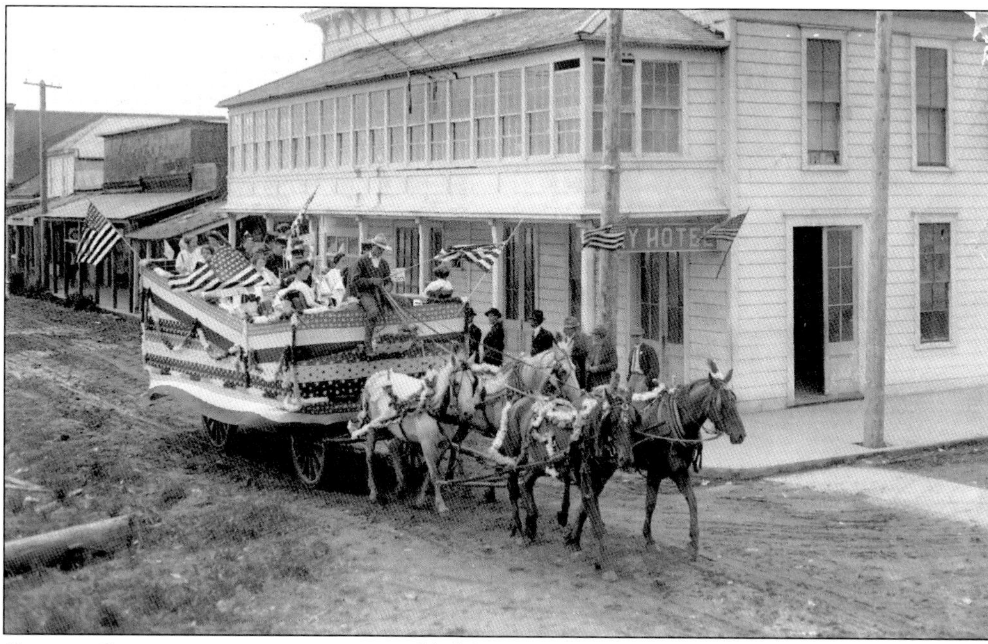

Crescent City grew as more streets were added, but Front Street remained the primary thoroughfare. It was widened with the addition of a sea wall to keep driftwood and debris from washing onto the street. The Fourth of July parade always proceeded along Front Street.

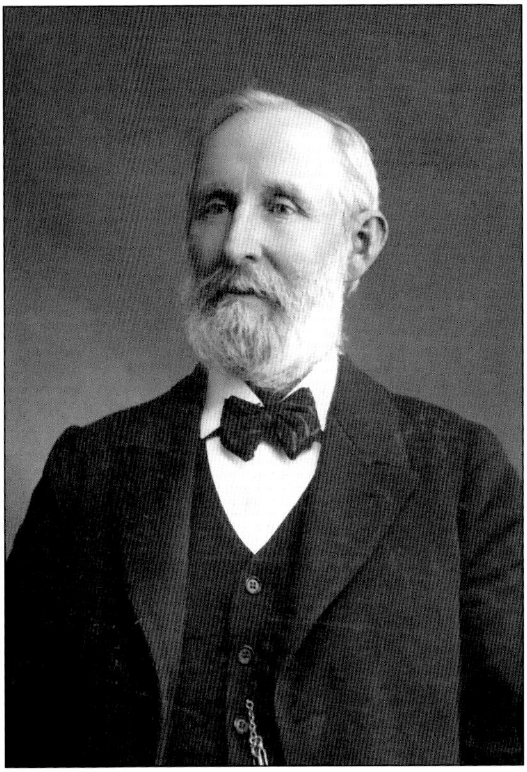

Jacob Marhoffer was the bookkeeper and general superintendent of Hobbs, Wall and Company and also ran the Hobbs Wall Store. He worked for the company from 1868 until 1900 when he became the first president of the first bank of Del Norte County.

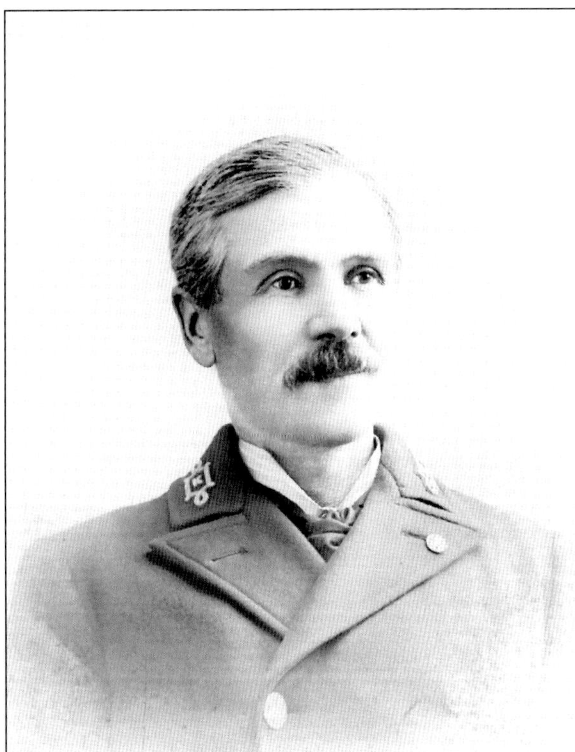

John Heatley Jeffrey was a captain in the 56th Massachusetts Infantry during the Civil War. He married Nellie Hamilton on January 24, 1868, and immediately after the ceremony, the couple left for California by way of the Isthmus of Panama. Captain Jeffreys was appointed keeper of the light station at Crescent City in 1875. He remained in that position until 1914.

Nellie Jeffrey was appointed "assistant light keeper" by the Light Station Service to help her husband run and maintain the light station. In September 1882, when she was informed that her position would no longer be funded due to budget constraints, she still assisted her husband. The Jeffreys raised four children while at the light station.

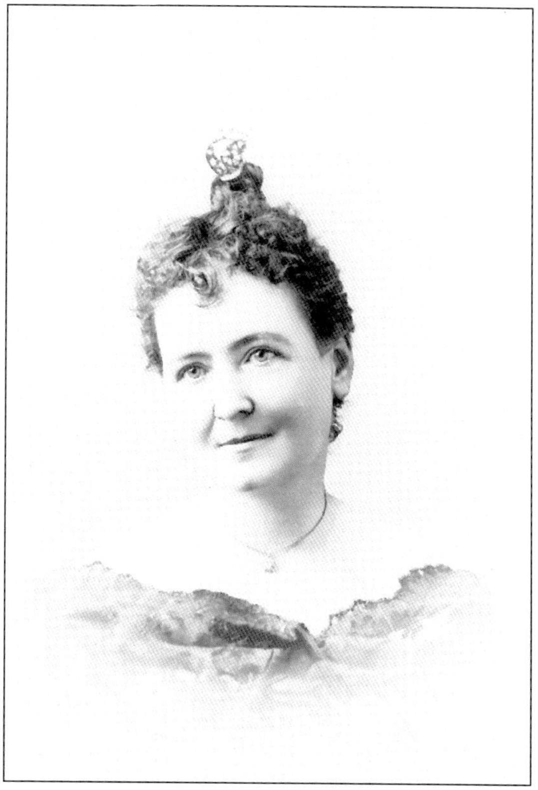

It took years of studies and discussion to determine the best site for the St. George Reef Light Station before finally settling on Seal Rock. In October 1881, a surveyor assessed the area and plans were then drawn up in San Francisco. In 1882, Congress made the first appropriation of funds and construction began.

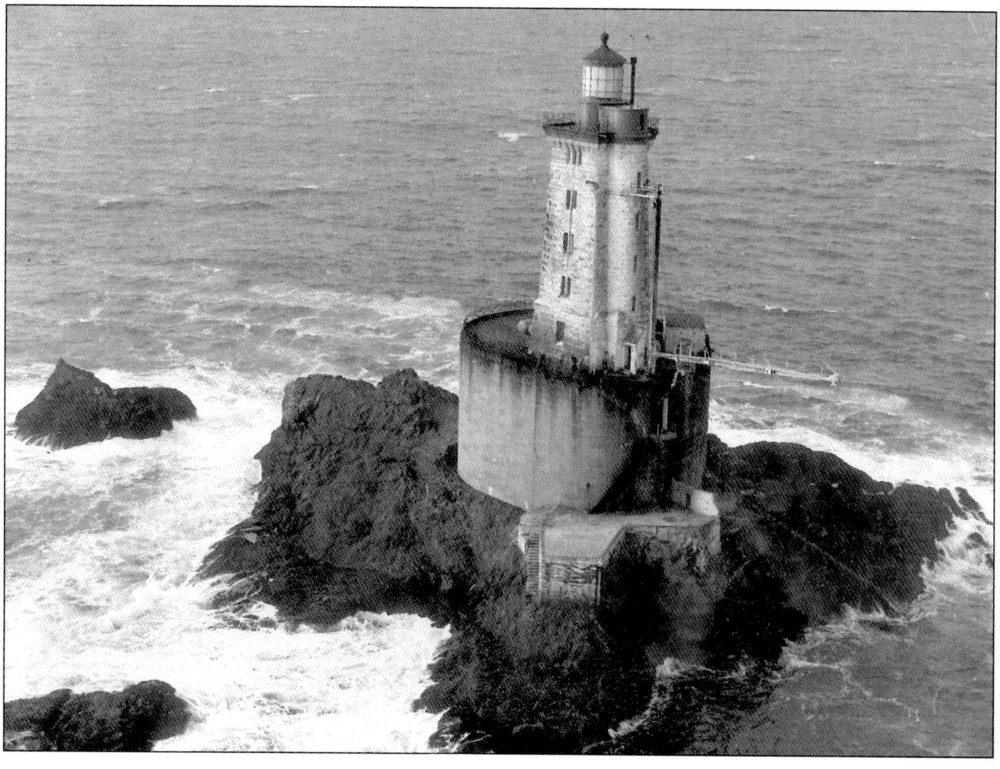

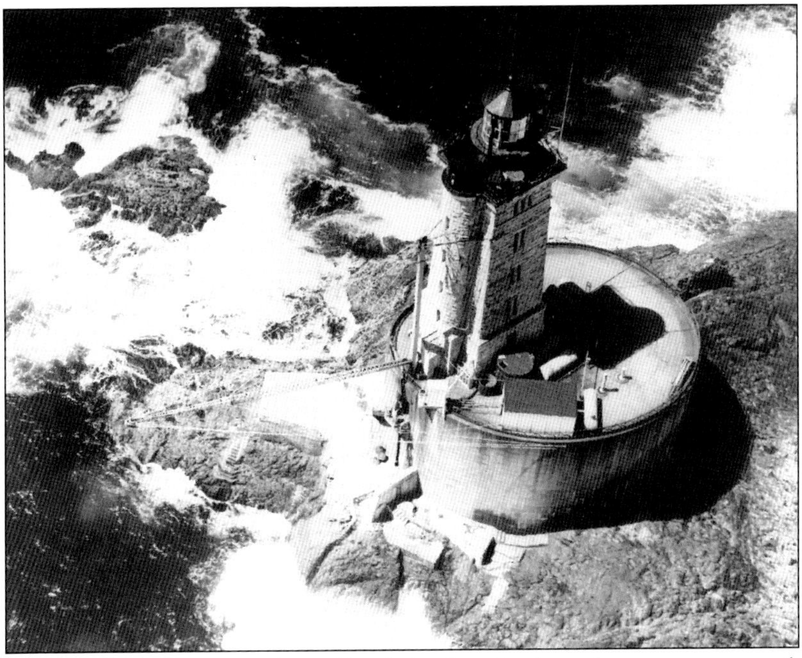

Because of high surf conditions, work could only be done in the calmer summer months, but the St. George Reef Light Station was finally completed in October 1891. At a cost of $704,634, it was the costliest light station ever built—and was considered one of the finest. The St. George Reef Light Station was in operation until May 13, 1975.

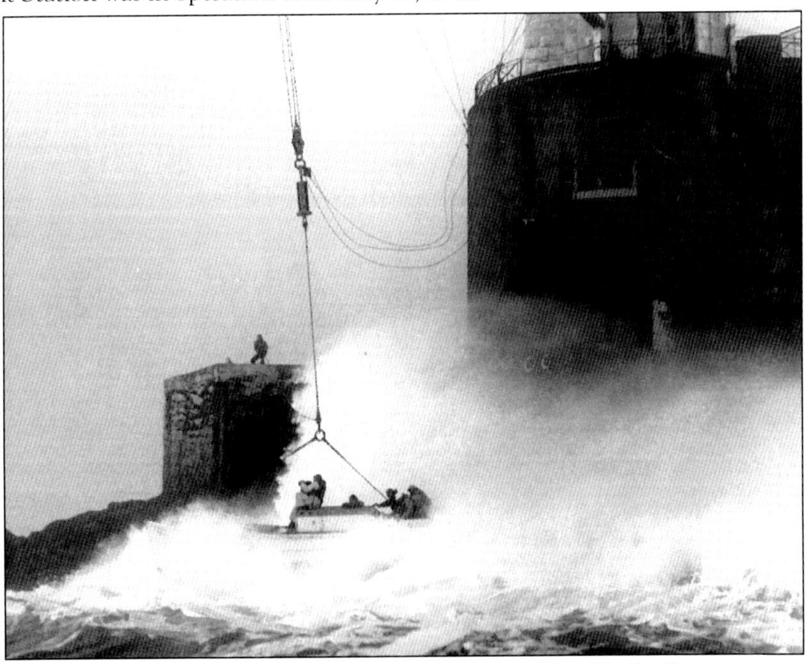

One of the most dangerous aspects of life on the St. George Reef Light Station was getting on and off the station. The surf never permitted a boat landing on the islet. Nets attached to the boom were lowered and men and supplies were loaded into them and hoisted up. Sometimes the station boats were hoisted to the top of the pier, 66 feet high, by the boom.

The lens for the St. George Reef Light Station was a first-order Fresnel, made in France at a cost of $15,000. It was shipped to San Francisco before being transported up the coast to the light station. The lens was lit for the first time on October 20, 1892.

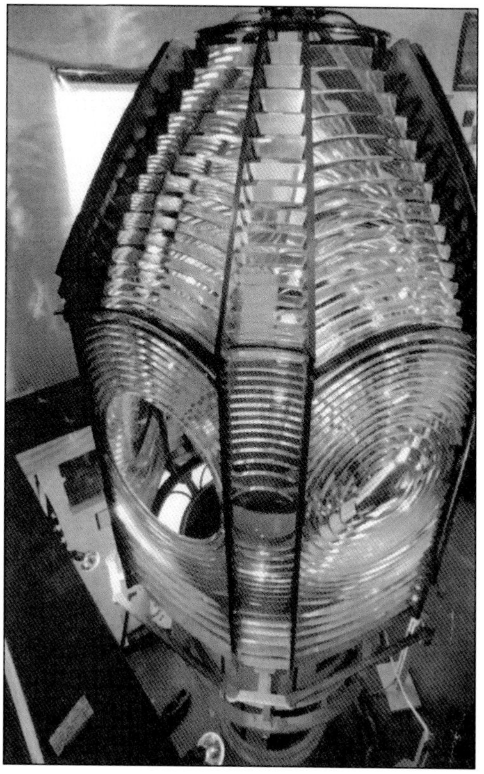

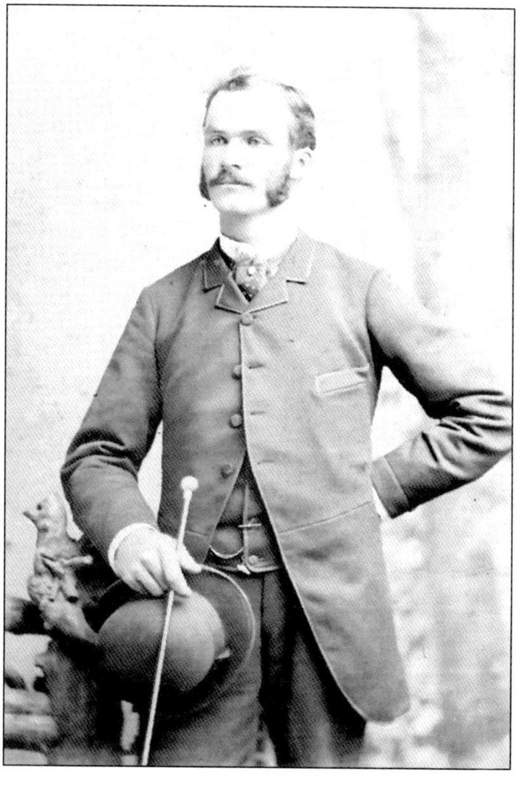

James McNulty moved to the Smith River ranch of his grandparents with his widowed mother when he was 18 months old. She then married William Hamilton, a widower who was to become an attorney. James finished school in Crescent City and tried bark scaling and surveying before assisting his stepfather with briefs and title searches. This caused him to decide to study law, and after completing his studies, he opened a law office in Crescent City.

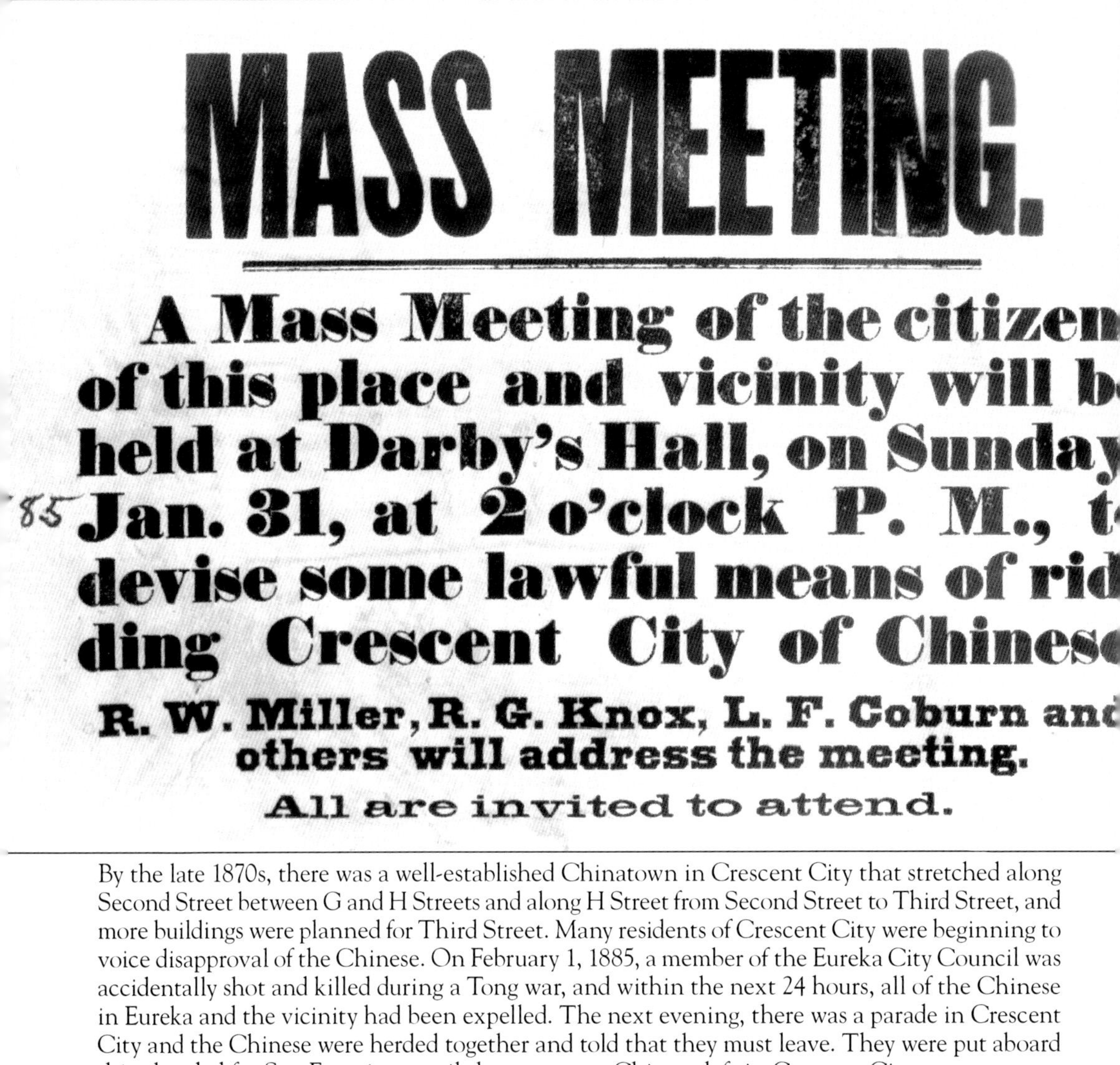

MASS MEETING.

A Mass Meeting of the citizen of this place and vicinity will b held at Darby's Hall, on Sunday '85 Jan. 31, at 2 o'clock P. M., t devise some lawful means of rid ding Crescent City of Chines

R. W. Miller, R. G. Knox, L. F. Coburn an others will address the meeting.

All are invited to attend.

By the late 1870s, there was a well-established Chinatown in Crescent City that stretched along Second Street between G and H Streets and along H Street from Second Street to Third Street, and more buildings were planned for Third Street. Many residents of Crescent City were beginning to voice disapproval of the Chinese. On February 1, 1885, a member of the Eureka City Council was accidentally shot and killed during a Tong war, and within the next 24 hours, all of the Chinese in Eureka and the vicinity had been expelled. The next evening, there was a parade in Crescent City and the Chinese were herded together and told that they must leave. They were put aboard ships headed for San Francisco until there were no Chinese left in Crescent City.

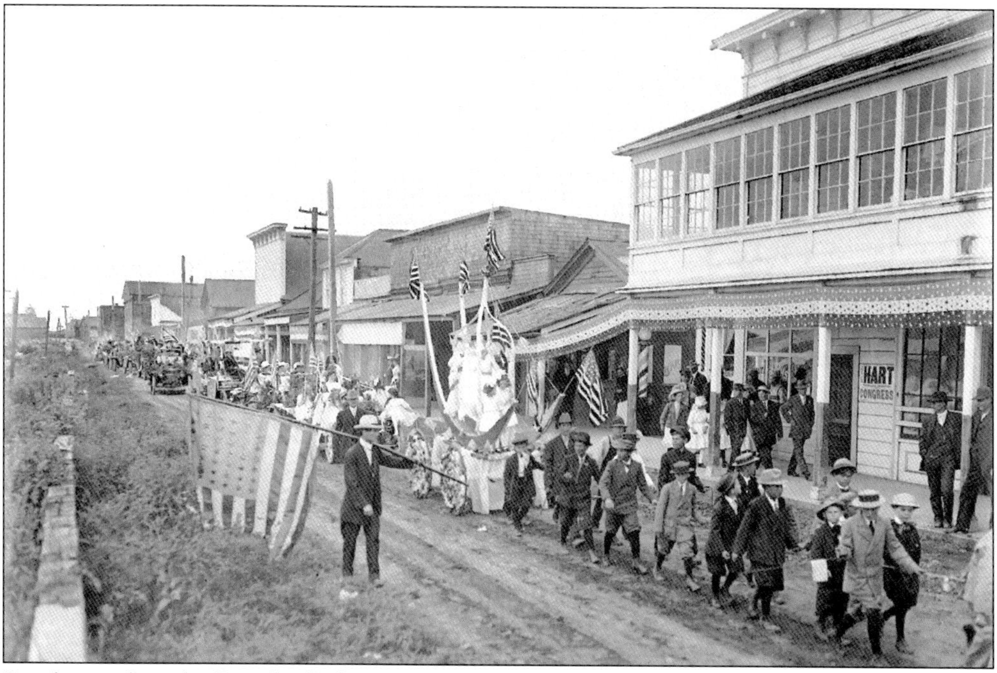

People march in the Fourth of July parade along Front Street in front of the Bay Hotel. A sea wall of split redwood bolts a foot thick had been constructed along the ocean side of the street, seen at left, which was capped with heavy planking. Front Street was now 60 feet wide.

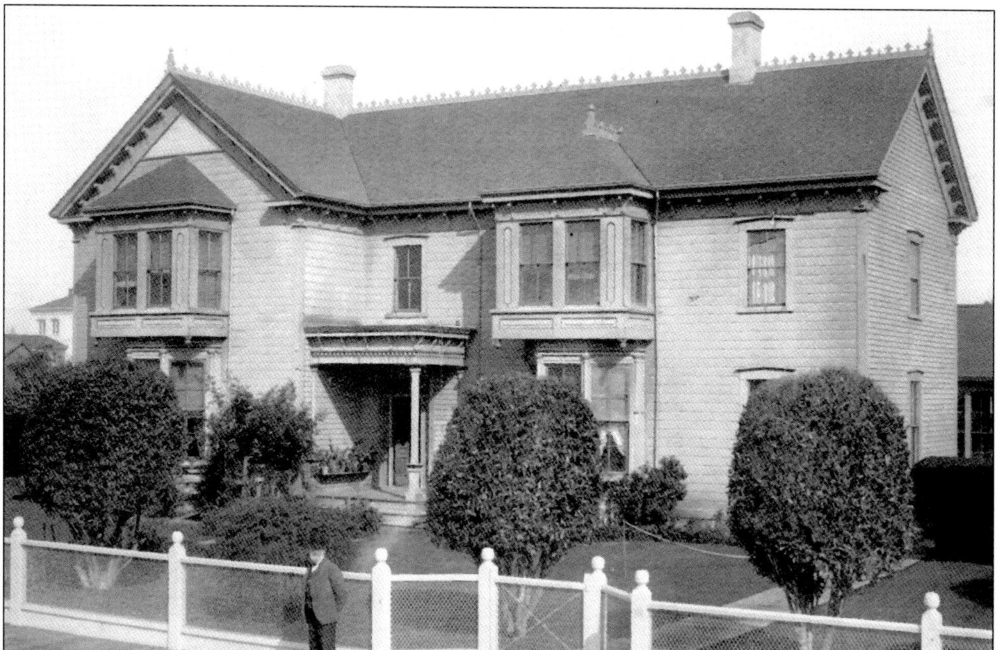

Jacob Marhoffer was general superintendent for Hobbs, Pomeroy and Company, which later became Hobbs, Wall and Company. In 1871, he married Ln Mason, daughter of Dr. Edgar Mason. Their home was built in 1880 on the corner of Third and K Streets and was considered one of the finest homes in Crescent City.

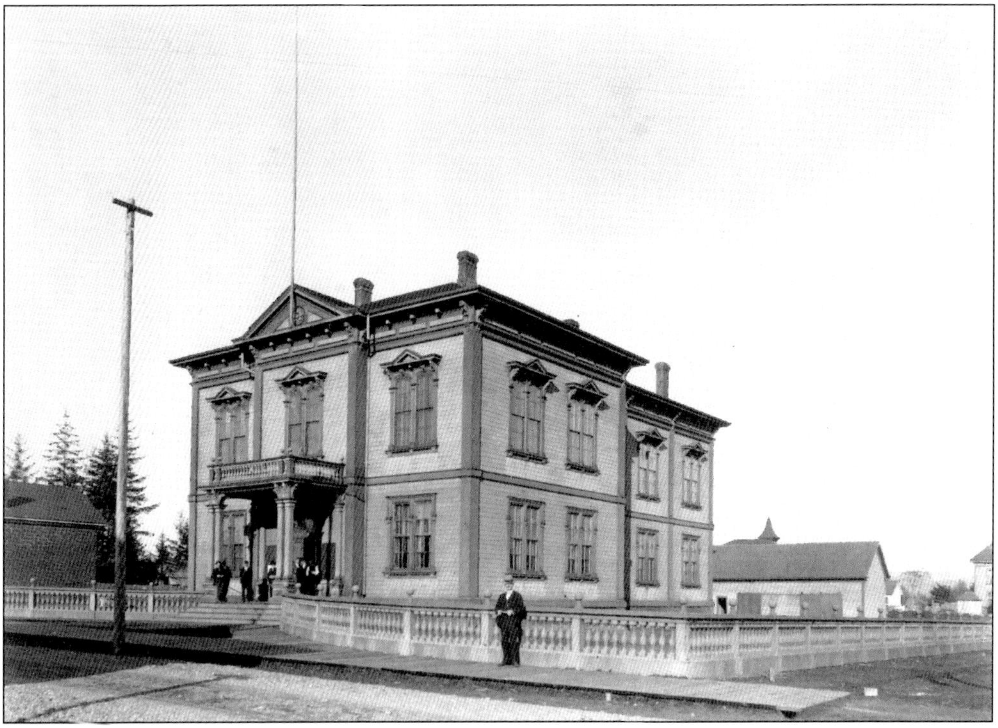

The Del Norte County Courthouse was constructed in 1882. It was a very impressive wooden structure with a great deal of fine detail work—the pride of the county.

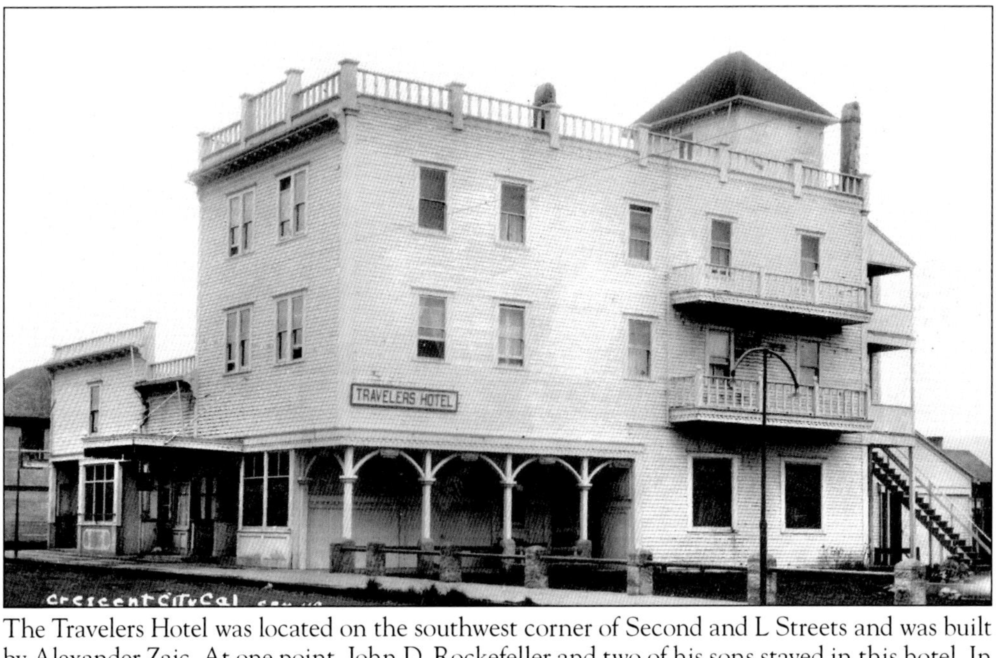

The Travelers Hotel was located on the southwest corner of Second and L Streets and was built by Alexander Zaic. At one point, John D. Rockefeller and two of his sons stayed in this hotel. In 1942, it was torn down and the lumber sold.

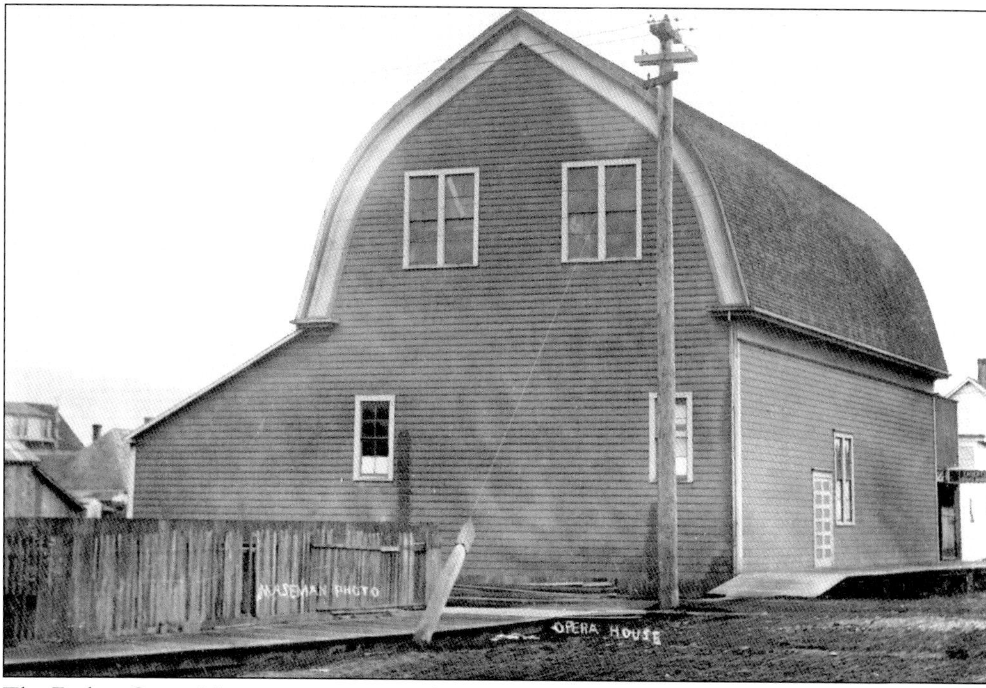

The Endert Opera House was constructed in 1886 by Joseph Endert and Joseph Capprice on the southwest corner of Third and J Streets. The theater was upstairs, and downstairs there was a dance hall and skating rink.

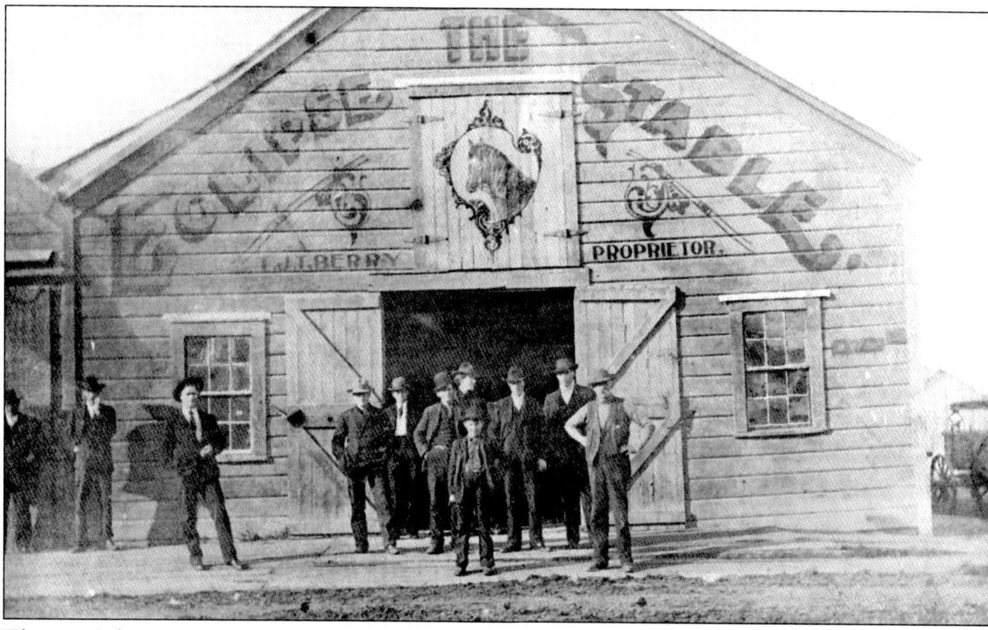

Thomas Johnson Turner Berry was born in 1858 in Iowa. In 1878, he arrived in Crescent City where he became connected with Frank Burtschell in his livery stable. In 1890, Berry took over the business and called his new business Eclipse Livery and Feed Stable. In 1901, Berry was elected assemblyman, and he was reelected in 1907. The Eclipse Livery and Feed Stable was located on the northwest corner of Second and I Streets.

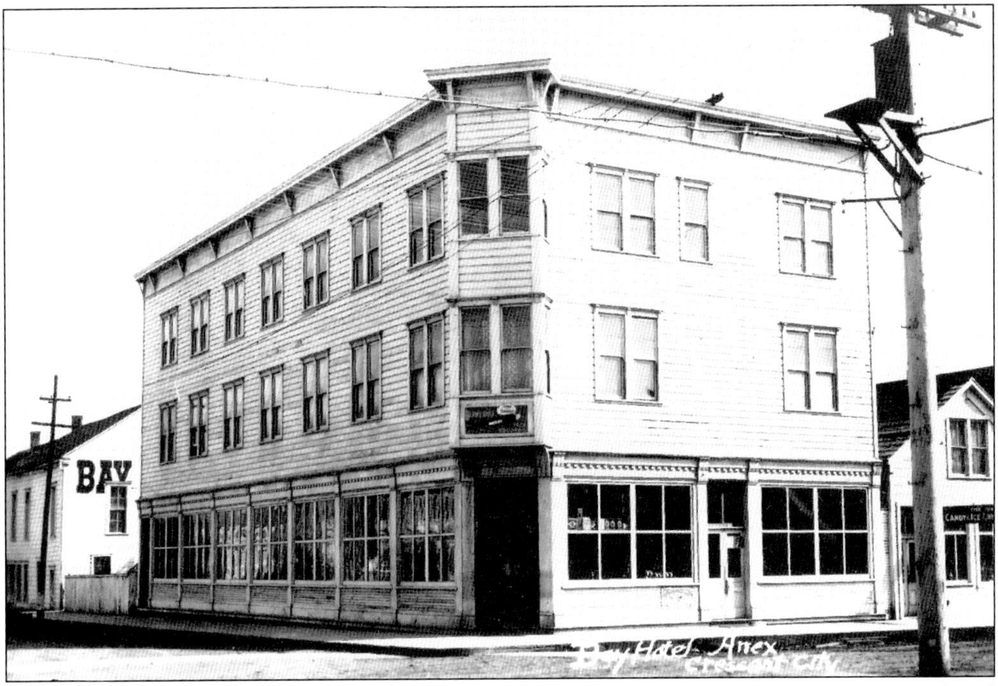

Francis Burtschell renovated the Bay Hotel in 1885; the entire front section was removed and relocated across the street. A new front was added to the Bay Hotel, and the old front section was expanded and remodeled to become the Bay Hotel Annex. The annex was destroyed by the 1964 tsunami and replaced by the new post office.

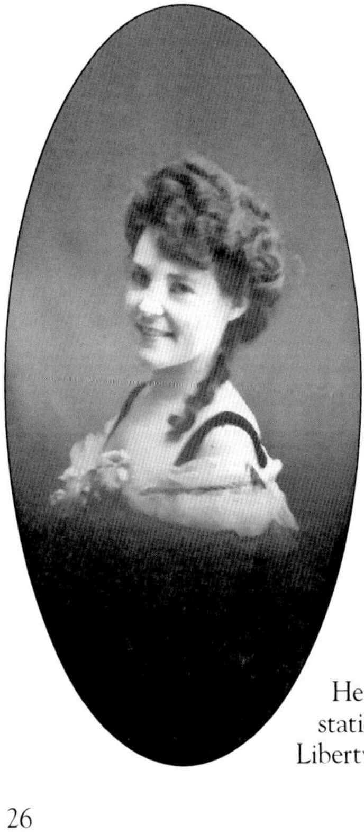

Helen Jeffrey was the daughter of John Jeffrey, the Crescent City light station keeper, and his wife, Helen "Nellie" Jeffrey. Helen was Miss Liberty on many of the Fourth of July parades in Crescent City.

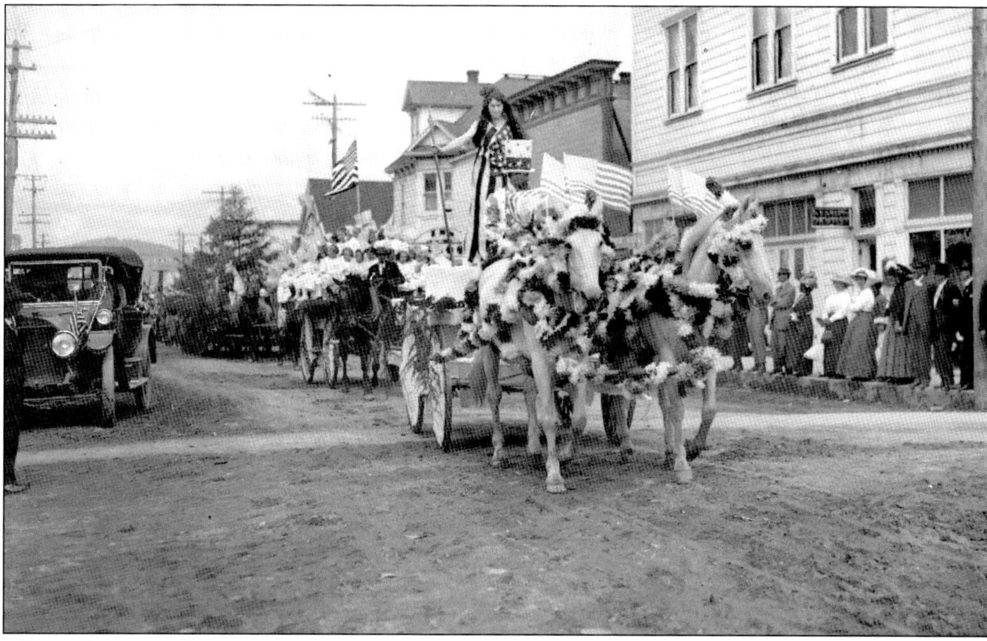

About the time the Bay Hotel was remodeled, Front Street also got a face lift. The street was widened to 60 feet, and a new sea wall was constructed. As seen here, Front Street was still a main part of the Fourth of July Parade route.

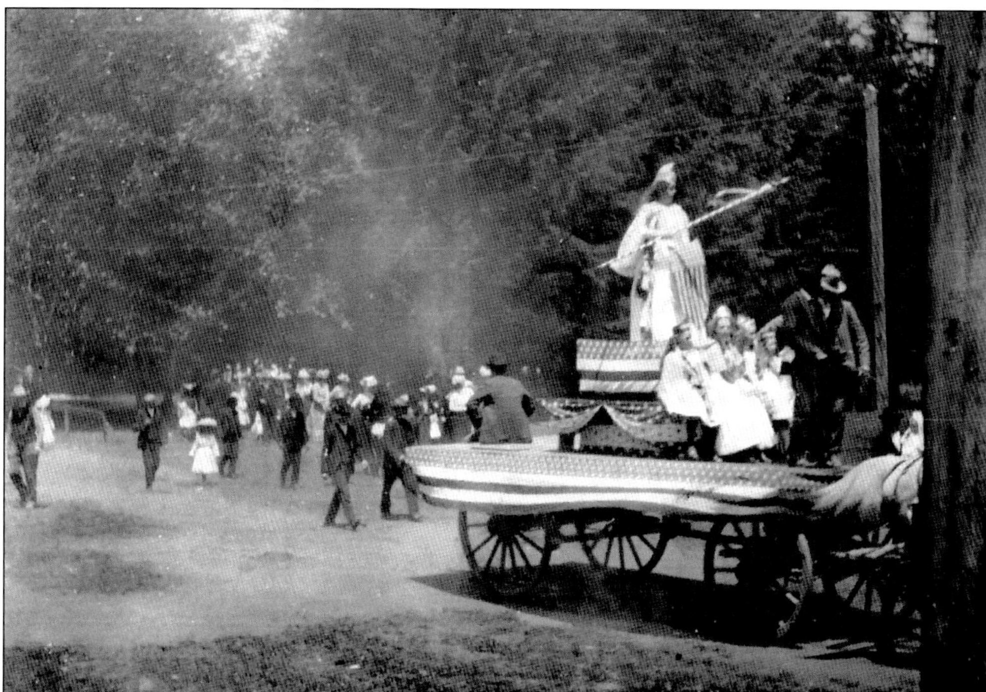

The Fourth of July parade always ended at the Citizens Plaza Park; Helen Jeffrey was Miss Liberty on this float. The parades were always followed by a barbeque picnic and a Crescent City Band concert.

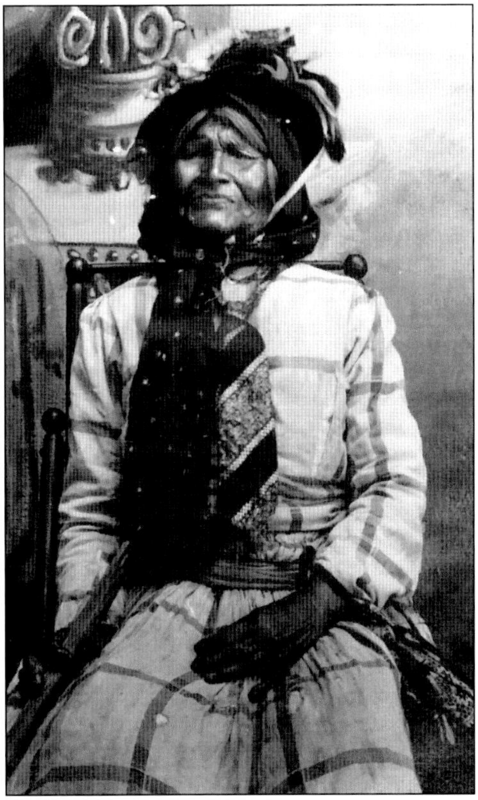

Buttons was a Tolowa Indian woman seen frequently in Crescent City. She was very friendly and loved people and would sing and do a dance if someone asked her. She was often paid with buttons, which she sewed on to her clothes. This picture was taken in 1890.

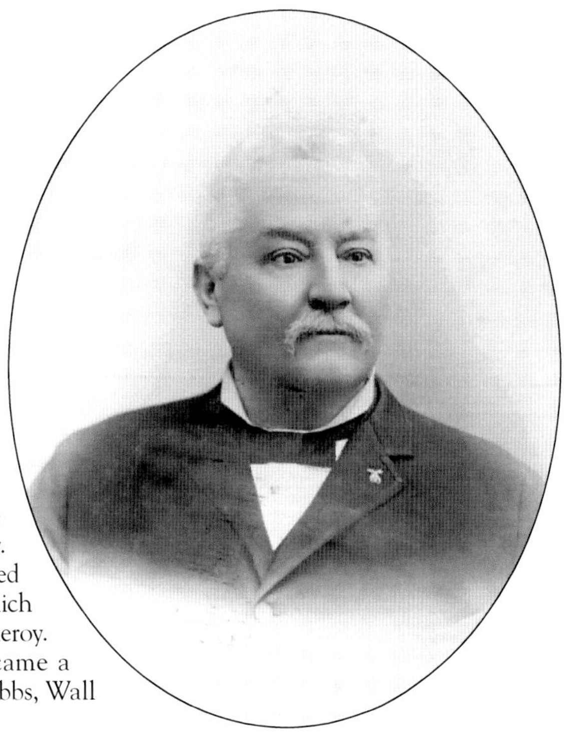

Joseph G. Wall was the first agent for the Wells Fargo and Company in Crescent City. He became involved in lumbering and worked with the Hobbs, Gilmore and Company, which was owned by Caleb Hobbs and David Pomeroy. When Pomeroy died in 1893, Wall became a partner and the business was renamed Hobbs, Wall and Company.

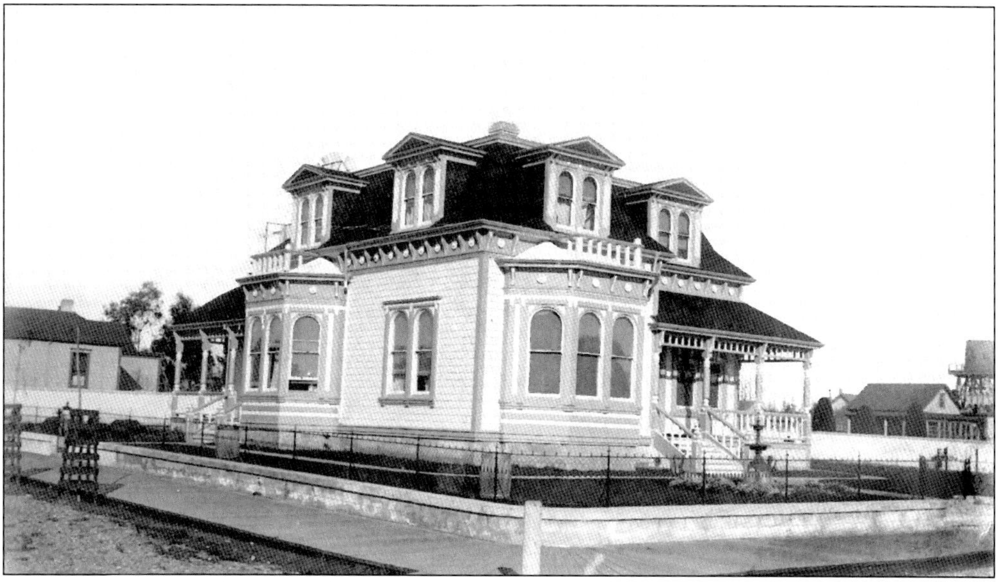

Joseph Bernhardt Endert arrived in Crescent City in 1871 as a man of many talents that included performing as an acrobat and trapeze artist, becoming a deputy sheriff before being elected as sheriff, and serving as a tax collector. In 1886, he built the second theater in Crescent City before establishing the first Del Norte County Bank. He built his home in 1893 on the corner of Third and J Streets—one of the finest in Crescent City.

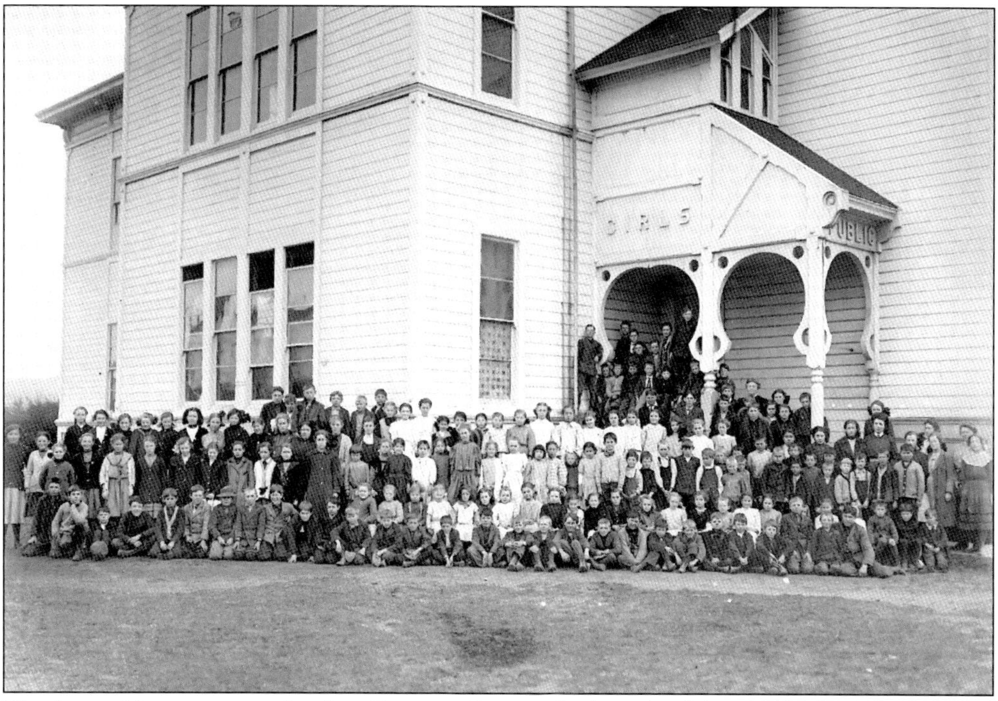

The first public grammar school in Crescent City was built on land donated by Dr. Edgar Mason, located on H Street where the Del Norte County Court House now stands. It was home to the first high school class in 1891 after the McGowen Act authorized the establishment of county and district high schools. It housed the high school until a new one was built.

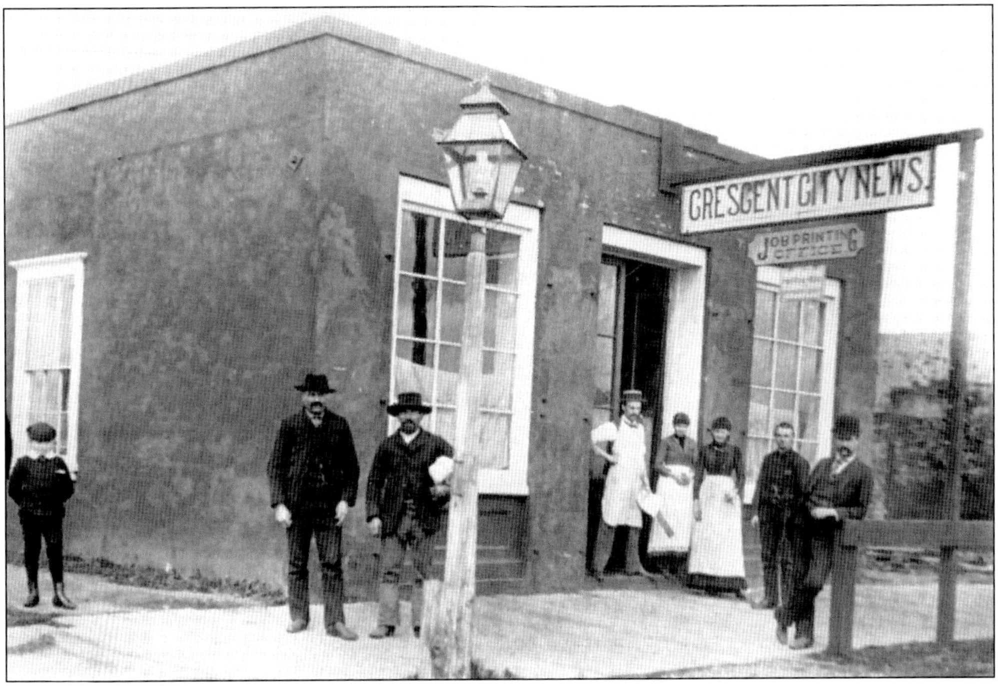

The *Crescent City News* was established in 1892 by John L. Childs when he decided to run for public office, using the newspaper to express his political views. It was printed every Thursday on a Franklin type press with hand-set type. In 1909, Childs sold the newspaper to Tommy Thompson, who continued to publish it until the paper was consolidated with the *Argus and Del Norte Record* to become the *Del Norte Triplicate*.

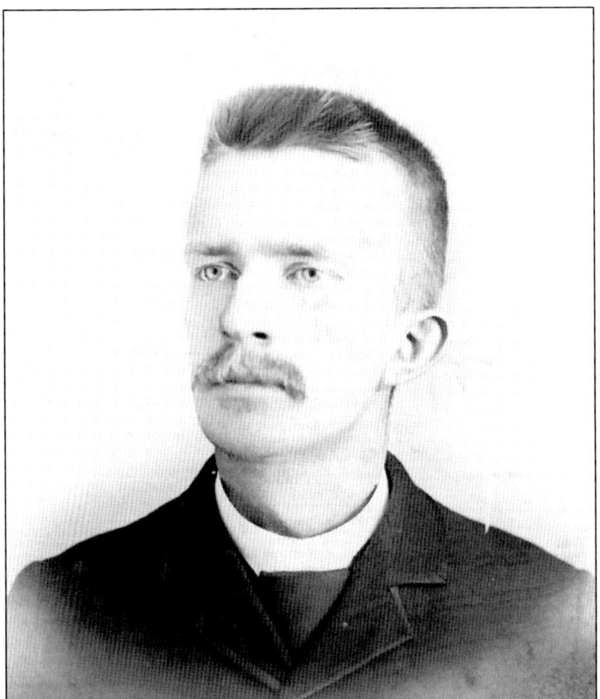

John L. Childs moved to Crescent City in 1892 and was a teacher at the Lincoln School near Fort Dick. The next term he became principal of the Crescent City Grammar School; he was elected county clerk the same year. He also studied law and was admitted to the bar in 1896. In the fall of 1897, he was elected district attorney, and in 1903, he became a superior court judge and served as such for 18 years.

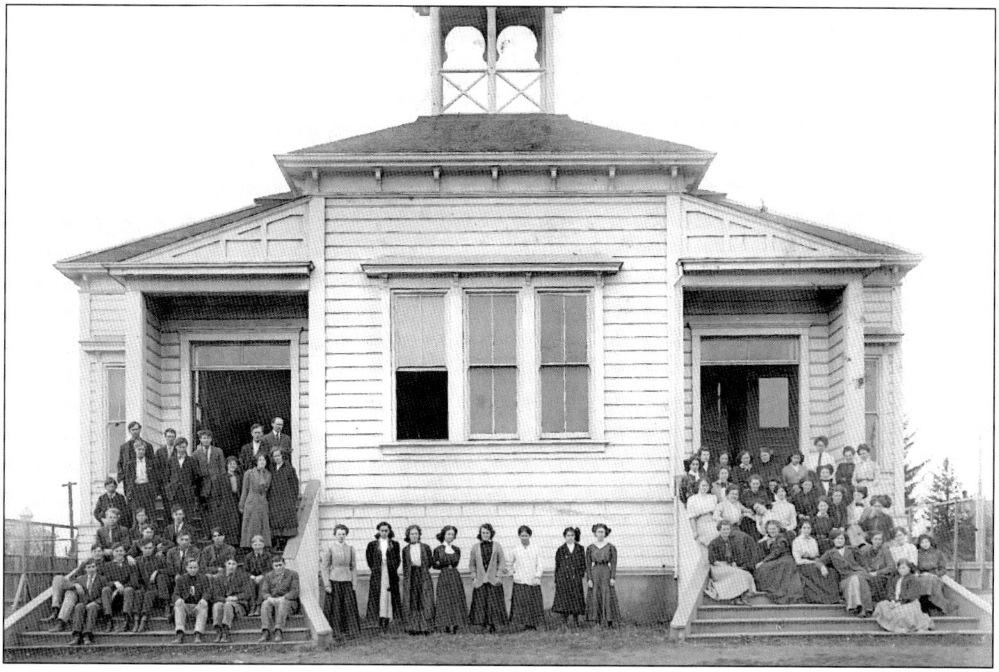

In 1891, the McGowan Act authorized the establishment of county and district high schools and a new high school was organized in Crescent City. Classes were at first held in vacant rooms in the grammar school, until land was purchased and money raised through taxation and donations for the construction of a high school. Located on J Street between Fifth and Sixth Streets, it was completed on August 19, 1895, with the class of 1896 its first graduates.

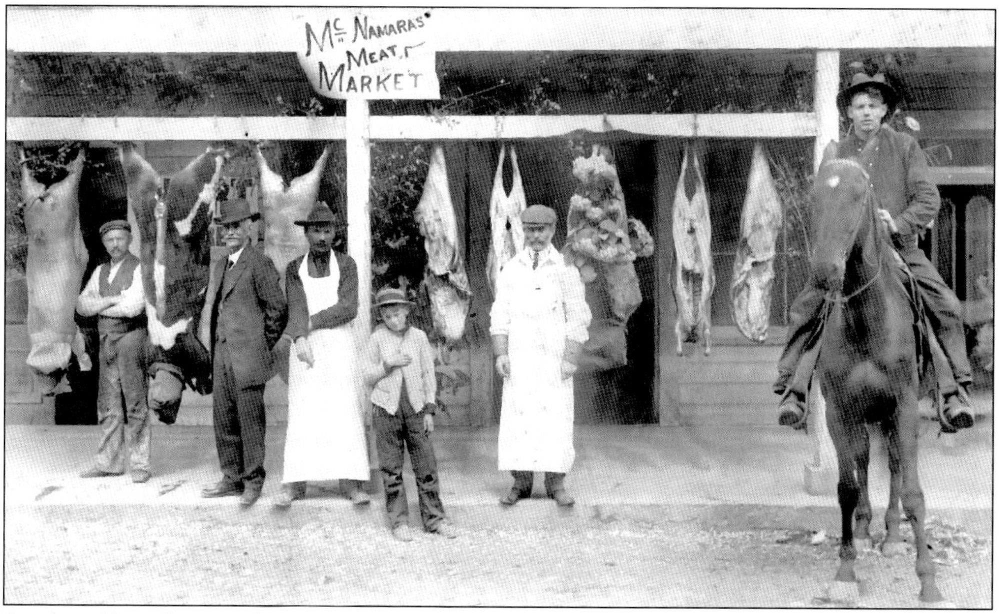

Butchers Emetsburg and McNamara were located on Second Street between H and I Streets. They advertised as dealers in livestock, butter, and eggs and sold all cuts of beef and pork as well as many kinds of sausage. By the early 1900s, McNamara had become the sole owner of the market, which became known as the McNamara Meat Market.

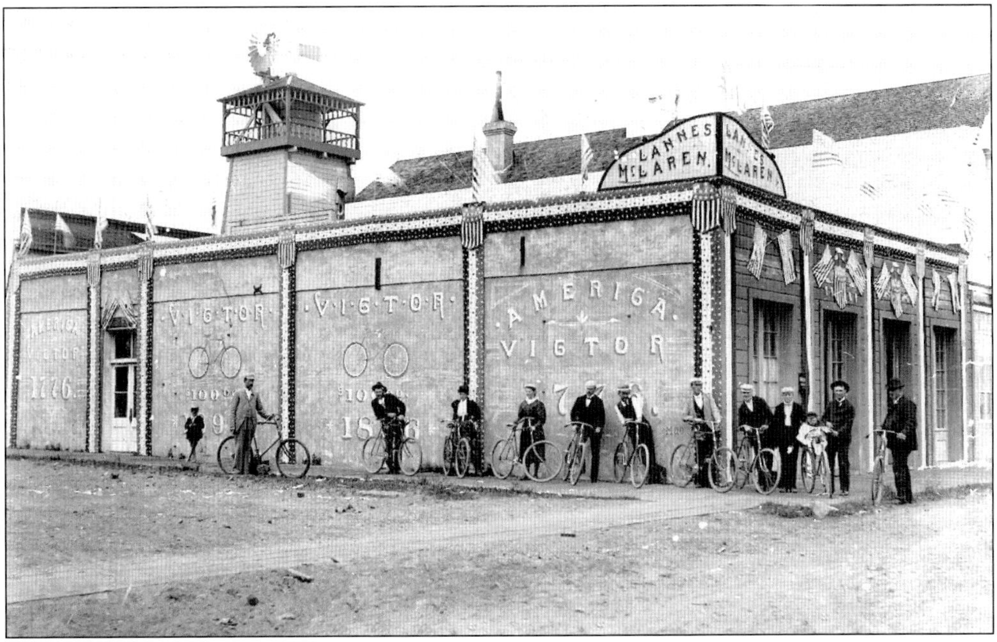

A typical Sunday morning scene during nice weather is captured here. The McLaren-Lannes store was on Front Street between H and I Streets and sold groceries and dry goods, millinery, men's and boy's clothing, hats and shoes, home furnishings, hardware, and crockery. It began as a boot and shoe store.

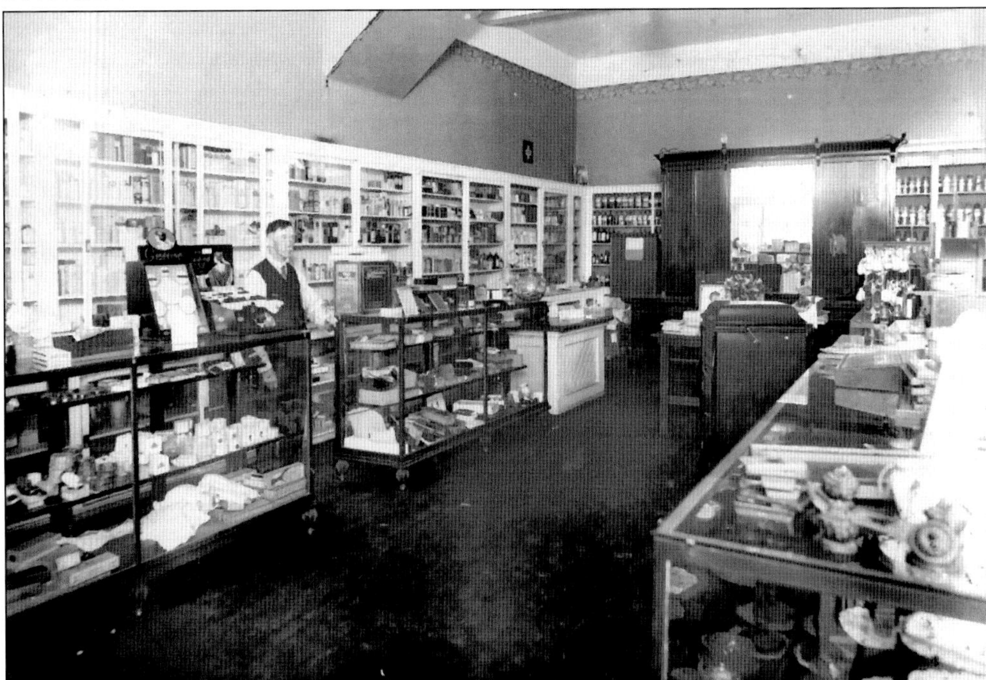

As the McLaren-Lannes store grew and expanded, it was divided into numerous specialized departments that offered a wide variety of products within their area of expertise—it had become a department store.

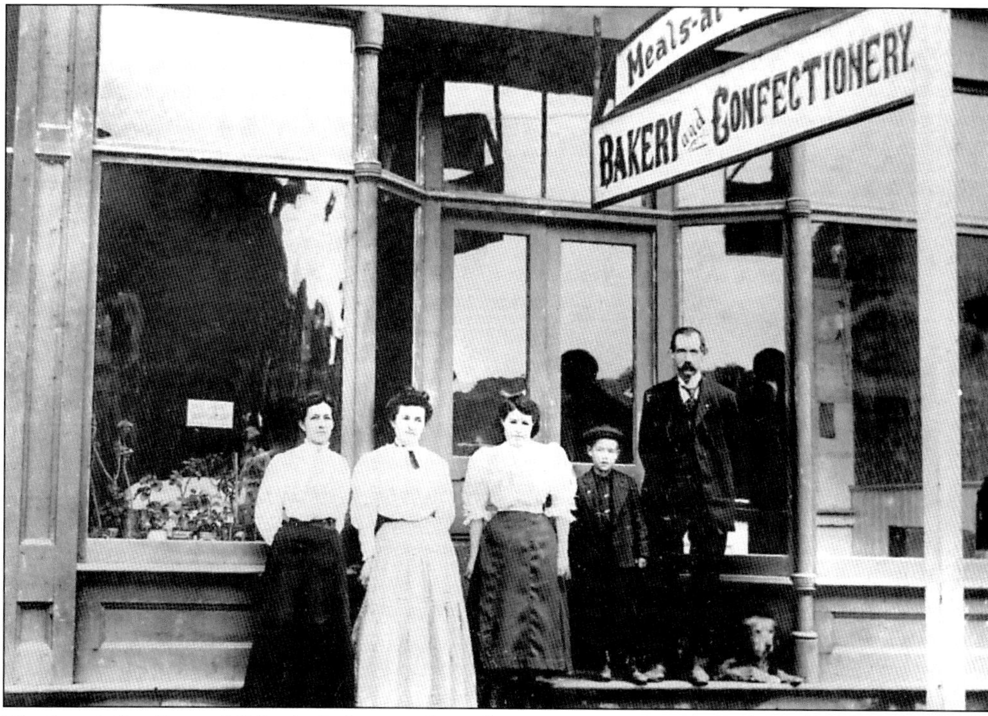

The Lewis family established a bakery and confectionery store on Second Street that also housed a restaurant. At the time, there were many single men working in the timber industry and retail field who enjoyed good, home-cooked food. There was also a large demand for baked goods and candies by the local families; thus the Lewis establishment was very popular.

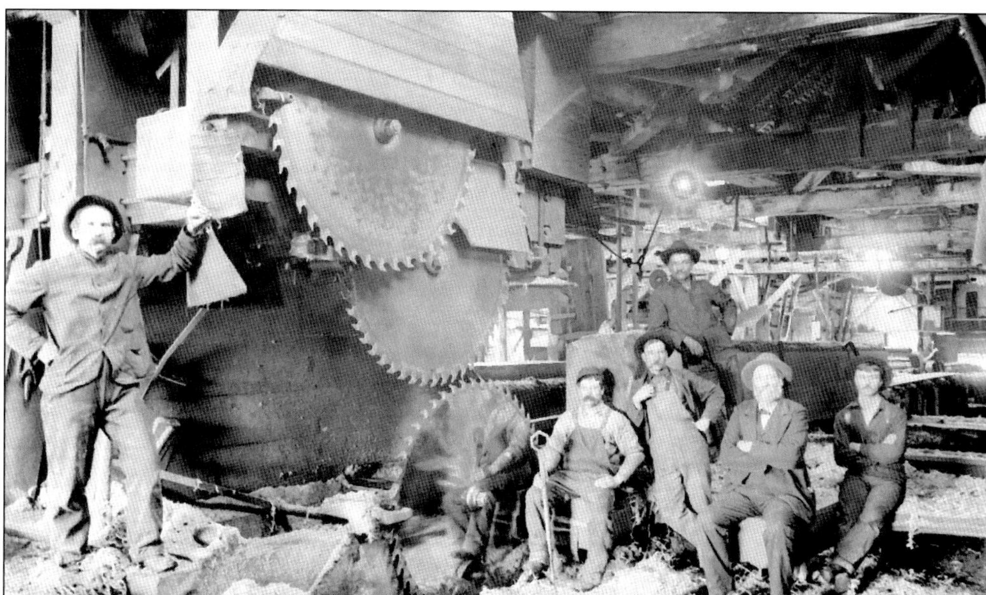

When Joseph Wall became a partner of the Hobbs, Wall and Company sawmill in 1893 there was major expansion to increase production; old equipment was upgraded and new equipment was added. Greenleaf Curtis, the sawmill foreman, is pictured second from the right.

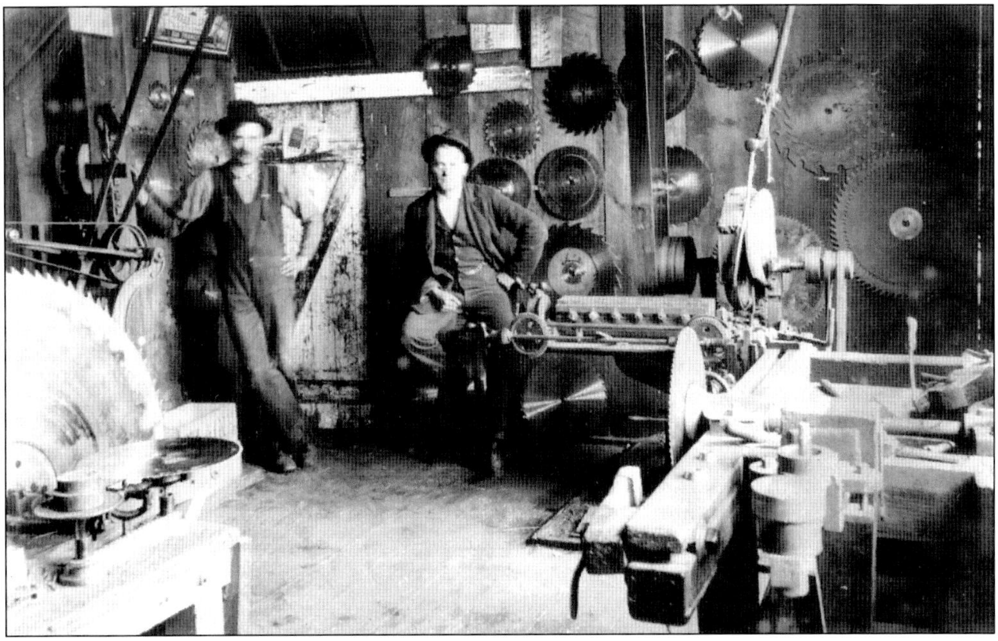

This is the filing room of the Hobbs, Wall and Company Box Factory as it looked in 1898. The next year, new equipment was installed and the box factory was modernized and expanded to increase production to meet a growing demand for wooden crates.

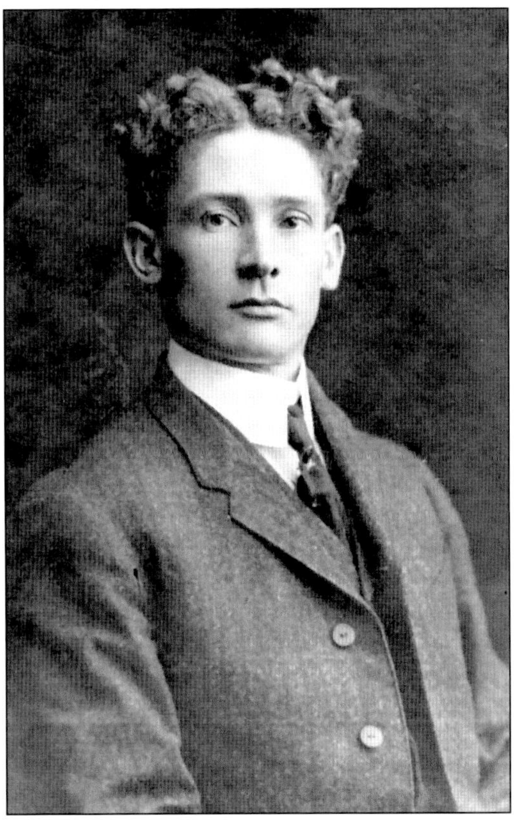

Dr. Ernest Fine was one of the early physicians in Crescent City when he arrived in 1899. His first office was in a one-room shack on the corner of Second and J Streets. During the rainy season, he had to travel to many of his patients, as the roads were very poor and became impassable for his patients. Many of his housecalls were made on horseback.

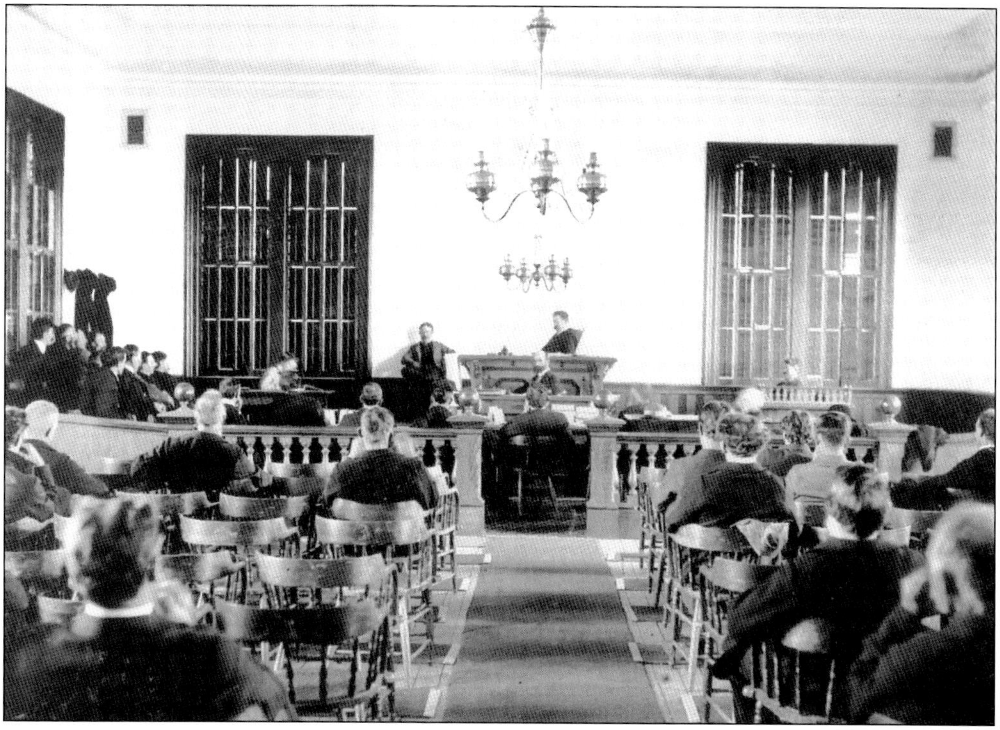

The Del Norte County Courthouse was well appointed and was a showplace featuring a great deal of well-executed woodworking. Judge Cutler was in charge of the courtroom in 1900, a time when the phrase "no law north of the Klamath" was popular. In other words, the law was very lax. Most of the trials dealt with local issues.

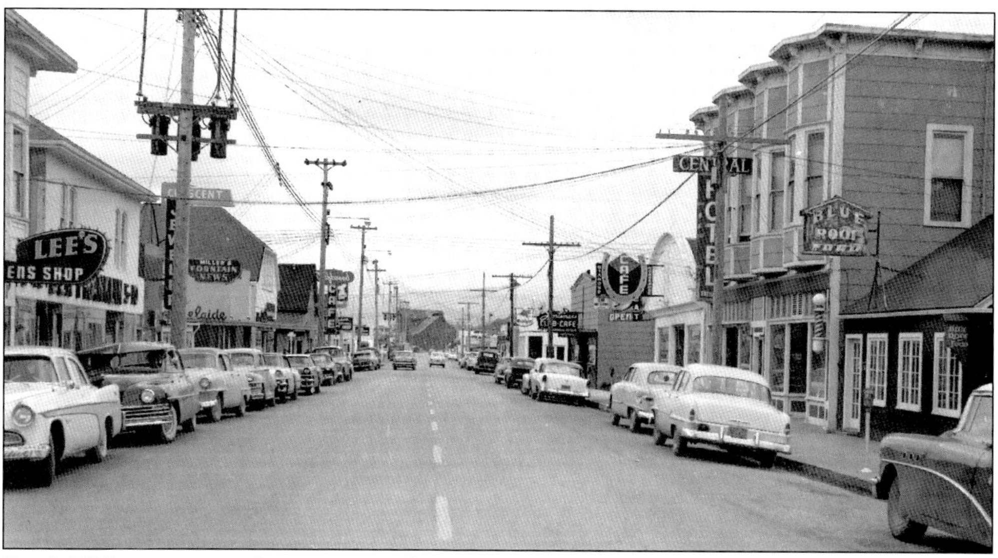

Frank Williams operated grocery, confectionery, and jewelry stores. As his business prospered, he had a building constructed on Second Street at I Street, known as the Williams Building. It housed his jewelry shop and a bank on the first floor, an assay office on the second floor, a law office, and the public library. Many years later, the building became the Central Hotel. The Williams Building is on the right.

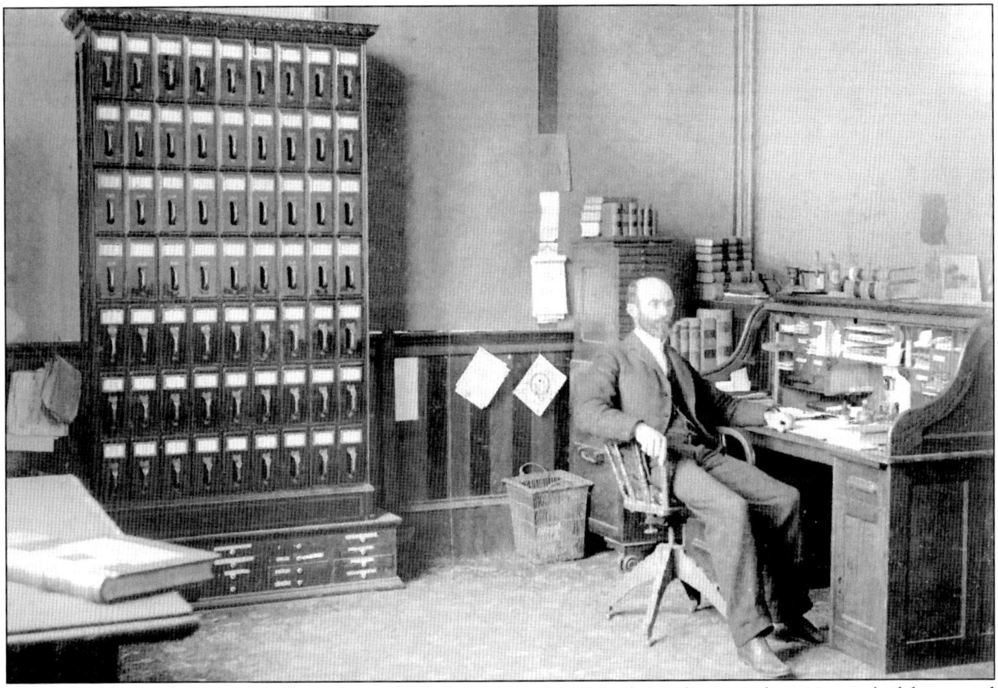

James McNulty was a founding attorney of the firm of Hirsch and McNulty. He scaled logs and did surveying when he finished school and finally decided to go into law after working with his stepfather, who was also an attorney. He served as county clerk and was the City Attorney for a number of years. The large wooden structure was the filing system of the day.

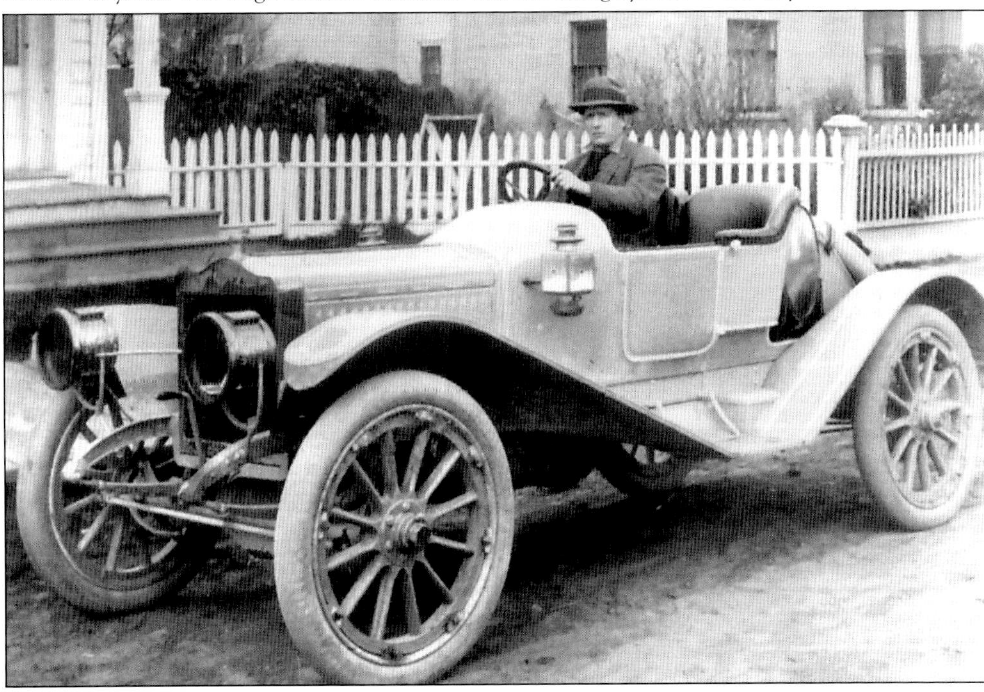

Dr Ernest Fine acquired one of the first automobiles in Del Norte County in 1905. It was a one-seat Ford roadster. It was painted bright red and was powered by a four-cylinder engine.

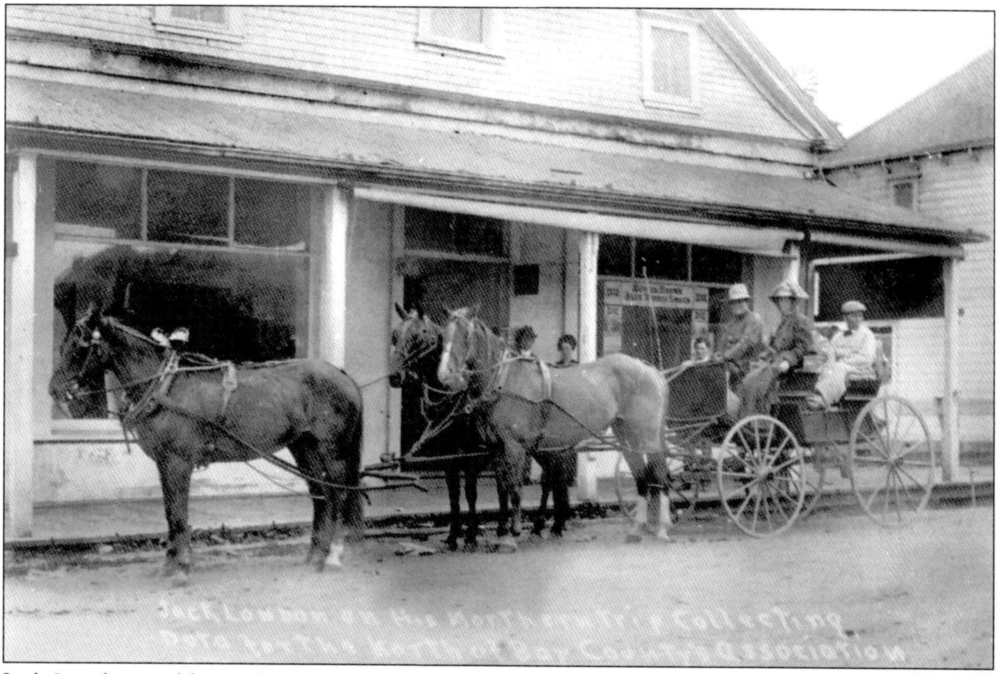

Jack London and his wife traveled through Del Norte County so he could write articles about the northern most parts of California. They stayed overnight in Crescent City and this picture was taken in front of the X. A. Phillips Store. Phillips used the picture for advertising and gave a free copy to all of his customers. Jack London wrote an article about the wilds and beauty of northern California, which appeared in the September 1911 issue of *Sunset* magazine.

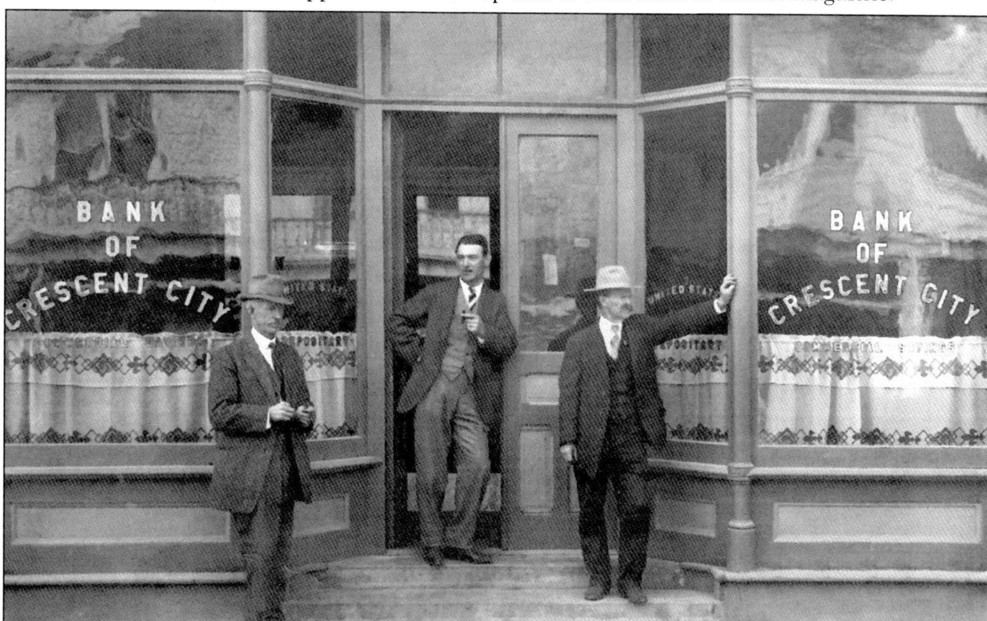

The first Bank of Crescent City was established in 1900 by Joseph B. Endert and four other partners. Located on the first floor of the Williams Building on Second Street, the bank was later sold to the Bank of Italy.

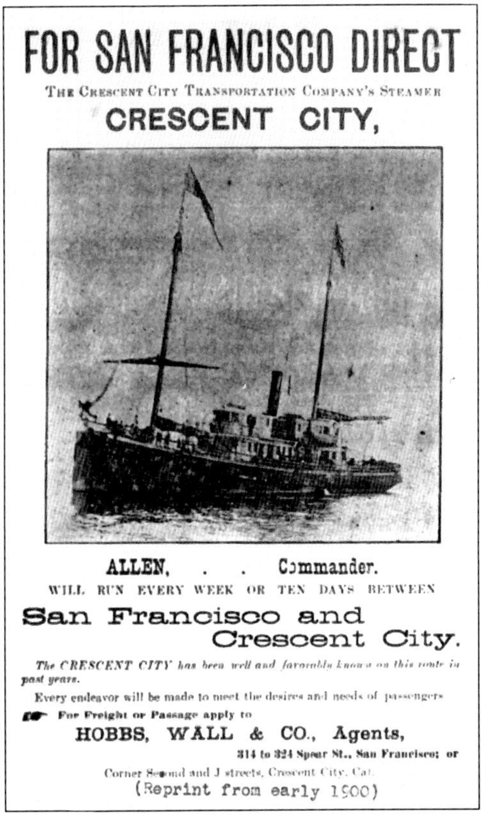

Most of the passenger and merchandise traffic into and out of Crescent City was by ship. By the early 1900s, ships arrived from and left for San Francisco on a fairly regular schedule every 7 to 10 days.

The Crescent City band poses for pictures before a concert performance at Citizens Plaza. Concerts were popular Sunday activities during the summer and always attracted a large number of people. It was an important way of socializing with friends and family.

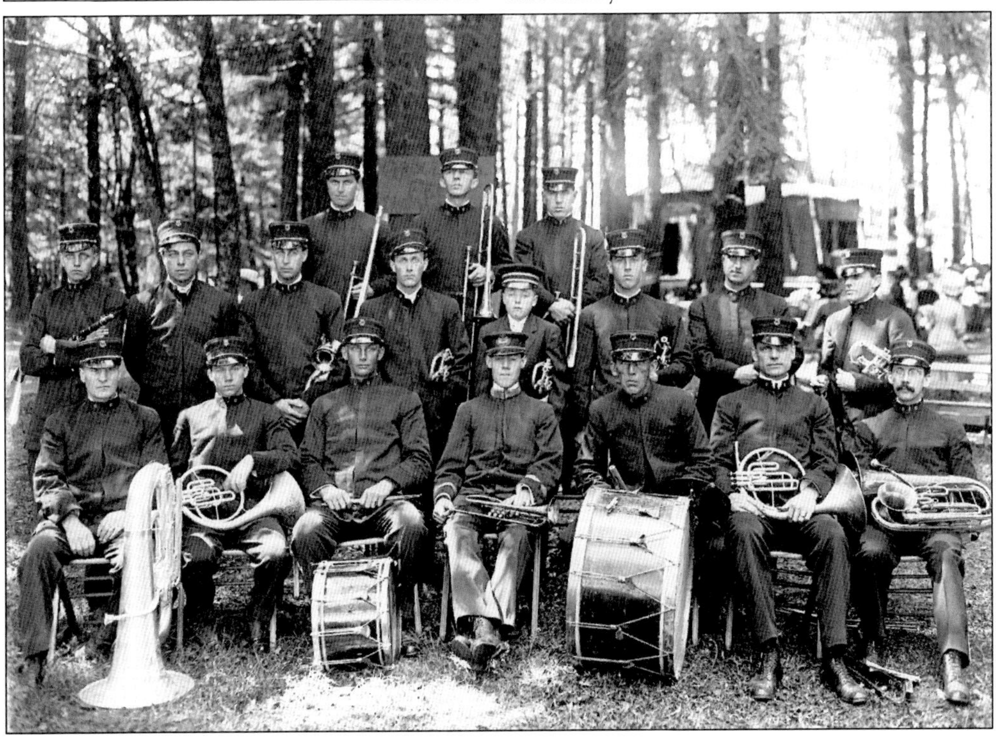

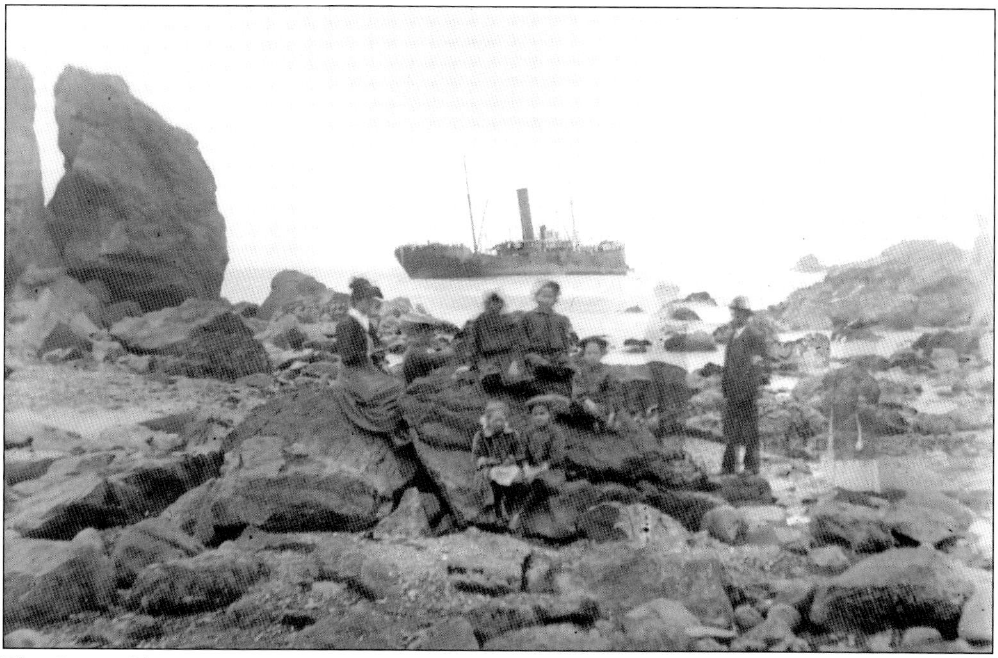

The *Queen Christina*, a tramp steamer, was one of the largest freighters on the Pacific coast. On October 19, 1907, the *Christina* sailed from San Francisco for Portland, Oregon. The next morning, in thick fog, she ran aground on the rocky shoal just south of Point St. George. She was stuck fast and abandoned. An early storm a few days later caused a split in the plates on the port side and the *Christina* could not be salvaged.

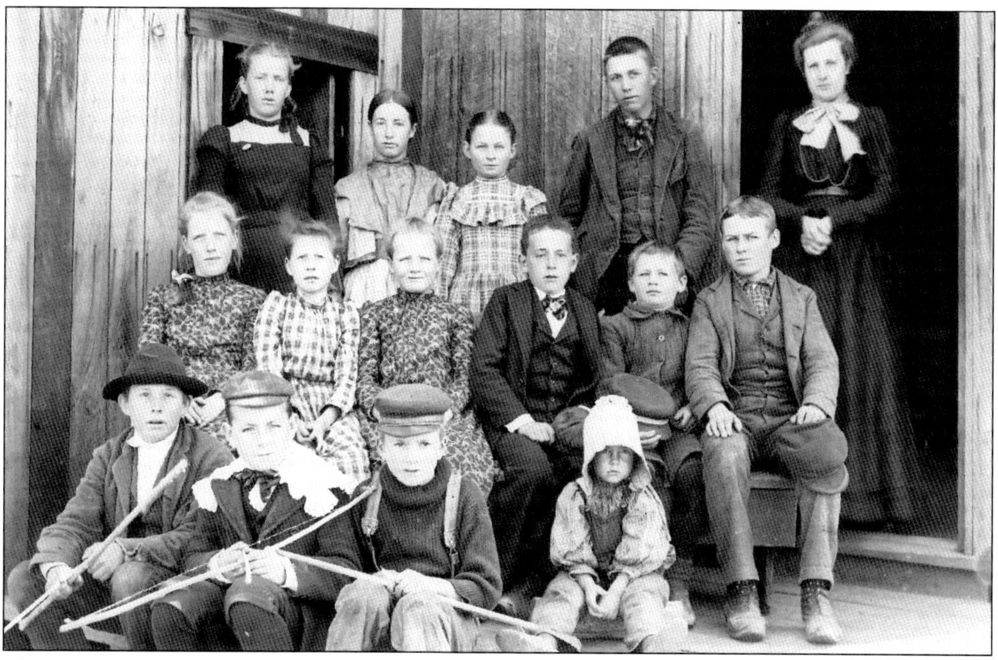

This is a class picture of the old Pine Grove School, located on the road from Crescent City to Fort Dick on what is now Northcrest Drive. The old school was torn down and replaced with the current Pine Grove School.

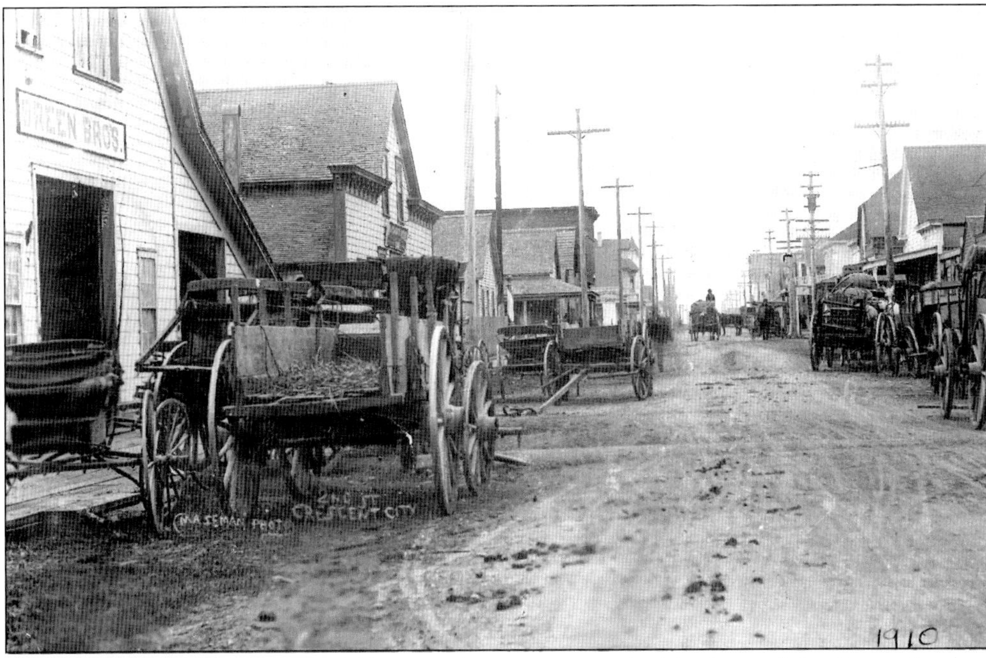

This scene looks east on Second Street with a carriage parked in front of the Breen Brothers Livery and Feed Stable. The Breen brothers, Will and Jack, ran the business. Jack was elected sheriff in 1913 but remained active in the livery business.

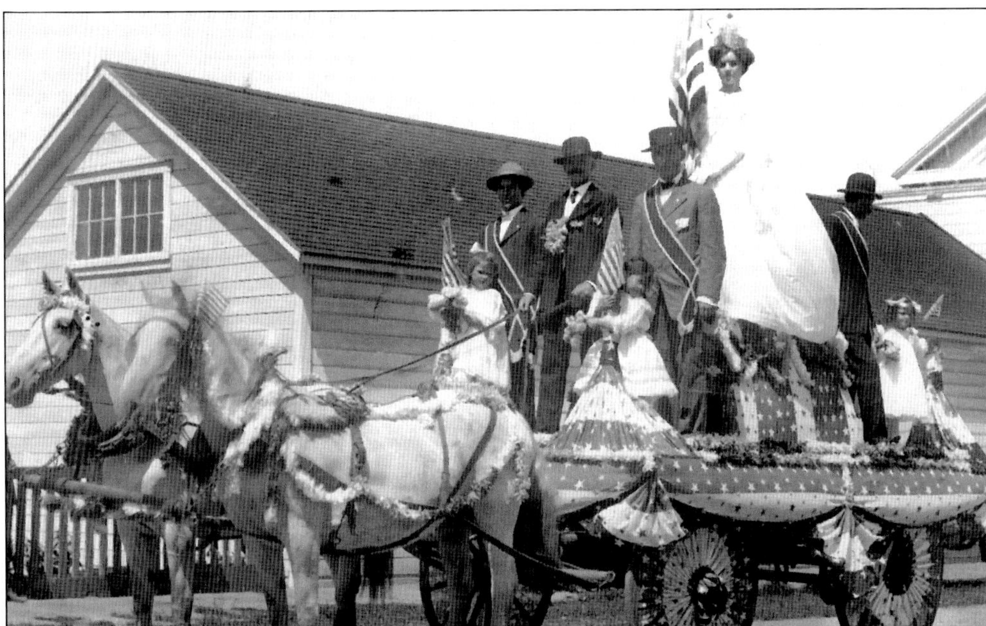

The Fourth of July parades and associated celebrations were very much a part of Crescent City culture. They were very popular and very necessary to the people of the city and drew folks from all over the county. They had been a tradition since the mid-1850s.

Two

SMITH RIVER
THE EARLY YEARS

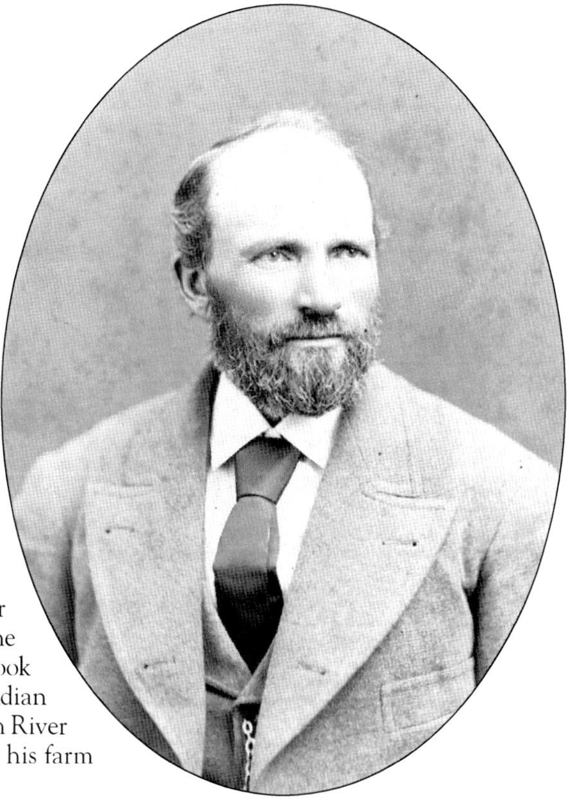

Henry Westbrook was born in Prussia in 1829. He immigrated to New York City in 1849, and in 1852 he started overland for Oregon. He worked a gold mine for a year before returning to farming for a while. He then decided to return to Sailor Diggings, but the day before he arrived, the Rogue River Indians declared war. Westbrook enlisted in the militia and fought in the Indian war. When it ended, he returned to Smith River and acquired 160 acres of land. By 1888, his farm consisted of 1,600 acres.

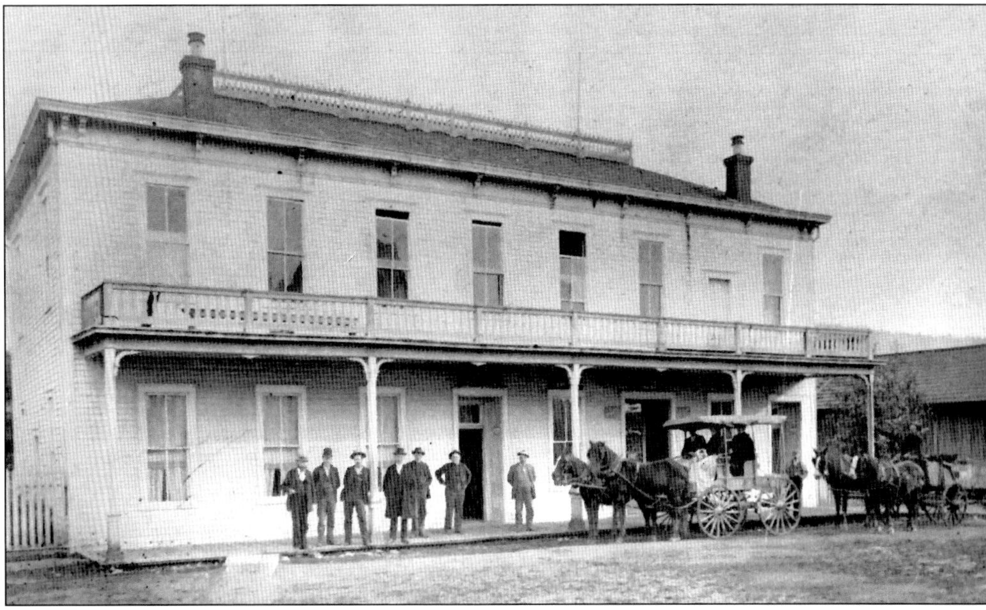

James Brooking left New Hampshire in 1839 at the age of 11 and spent eight years as a sailor before leaving the sea in San Francisco and becoming a miner. In 1856, he bought a ranch in Smith River and settled down. He built the Brooking Hotel in 1868, which housed the first post office in Smith River. Brooking was postmaster for 19 years and was justice of the peace for 21 years.

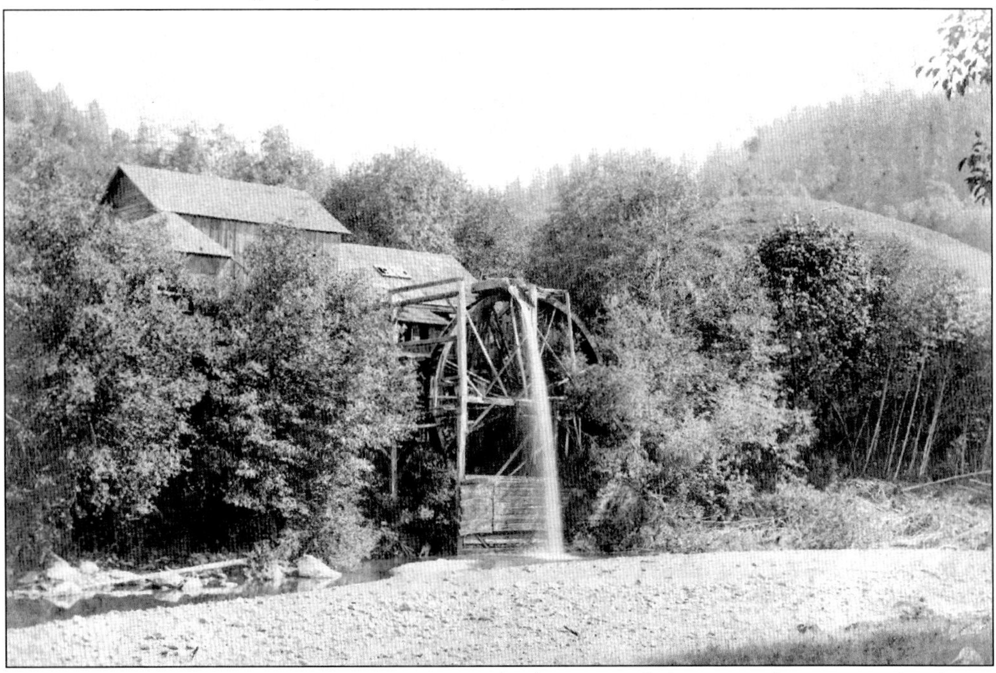

The first flour mill in Del Norte County was built on Smith River in the spring of 1859 on Rowdy Creek and was powered by a mammoth water wheel. In October, the mill was sold to N. O. Armington of Crescent City, who completed equipping it, and the first local grown wheat was ground into flour there in November of that year. The mill was shut down around 1885 as ranchers gave up growing wheat.

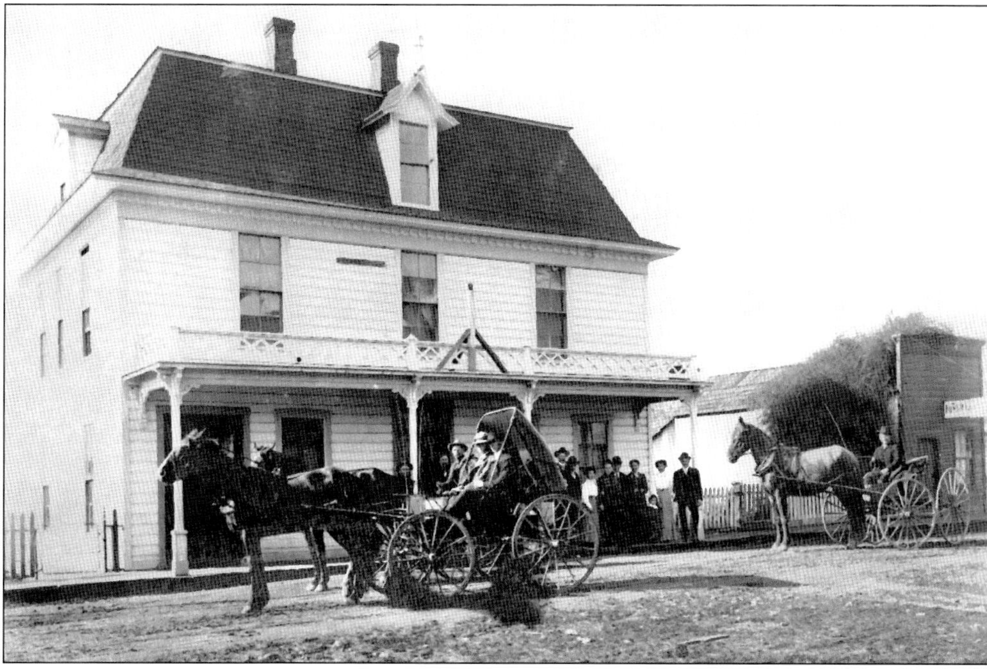

The Valley Hotel was built in 1883 by Daniel Otto, who sold it to James Andrew Jackson McVay in 1885. The hotel was on Fred Haight Drive. The hotel burned down around 1937.

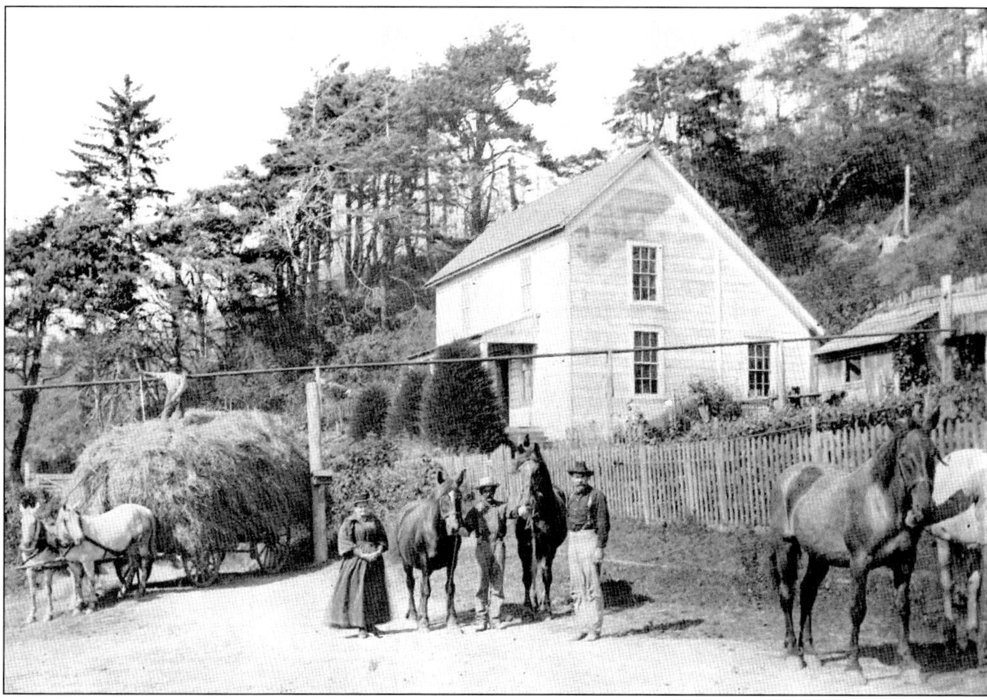

In 1881, Francis Burtschell acquired a 664-acre farm in Smith River. By 1893, it had grown to 992 acres and was a dairy ranch, which consisted of the main house, three large barns, and a huge dairy house. This is a picture of the Burtschell family in front of the farm even though they lived in Crescent City because the Smith River farm was leased out.

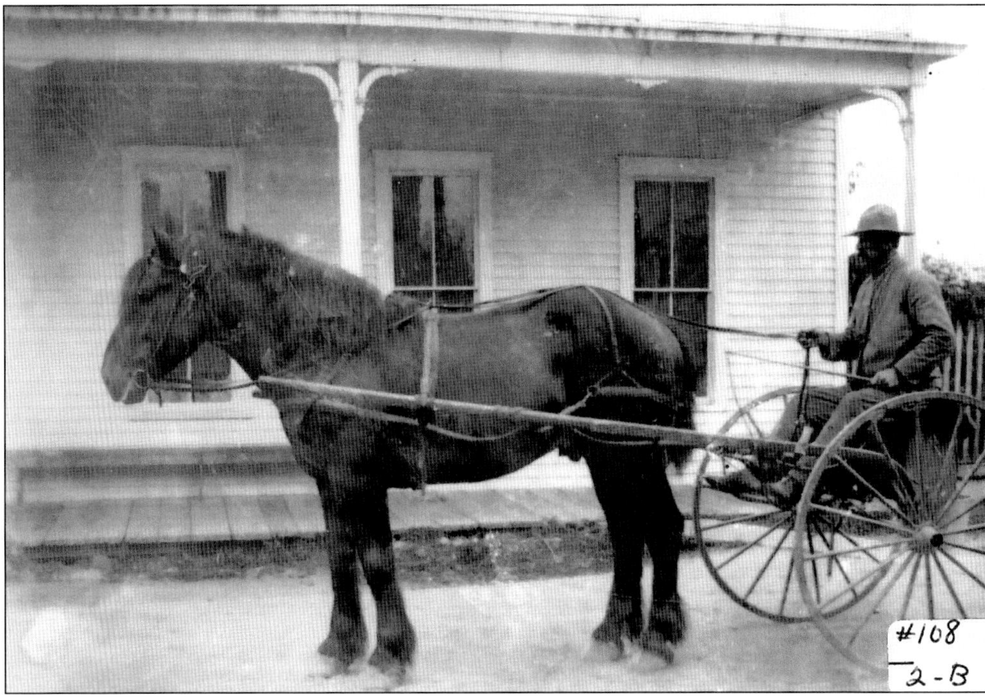

Thomas J. T. Berry arrived in Crescent City in 1878 and worked for Francis Burtschell in his livery stable. By 1890, Berry took over the business and called it the Eclipse Livery and Feed Stable. He had a number of thoroughbred horses, but his most prized one was Dexter Moore, shown here in front of the Brooking Hotel pulling a sulky driven by Berry.

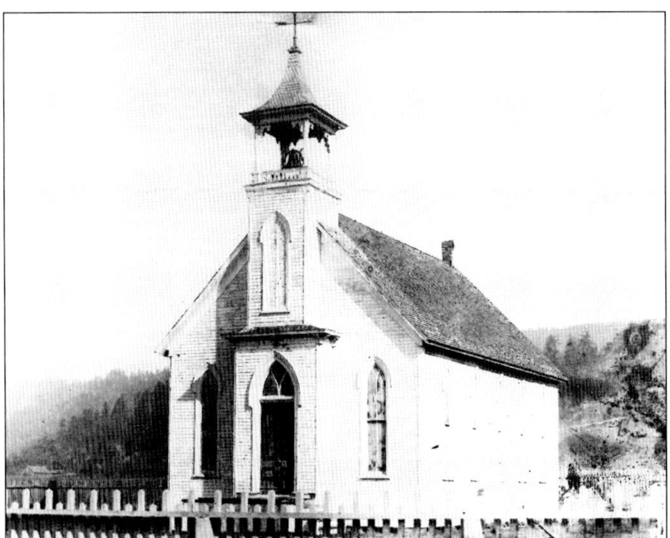

Construction of the Smith River Methodist Church began in 1878 and was completed in 1879. The church was dedicated on August 18, 1880, and stood almost 90 years before it was completely destroyed by fire in 1969. It was started by an arsonist who had also started a fire at St. Paul's Episcopal church in Crescent City, which was quickly put out. The arsonist was arrested the next morning in Brookings after he tried to start another fire at the Trinity Lutheran Church.

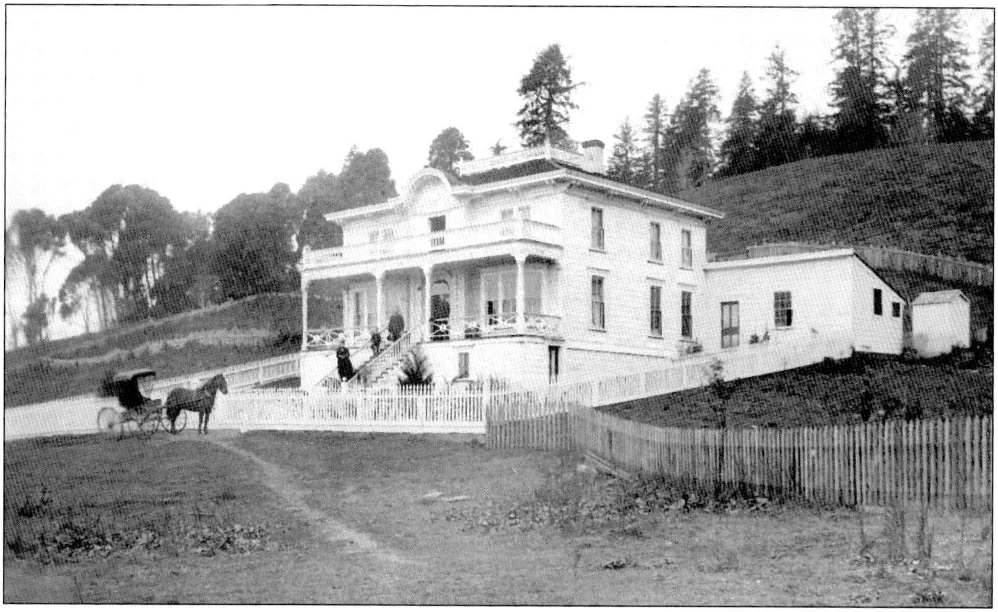

William Westbrook built this stately home on a rise with a commanding view of the Smith River Valley. It was considered one of the finest in Del Norte County. Westbrook's ranch consisted of over 1,200 acres and was located only one mile from Smith River Corners. He also owned a large supply store in Smith River Corners.

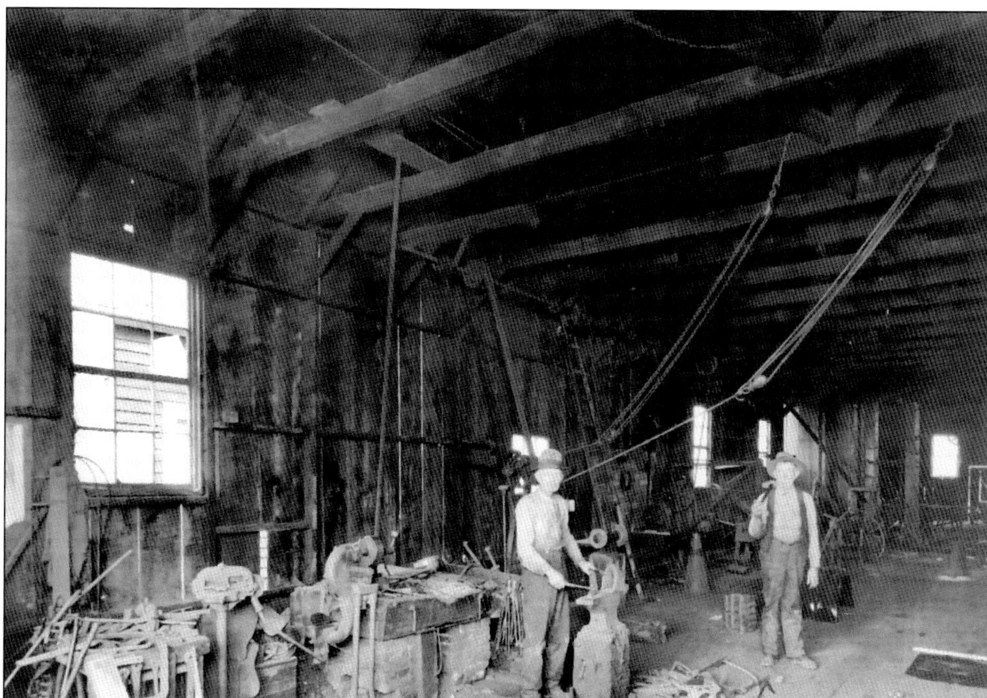

Carl "Cash" Lockwood was the owner and smithy of the Lockwood Blacksmith shop in Smith River Corners. He provided the repairs needed on equipment for all of the ranches in the Smith River Valley. His shop was located on Fred Haight Drive, which was the main highway at the time.

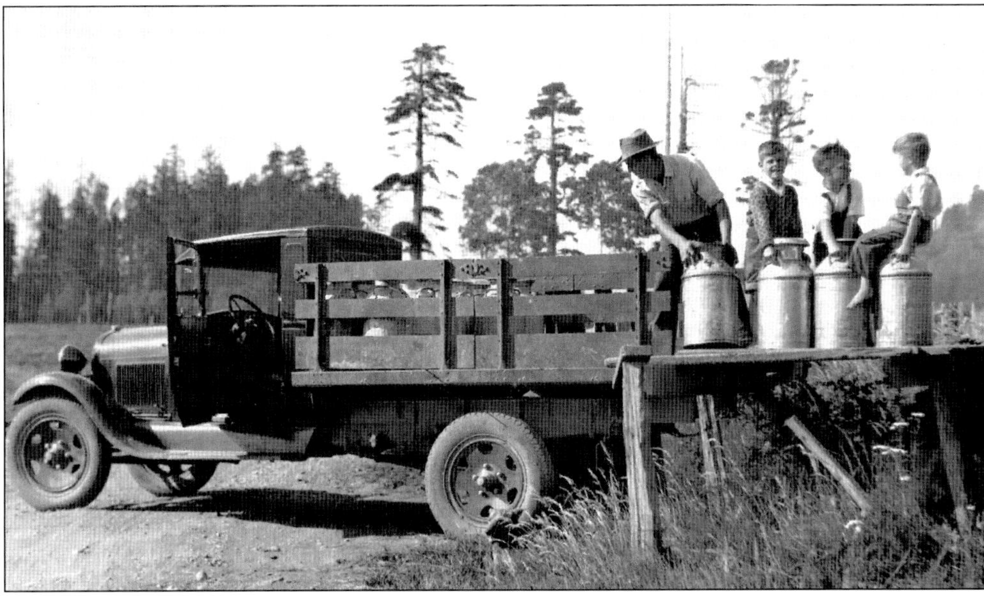

Taking the milk to the Crescent Creamery in Smith River was a daily task. Al Henry loads milk cans onto his truck with the help of two of his sons and a friend of theirs. The Crescent Creamery was owned by brothers William and Henry Westbrook, Thomas Duffy, and Francis Burtschell. The creamery could handle 40,000 pounds of milk a day, which was then turned into butter.

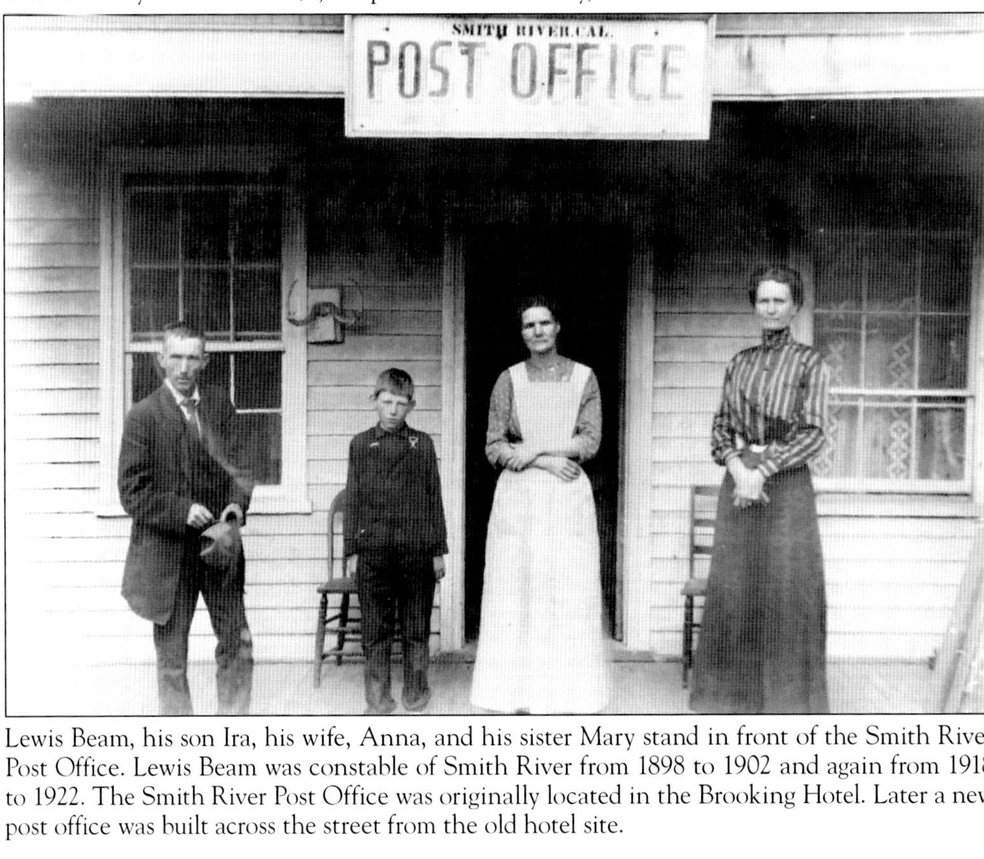

Lewis Beam, his son Ira, his wife, Anna, and his sister Mary stand in front of the Smith River Post Office. Lewis Beam was constable of Smith River from 1898 to 1902 and again from 1918 to 1922. The Smith River Post Office was originally located in the Brooking Hotel. Later a new post office was built across the street from the old hotel site.

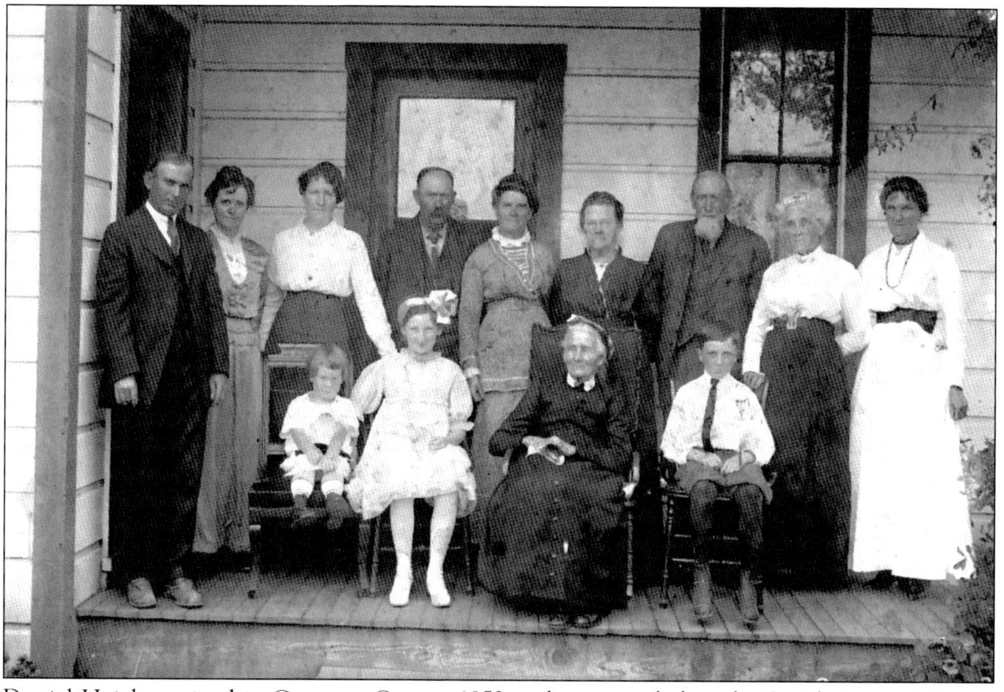

Daniel Haight arrived in Crescent City in 1853 and soon settled in the Smith River Valley as the first white settler. He married Fanny McVay Adams in 1868. This photograph was taken on the porch of their home.

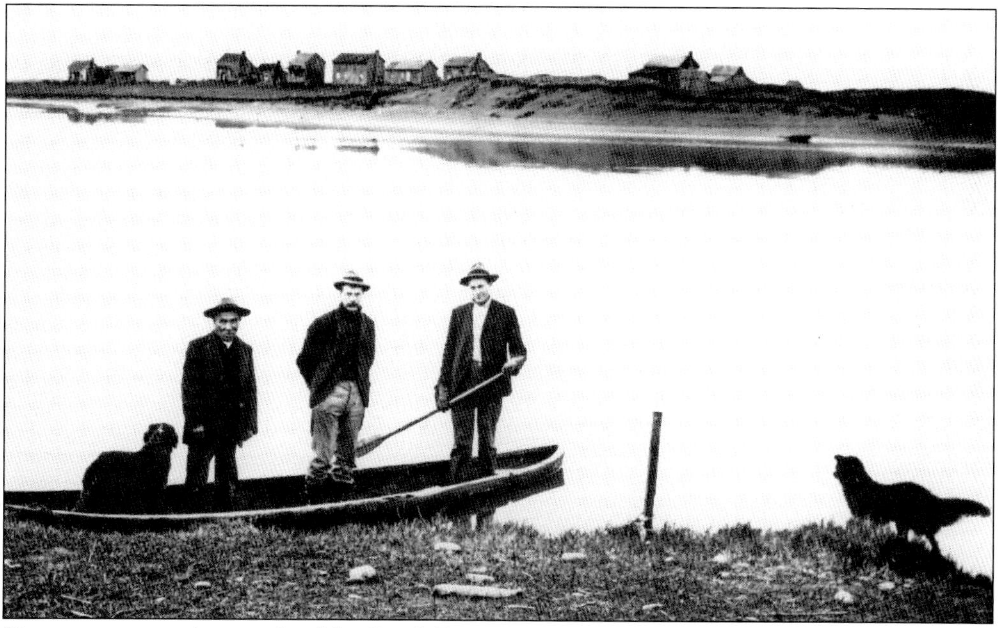

Canoe outings at the mouth of the Smith River were popular pastimes. The men in the boat are Rock Billy, E. Kamberg, and Ray Plaisted. In the background is Stundosen Village, a place the Tolowa had been allowed to develop on an island in the Smith River in 1892. By 1903, the island began to erode badly, and by 1906, all that was left of the village was two houses. The Stundosen cemetery was relocated to the mainland.

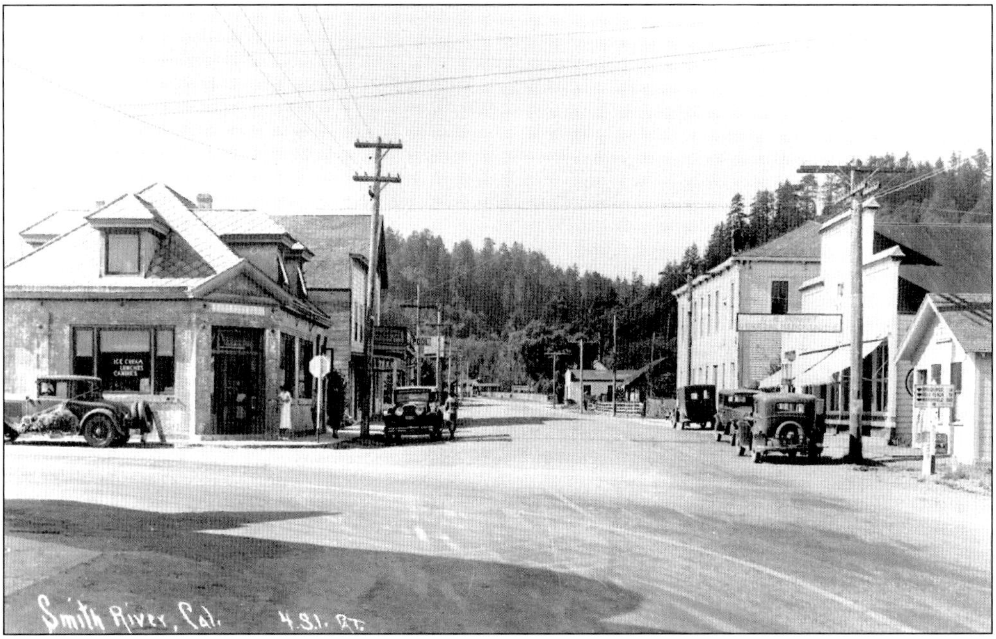

By 1908, the town of Smith River was a thriving ranching community. The store on the corner had originally been a bank but later became an ice cream parlor, restaurant, and candy store. The bank sign over the door was never removed.

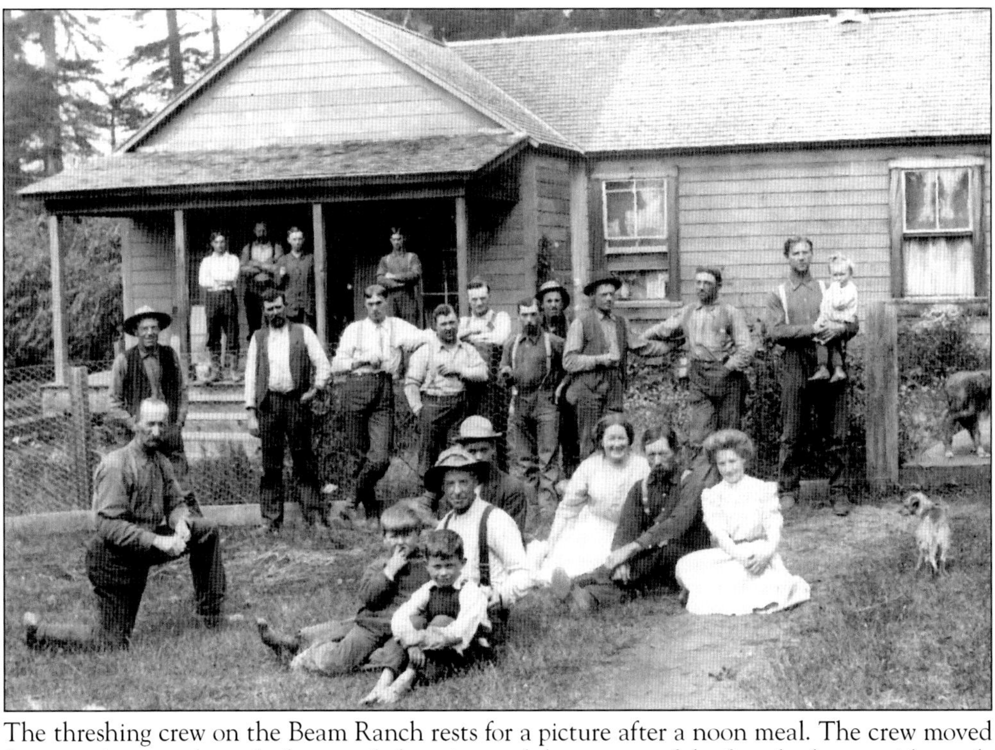

The threshing crew on the Beam Ranch rests for a picture after a noon meal. The crew moved from ranch to ranch, as the hay needed cutting and the women of the farm had to provide meals while they were working the ranch.

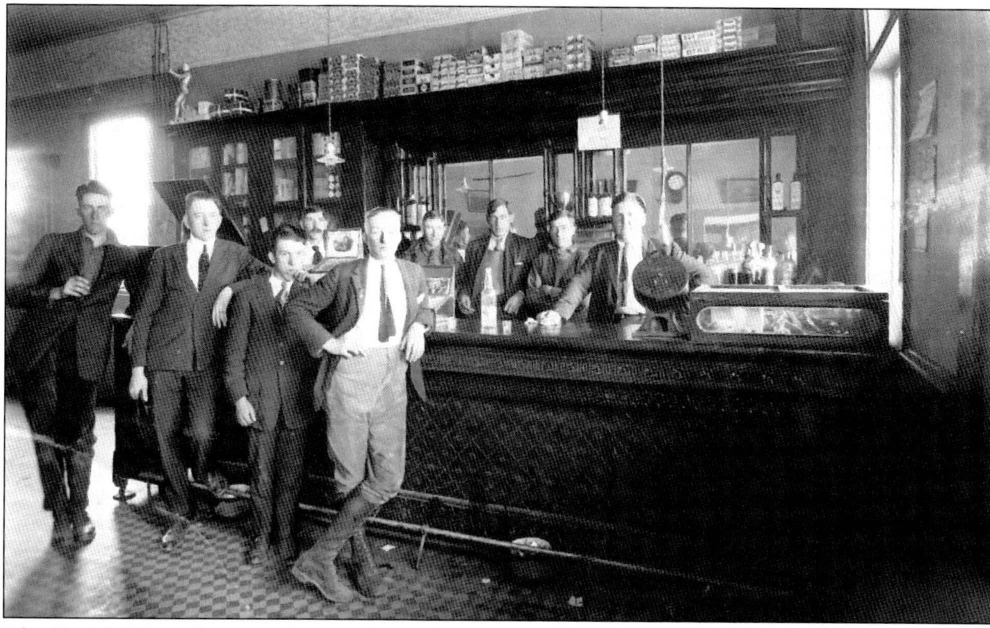

The Smith River Bar was the gentleman's watering hole. It was located in the billiards parlor building on Main Street. The clientele was usually well dressed, and everyone knew each other. It was a place to discuss local issues of the day and ranching news. Many business deals were also consummated here.

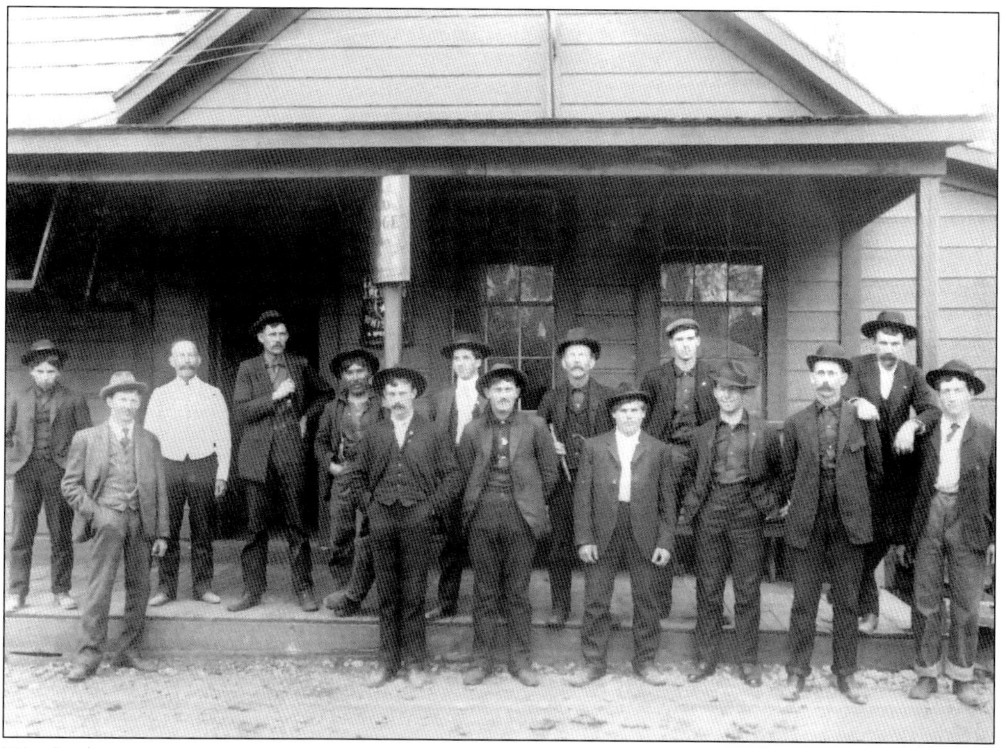

Wes Duley's was a boardinghouse and a bar in Fort Dick that catered mainly to loggers working in the area and local ranchers. Duley also owned a bar in Smith River.

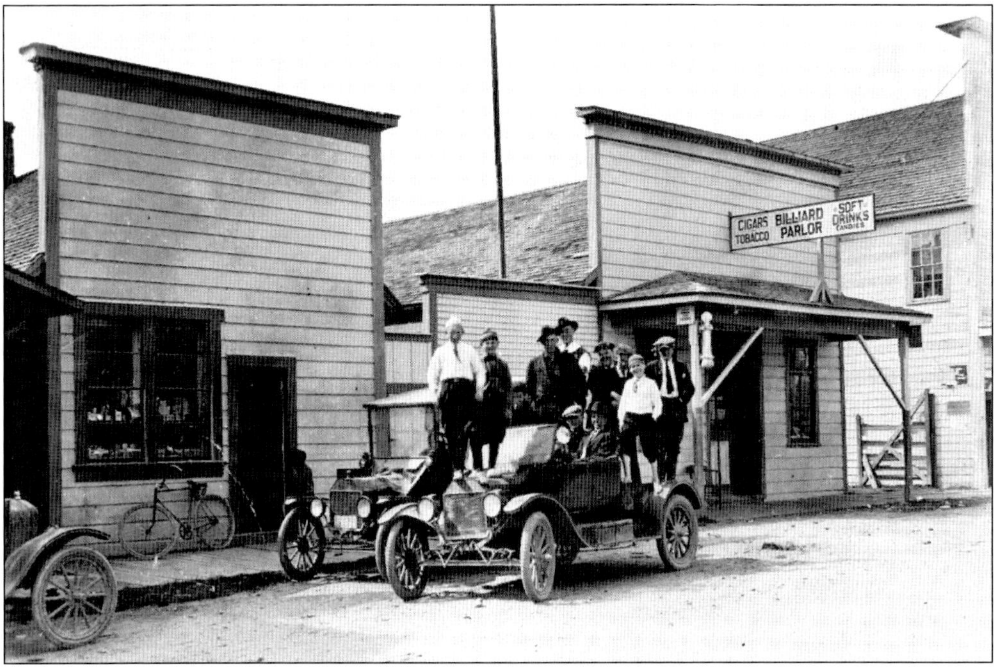

Main Street in Smith River is shown here in 1910 with the local billiard parlor in the background. This side of the street had a sidewalk and was the only place where the children could roller skate. Around 1937, a fire swept through part of downtown Smith River and destroyed all of the buildings shown in this picture.

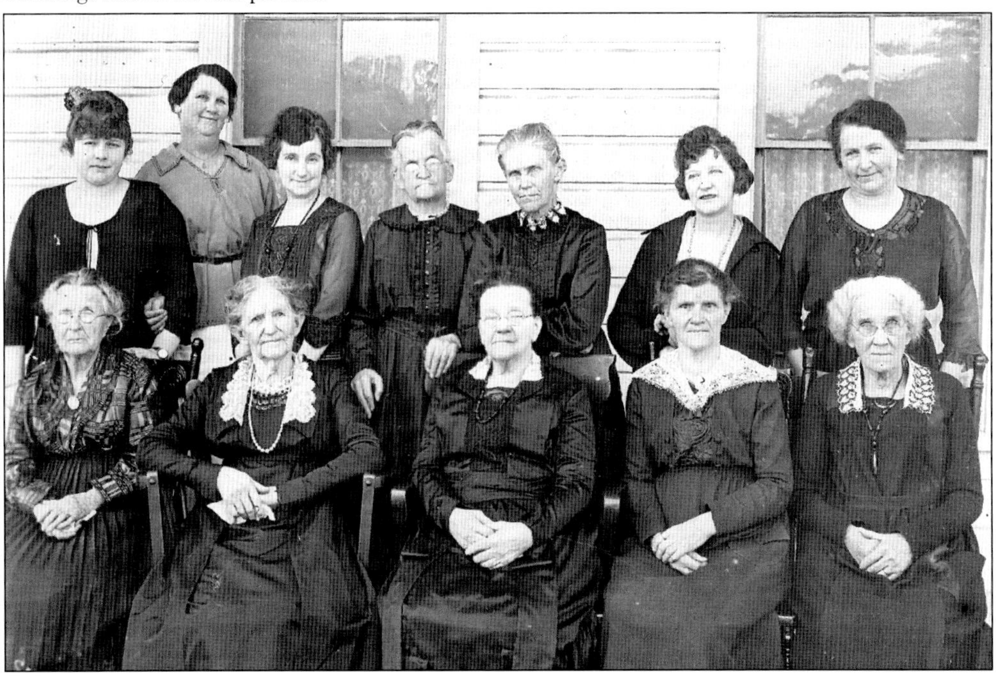

The Christian Woman's Society of Smith River was organized shortly after the Smith River Methodist Church was dedicated in 1880. The ladies organized and were in charge of many social functions for the church. This picture was taken in 1922.

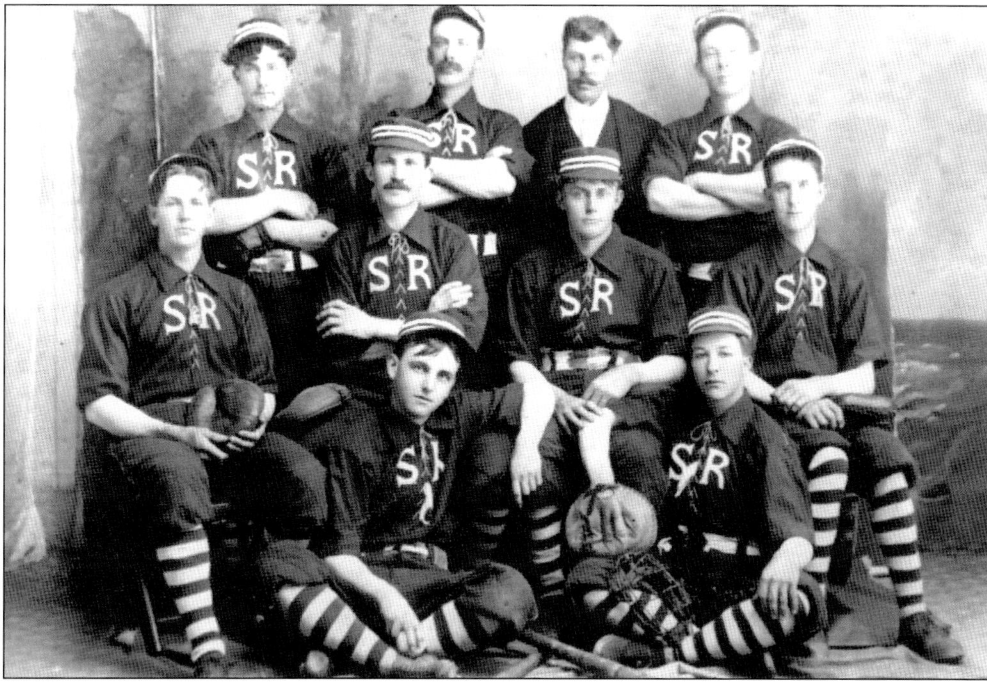

In the first part of the 20th century, baseball became the king of sports. Smith River had a very active team, and there were several teams in Del Norte County that played other squads from southern Oregon and northern California.

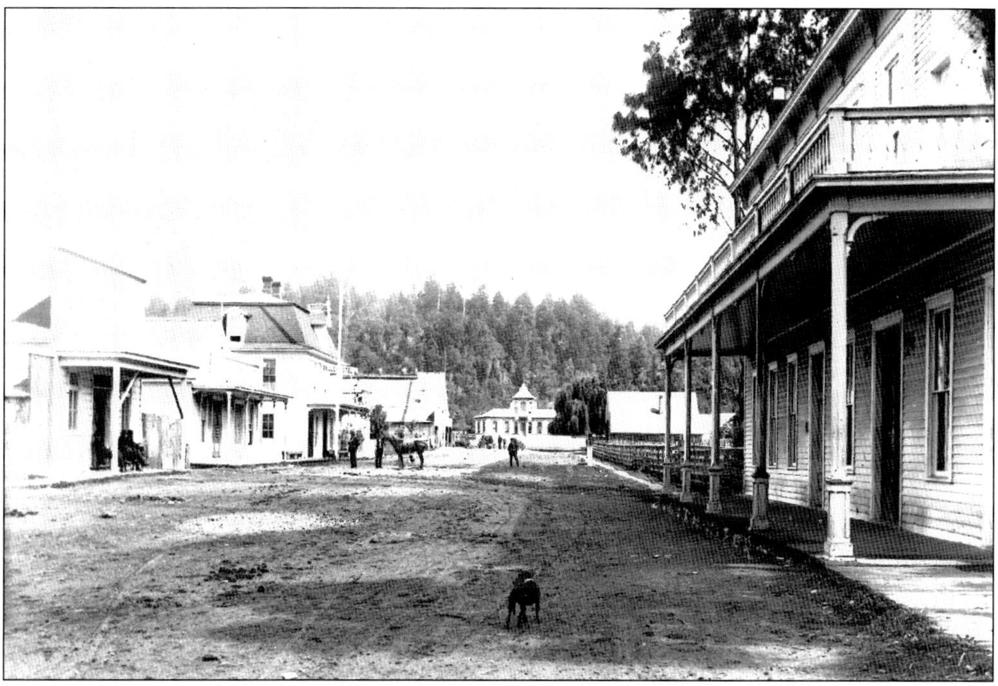

Main Street was a gravel-surfaced road originally called the Roosevelt, then it was Highway 101, and ultimately a route was constructed that bypassed town. The Brookings Hotel is on the right.

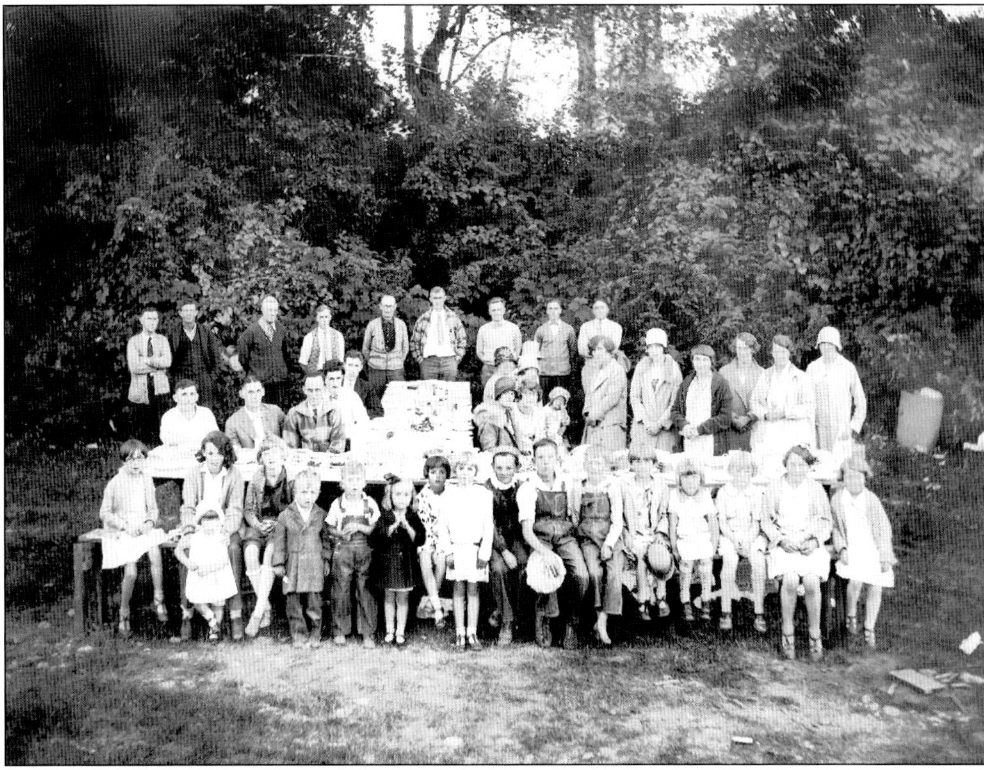

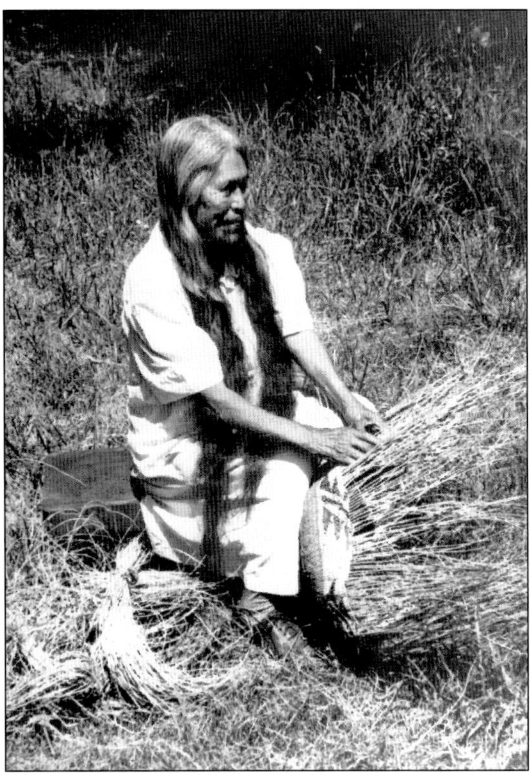

Employees of the Golden State Creamery and their families enjoy a summertime picnic on Rowdy Creek in 1928. The picnic was an annual event and lasted up to a week. Some families would pitch tents at the site and stay the entire time. The men would drive to the picnic site after work, while women would prepare meals and tend to the children.

Nellie Charlie, a Tolowa Indian, was an expert basket maker. She exhibited the fine skills necessary to produce the numerous intricate patterns used by the Tolowa weavers. She lived at the Smith River Rancheria.

Three

Del Norte Country Becomes Settled

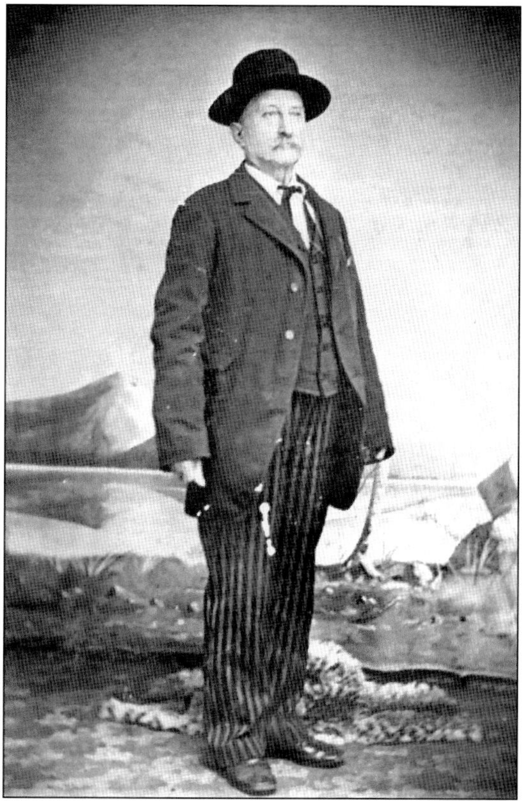

Horace Gasquet arrived in Crescent City from France in 1853. His first venture was carrying goods and supplies by pack train from Crescent City to the interior and mines operating there. In 1857, he purchased Mace's Ferry and Station located at the mouth of the North Fork of the Smith River. He also bought 160 acres on the north side of the Middle Fork and 160 acres on the flat on the south side of the river. Thus was born the village of Gasquet.

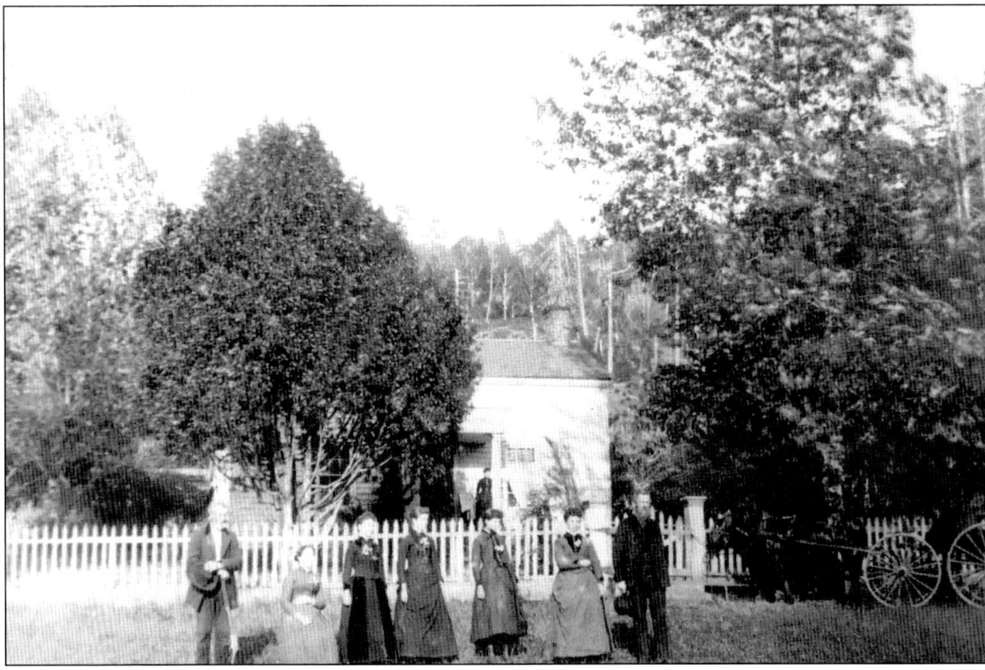

John Nickel arrived in Del Norte County in 1855 with his mother and uncle. His father died of "the fever" (probably yellow fever) on the trip west from Ohio. John had just turned 18 and was not old enough to file a land claim for himself, so his mother and uncle both filed adjacent claims in Elk Valley and deeded them to John when he became of age. By 1876, John Nickel had built the land into a large and prosperous dairy ranch.

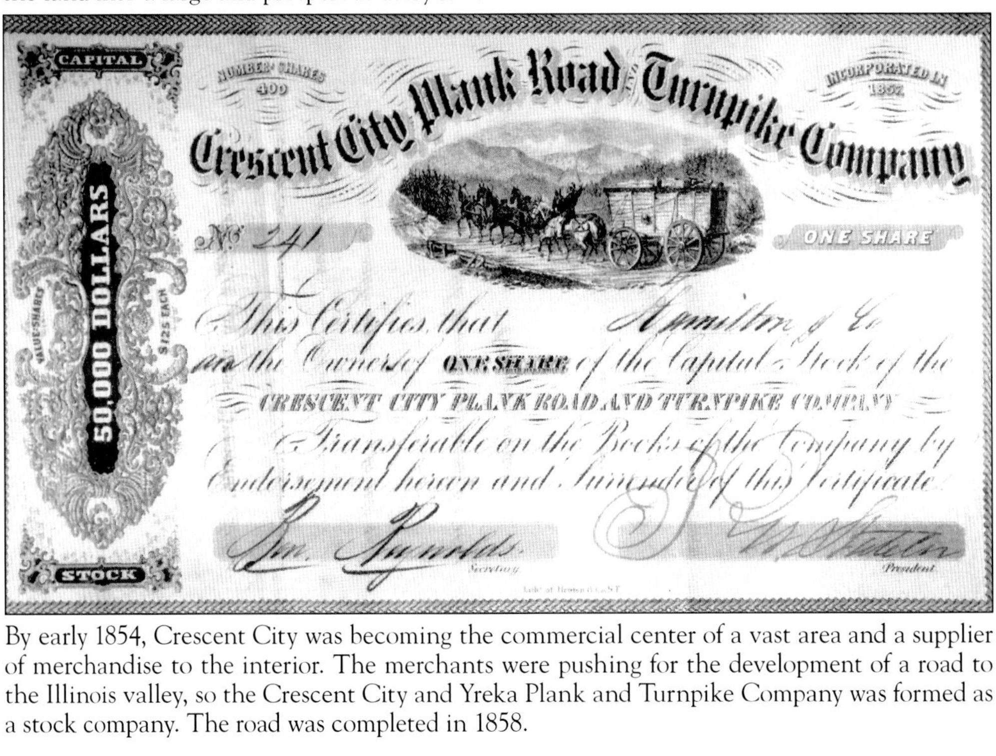

By early 1854, Crescent City was becoming the commercial center of a vast area and a supplier of merchandise to the interior. The merchants were pushing for the development of a road to the Illinois valley, so the Crescent City and Yreka Plank and Turnpike Company was formed as a stock company. The road was completed in 1858.

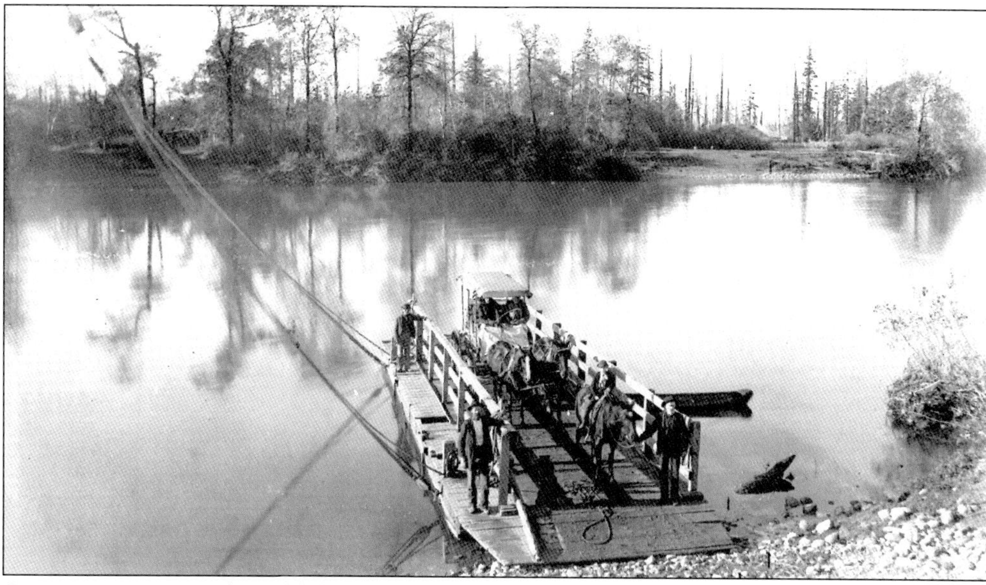

George Henry Peacock established a ranch on the first toll road in the county called the Peacock Station. He operated this ferry across the Smith River for a few years as well as a pack train to haul materials to the Oregon Territory. He sold the ferry operation and the land to the Baileys. At the time of this picture Henry Higgins was operating the ferry.

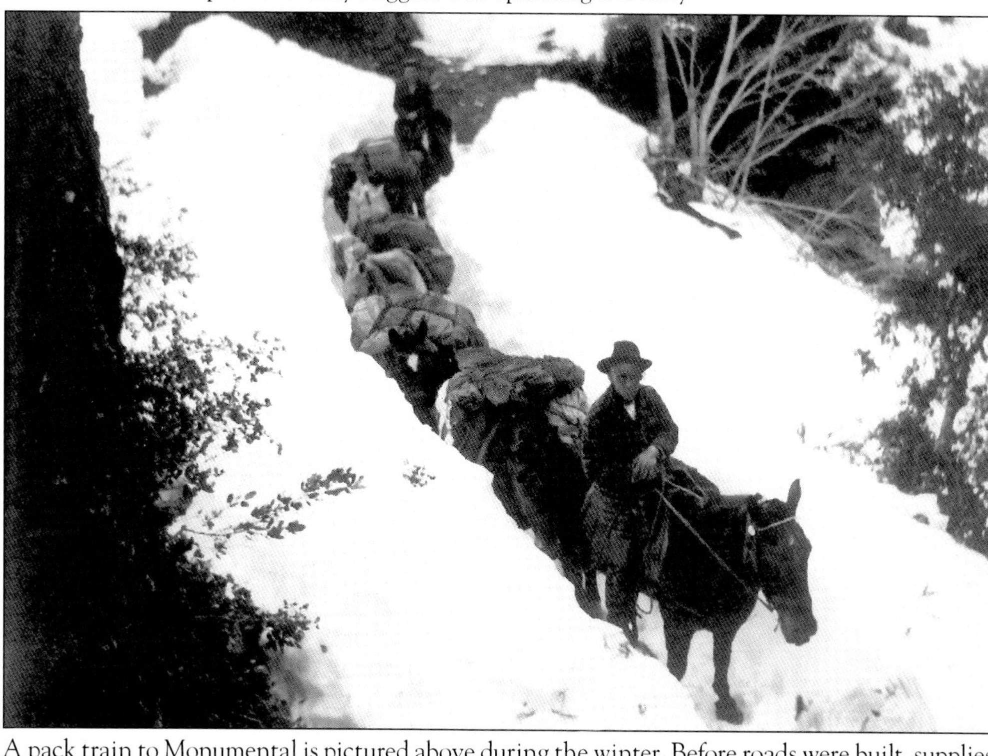

A pack train to Monumental is pictured above during the winter. Before roads were built, supplies and materials had to be brought to the mining towns by pack trains. They operated over narrow trails and were very difficult to manage during the winter months when there was a great deal of snow.

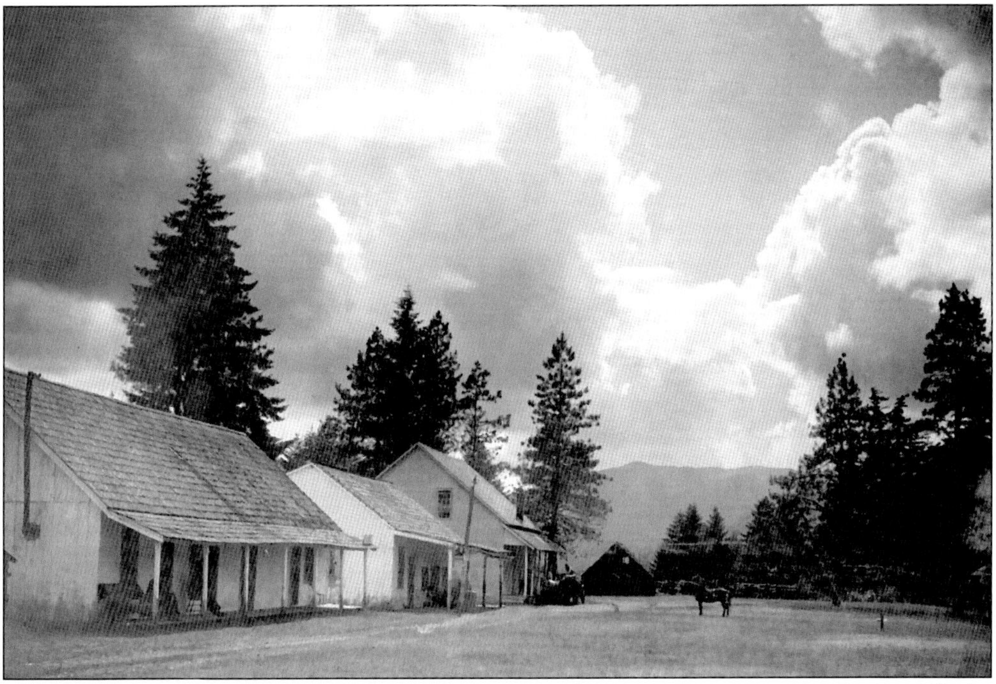

Horace Gasquet arrived in Crescent City in 1855 and became a citizen in 1860. In 1857, he purchased Mace's Ferry and Station, plus an additional 360 acres. The first building was a large cabin constructed in 1858, which provided travelers with lodging and a rest stop. His main business was transporting goods by pack train from Crescent City to the interior mines.

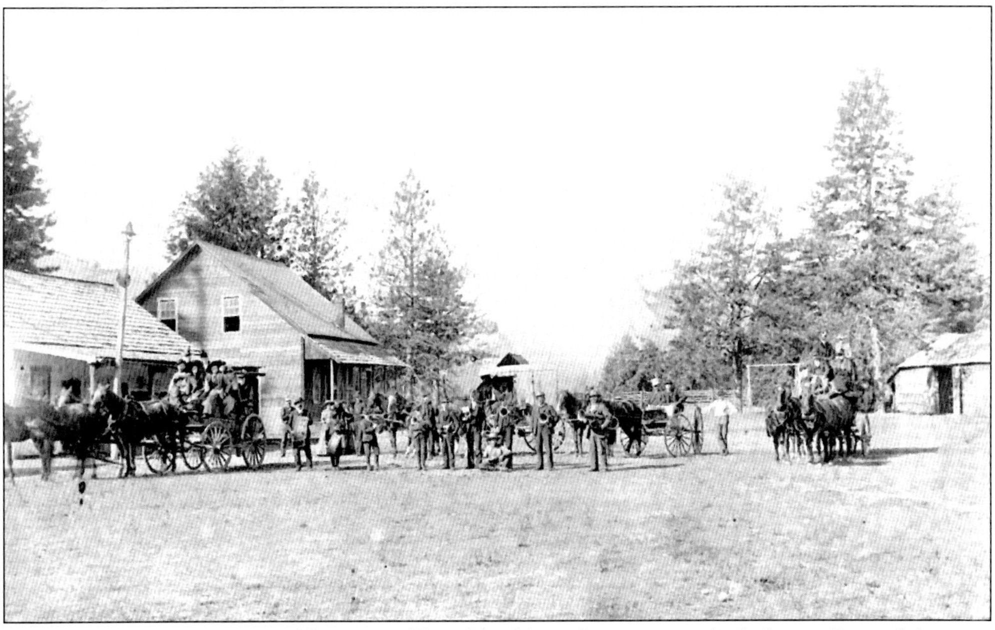

In 1860, Gasquet constructed his second hotel building that consisted of a lower floor of sleeping rooms. His next building, Redwood House, had bedrooms on the first floor and a dance hall on the second floor. As the popularity of the area and revenues increased, Gasquet expanded his village.

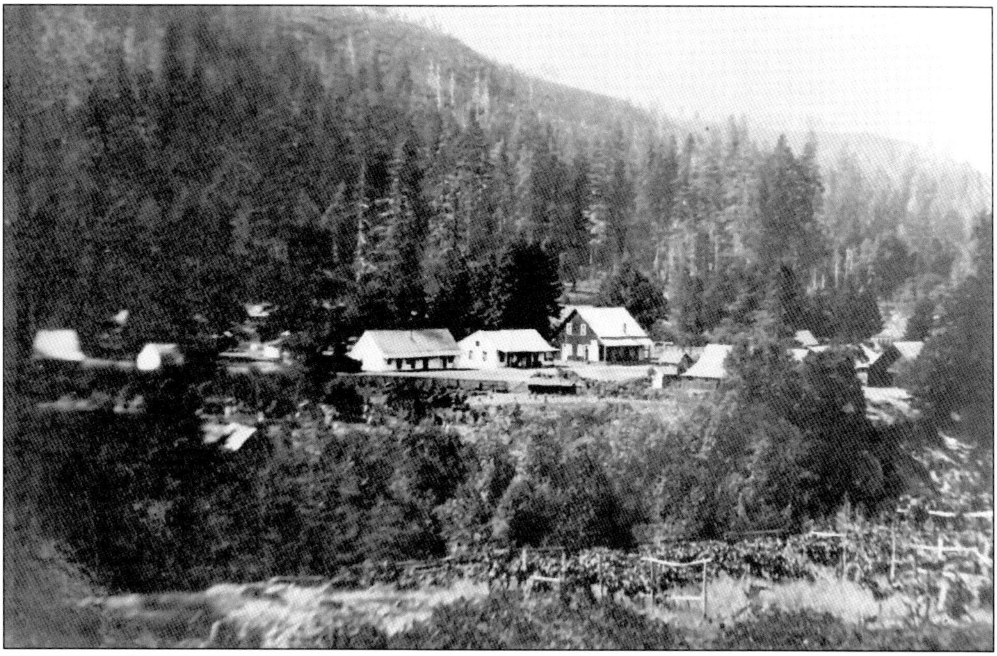

This view of Gasquet Village shows the extensive vineyards in the foreground. Horace Gasquet imported many different varieties of grapes from France to establish his vineyards, which produced excellent wines.

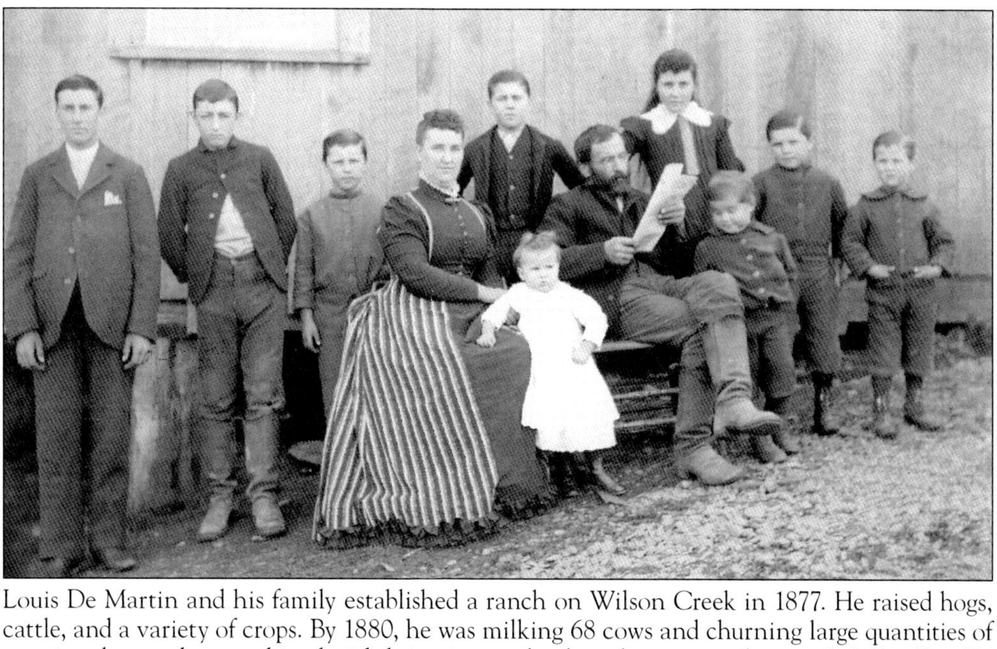

Louis De Martin and his family established a ranch on Wilson Creek in 1877. He raised hogs, cattle, and a variety of crops. By 1880, he was milking 68 cows and churning large quantities of premium butter that combined with brine in wooden barrels was stored in a side hill cellar. He also slaughtered hogs every two months, and the resulting ham, bacon, and lard was shipped to Crescent City along with butter on its way to San Francisco.

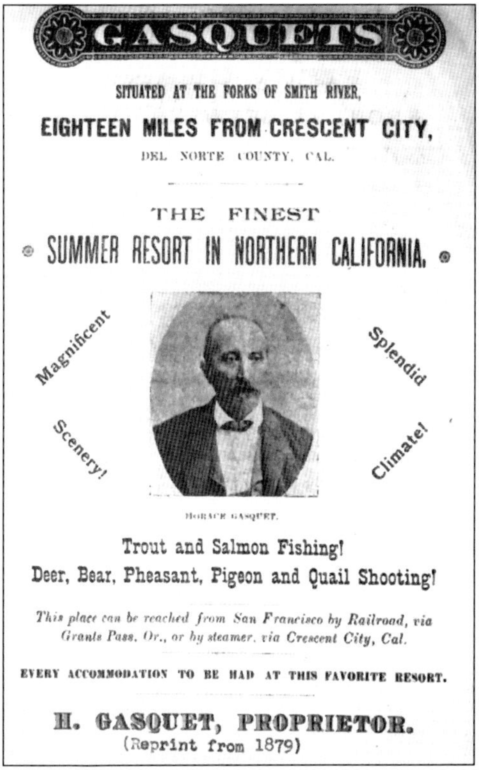

This advertisement for the Gasquet Resort was published in 1879. Gasquet Village became a well-known health spa and resort and drew guests from all over at a time when vacations were only for the wealthy and idle. Going on a trip to relax was frowned on by many, but for the less affluent, it was permissible to go to spas for health reasons.

By 1877, Gasquet had grown into a real village. There were several buildings occupied as hotels and sleeping rooms, and there was also a store, a saloon, a butcher shop, and a blacksmith shop. The winery was located at the back of the village. There were extensive vegetable and flower garden areas as well as a massive orchard.

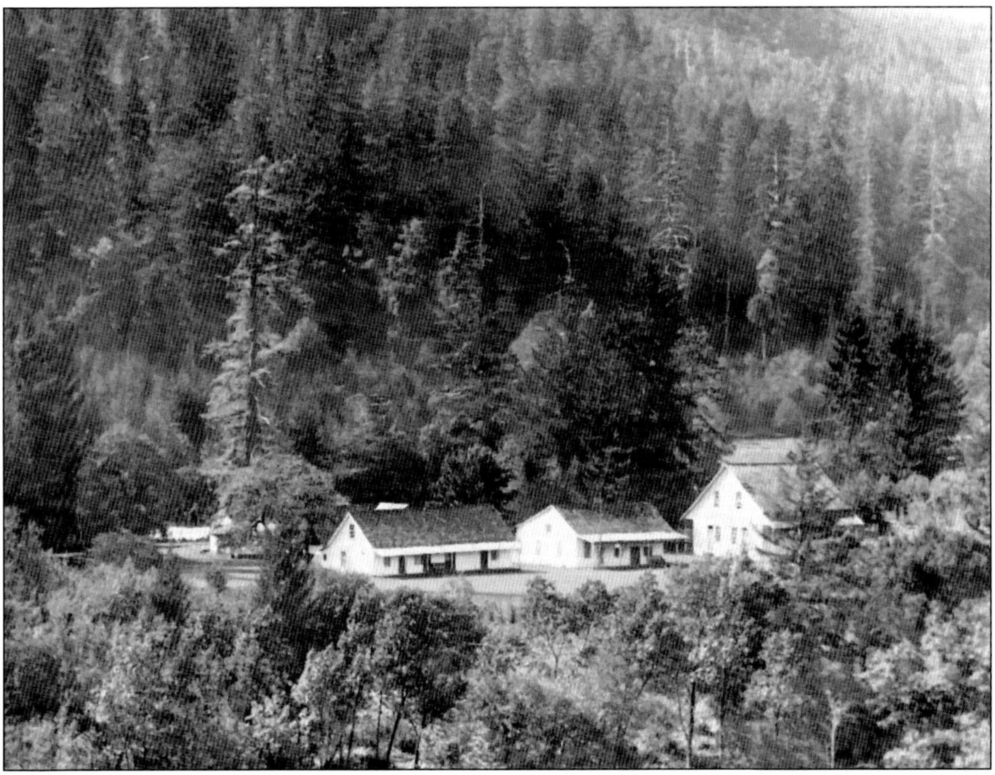

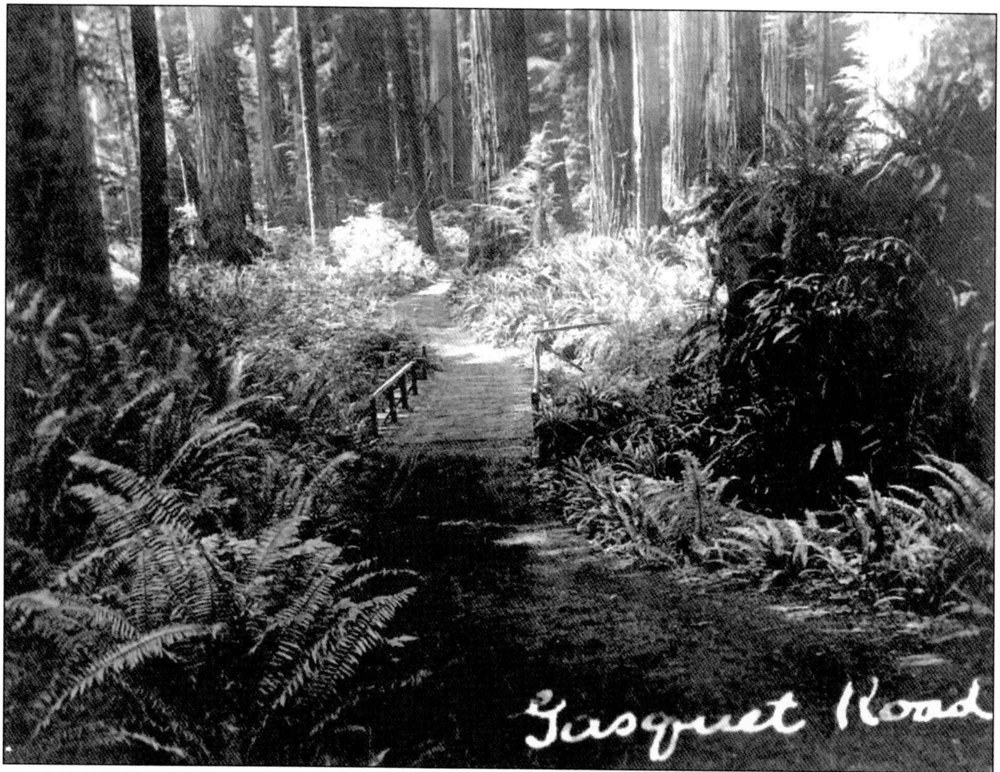

Horace Gasquet built a toll road to connect with old sections of the plank road. He began construction in 1881 with a labor force consisting of 60 Chinese laborers. They were supervised by George Dunn, who was a close friend of Horace. The road was completed in 1886.

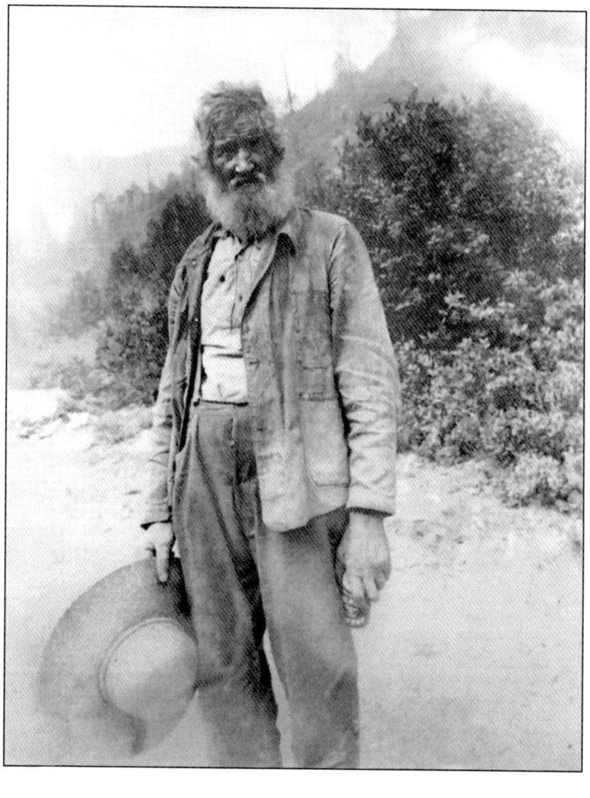

George Dunn was an Irishman and miner whom Horace Gasquet hired to supervise the construction of the Gasquet Toll Road. In 1890, Dunn built a stage station on the Gasquet Toll Road where Nine Mile Creek joined Partridge Creek. Partridge Creek was later renamed Patrick Creek, and Dunn's station became the Patrick Creek Station. Slowly he expanded his operation, adding several cabins. In 1906, Dunn was murdered by two men who believed he had a large stash of gold.

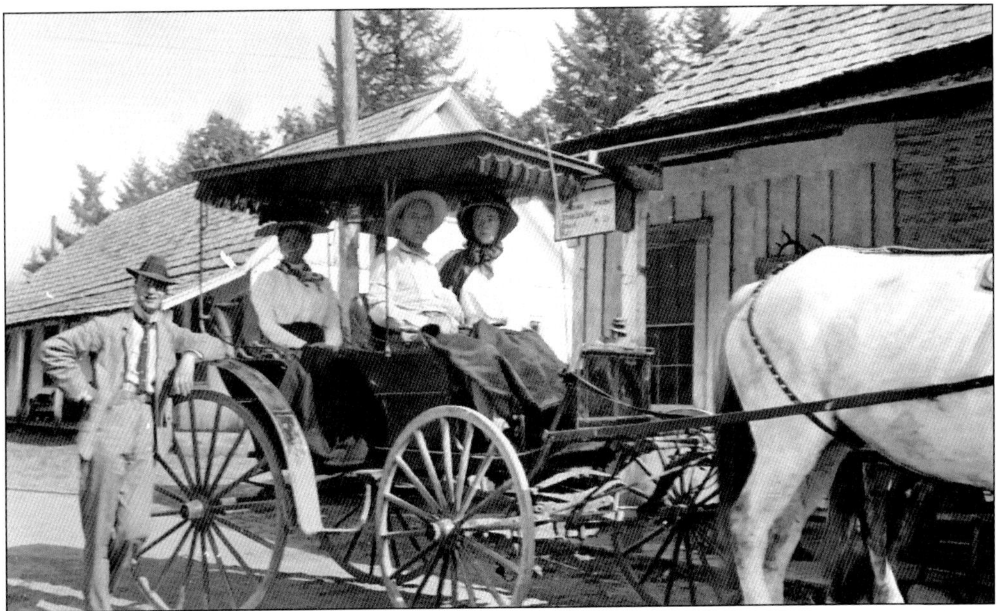

Gasquet Village was also a popular destination for a day trip from Crescent City or Smith River. Many people would take a leisurely drive to Gasquet Village to spend the day and enjoy the excellent food of Madam Gasquet.

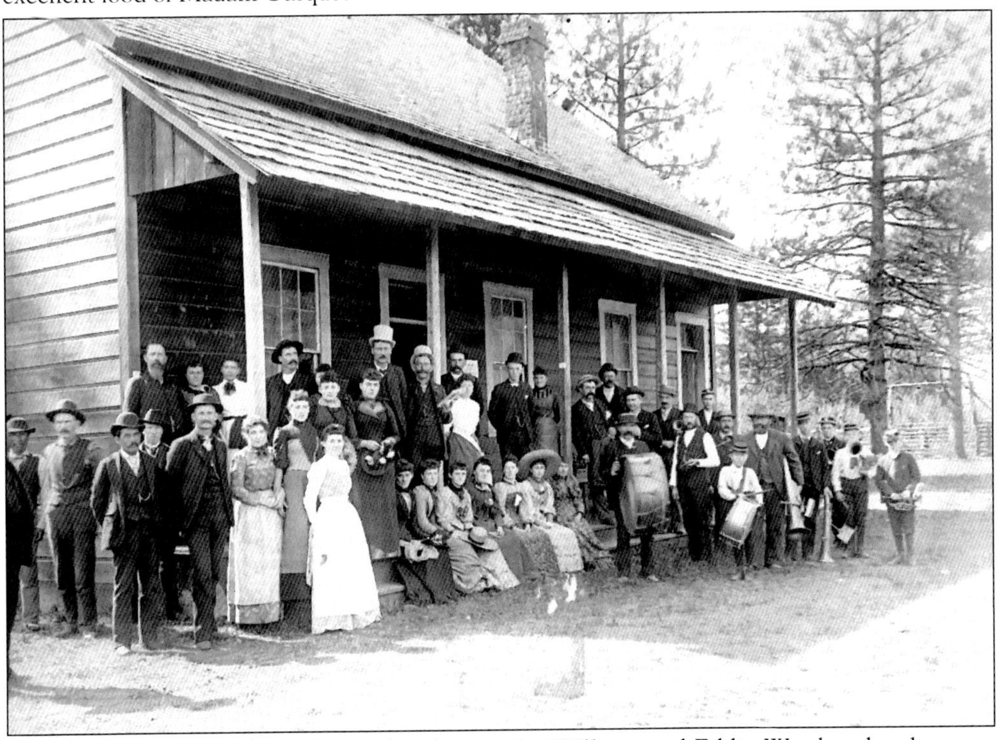

In 1883, the Gasquets hosted a weekend party for William and Eddie Westbrook, who were celebrating their wedding anniversary. William Westbrook is the tall man in the tall white hat. His wife, Eddie, is in front of him on the step. The Crescent City Excelsior Band provided the music for the weekend.

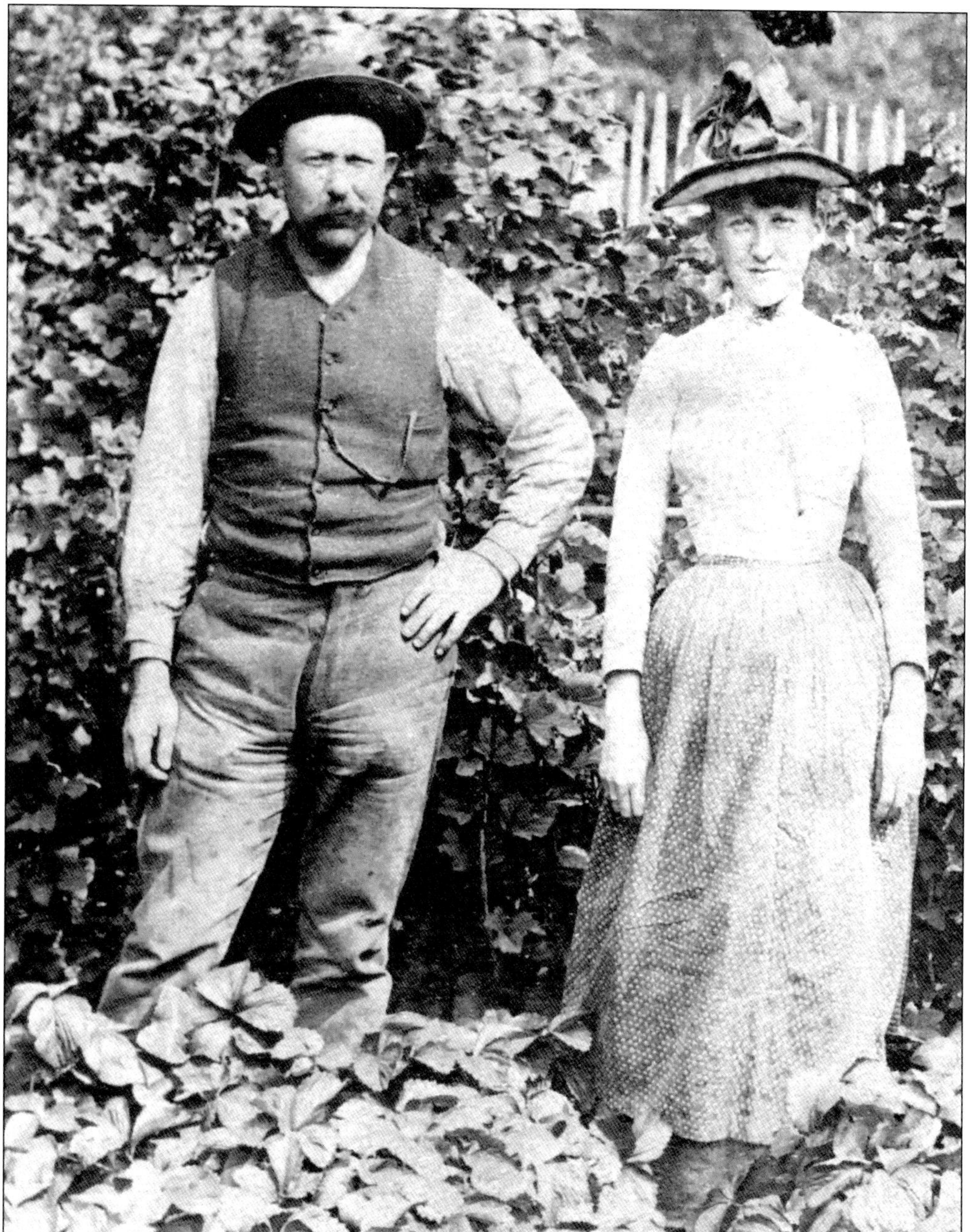

Between the two of them, Horace and Madeleine Gasquet developed a very successful business at Gasquet Village. Madeleine was skilled in the French method of cooking and also had a background in hotel management; thus, she oversaw the operation of the hotels and the kitchen. The Gasquet Resort was renowned for their excellent cuisine and warm hospitality and Gasquet Village became a well-known health spa that drew many patrons who visited on a regular basis. Horace was responsible for the vast financial empire he developed over the years that included not only the Gasquet Village, but the Gasquet Toll Road. He also had mercantile stores in Waldo, Oregon, and at Happy Camp and Gasquet Village, California—the first chain stores in California. He also had gold-mining interests at Happy Camp.

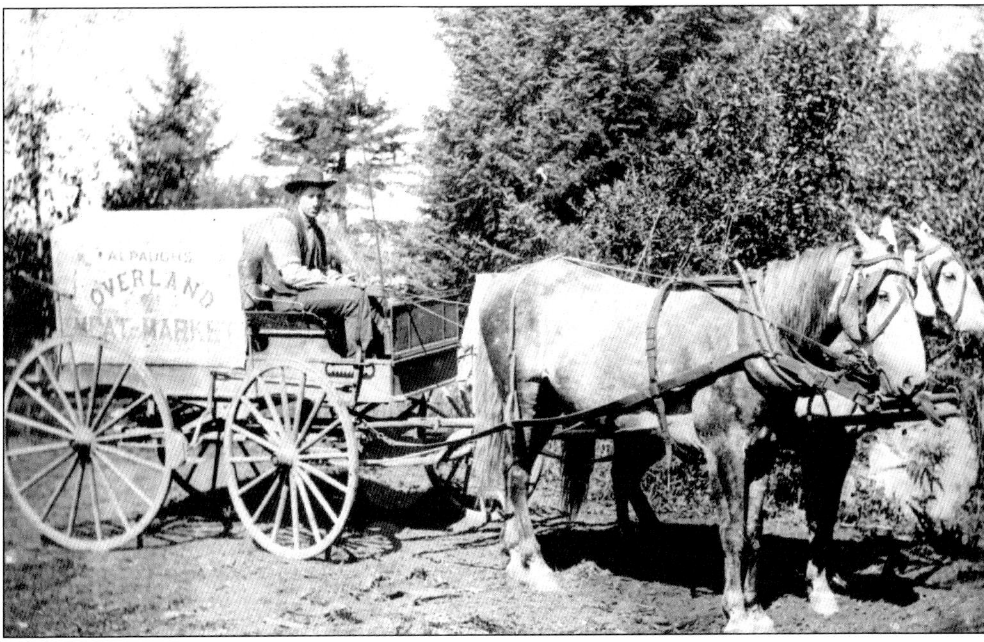

Jack Alpaugh operated a meat market out of Crescent City called the Alpaugh Overland Meat Market. He delivered beef, ham, bacon, and sausage to outlying areas and to the mining towns in his horse-drawn wagon.

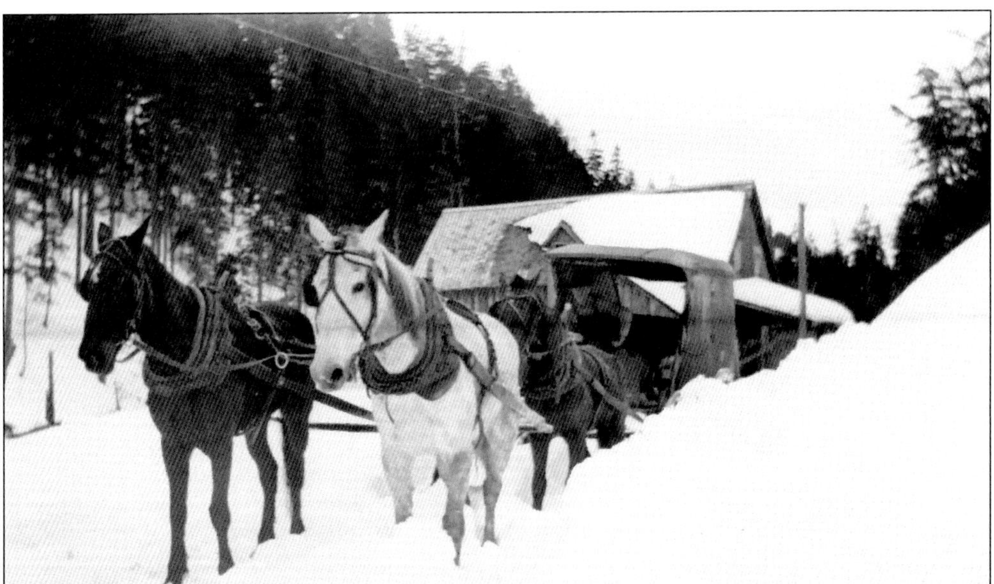

A delivery wagon arrives at Monumental. Delivering supplies was difficult and often dangerous during the winter months, and snow often made the trip impossible.

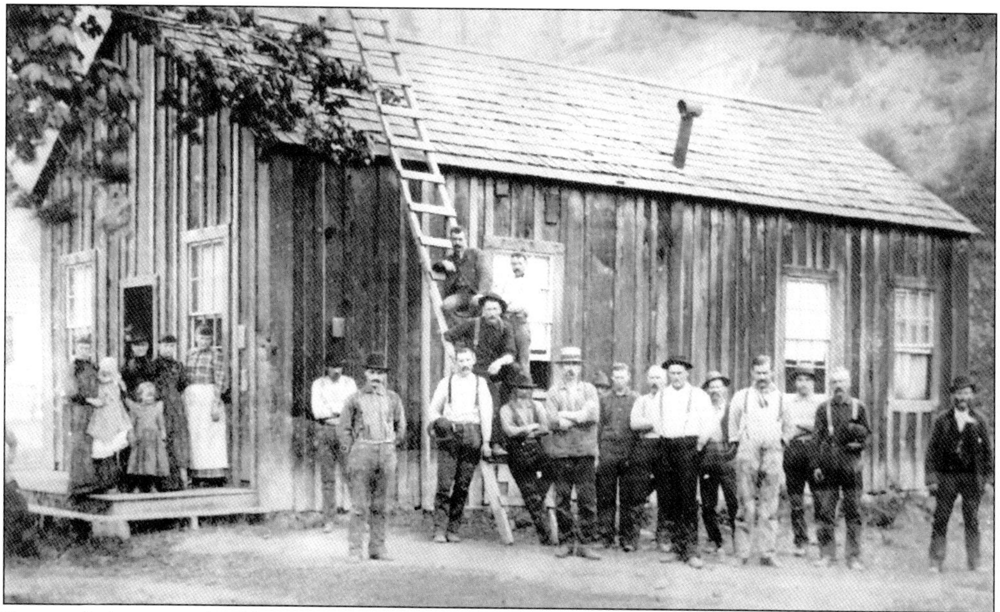

Pictured above is a building at the Low Divide Mine at Altaville.

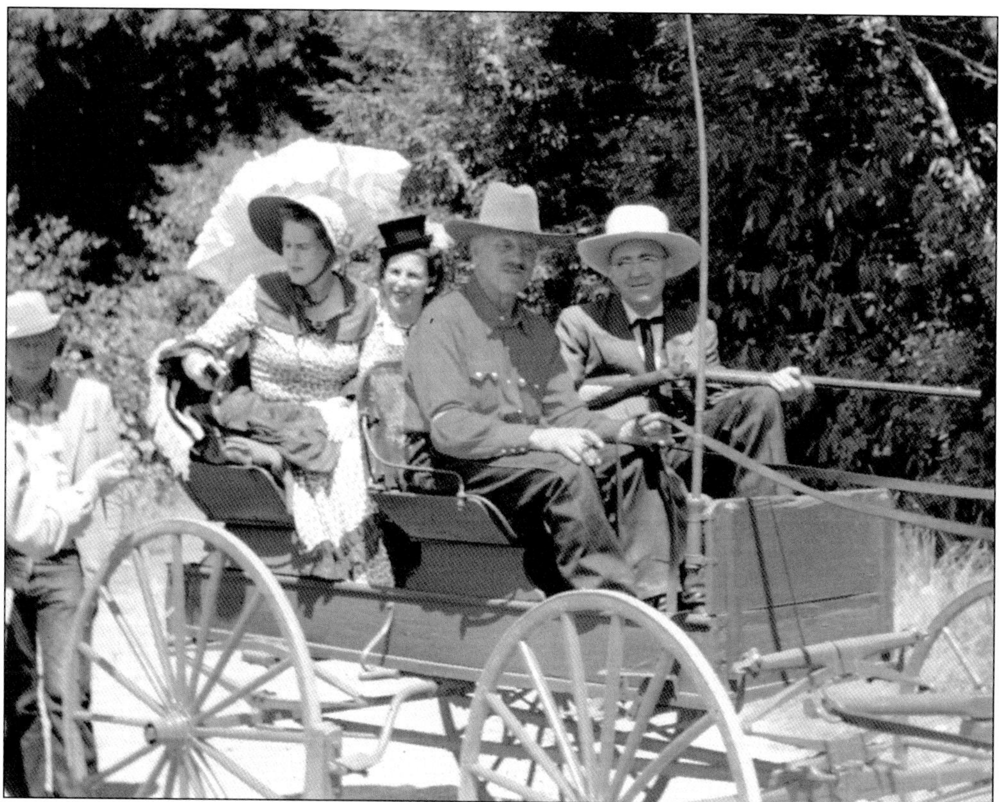

Sunny, Sunday summer afternoons were for outings, often drives in the country to visit friends.

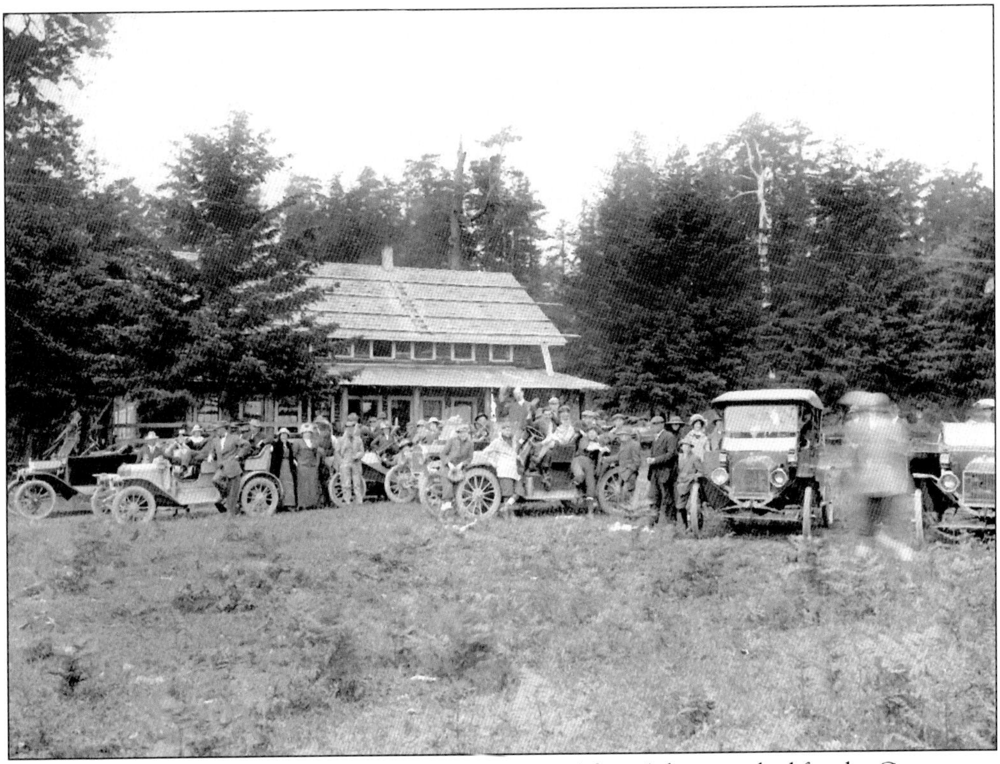

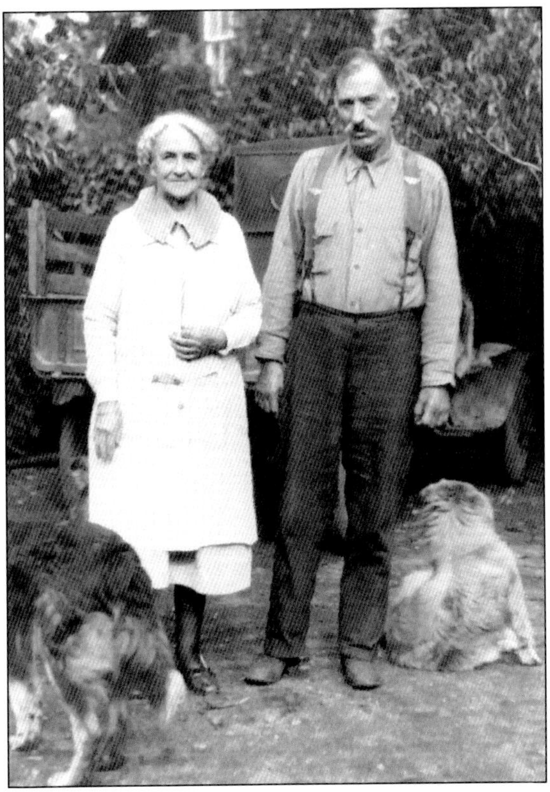

Mary Adams worked for the Gasquets at Gasquet Village as an assistant to Madam Gasquet for nine years. When Madam Gasquet died in 1889, Mary took over the operation of the hotels and kitchen of the resort. When Horace Gasquet died in 1896, Mary established the Adams Station, pictured above, on the Crescent City to Grants Pass Road.

The Adams Station became renowned for its excellent food and warm hospitality. Pete Peacock ran the stage coach station at Gasquet after driving one for years. Pete and Mary, pictured at left, were married in 1908 and ran the Adams Station together.

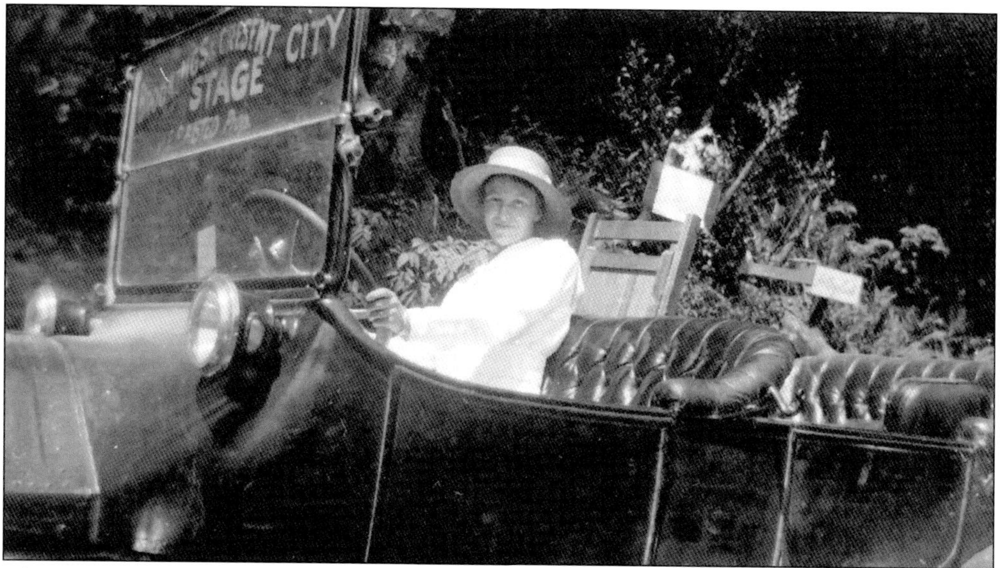

About 1912, automobiles came into use as stages between towns as the condition of roads improved. The Brookings and Crescent City Stage transported people and occasional merchandise between the two towns as weather permitted. Roads were still gravel and suffered during the rainy season.

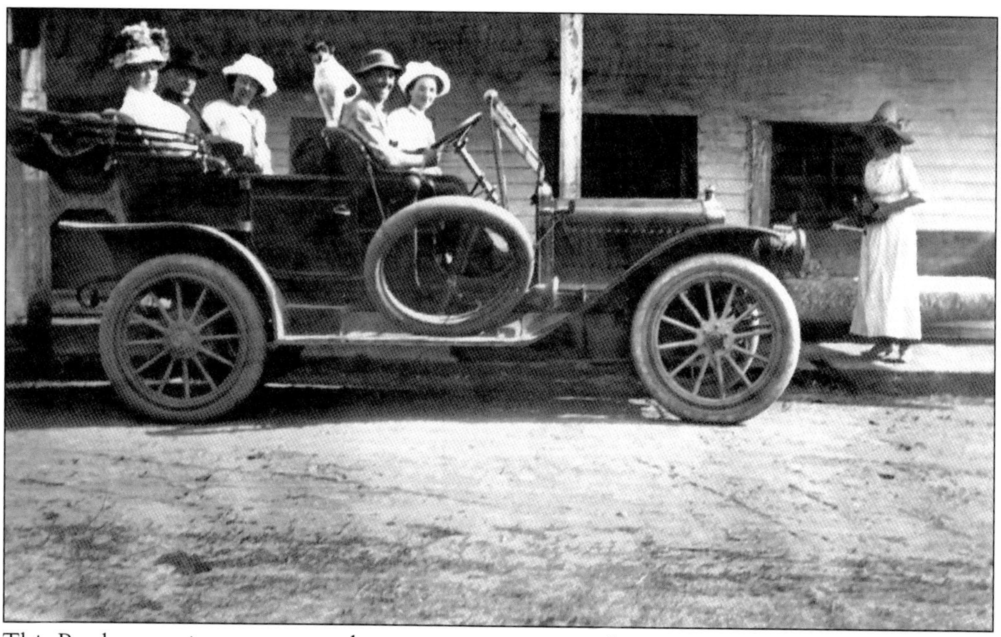

This Peerless touring car was used to transport passengers between Crescent City and points in Oregon when weather permitted—the age of the automobile had arrived. The touring cars were faster and much more comfortable than the old stage coaches, but winter travel over Oregon Mountain was impossible.

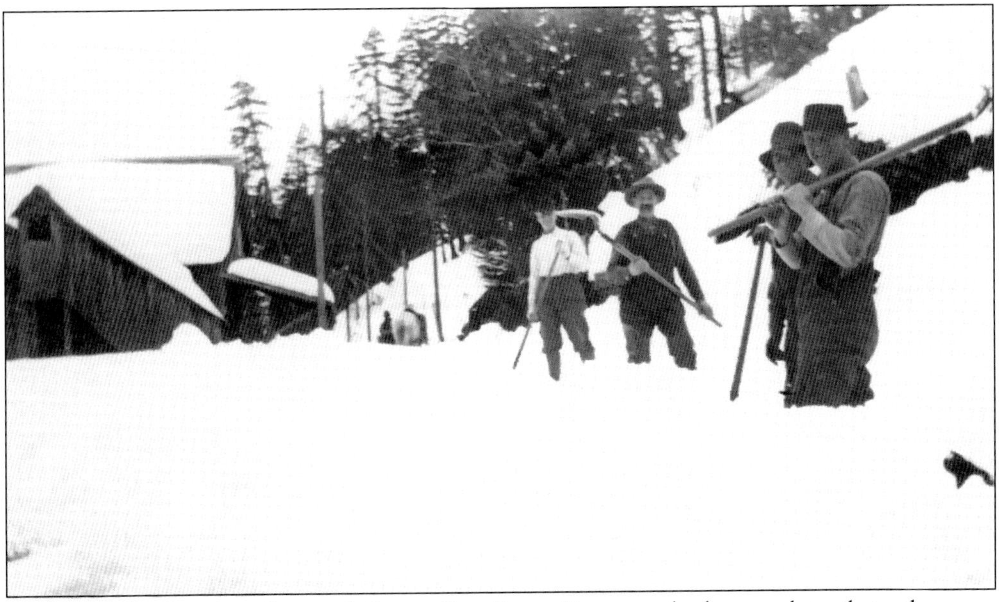

Men from the Crescent City and Grants Pass Stage Company had to mark trails in the snow on the mail route during the winter months. Deep snow often obliterated signs of the trail that made travel dangerous. As the mail delivery was by contract, the trails had to be marked with each snowfall.

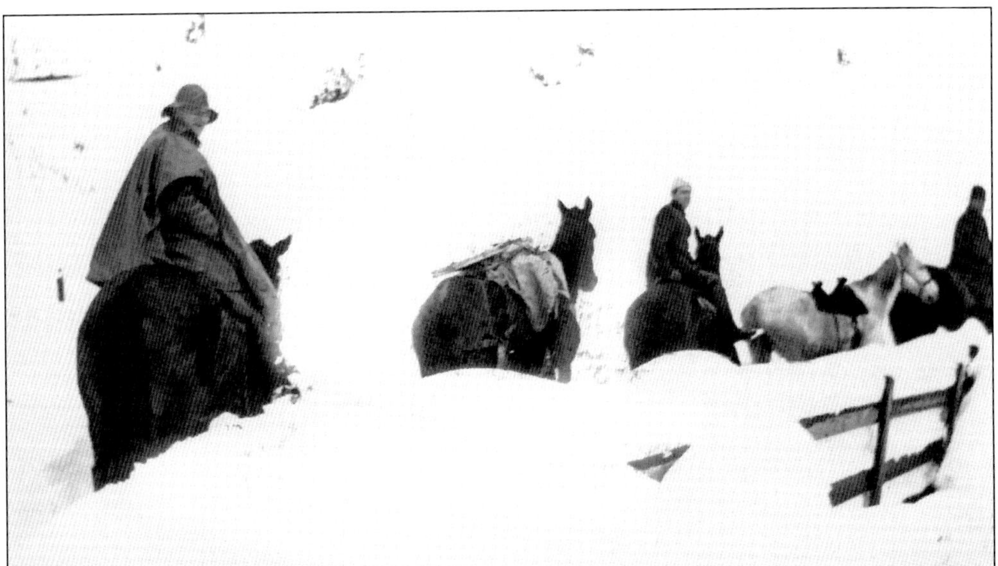

Riders with pack animals had to cross several bridges to deliver supplies to Monumental. During the winter heavy snows made the trip difficult and dangerous. This was part of the Crescent City and Grants Pass Stage Road in the late 1800s.

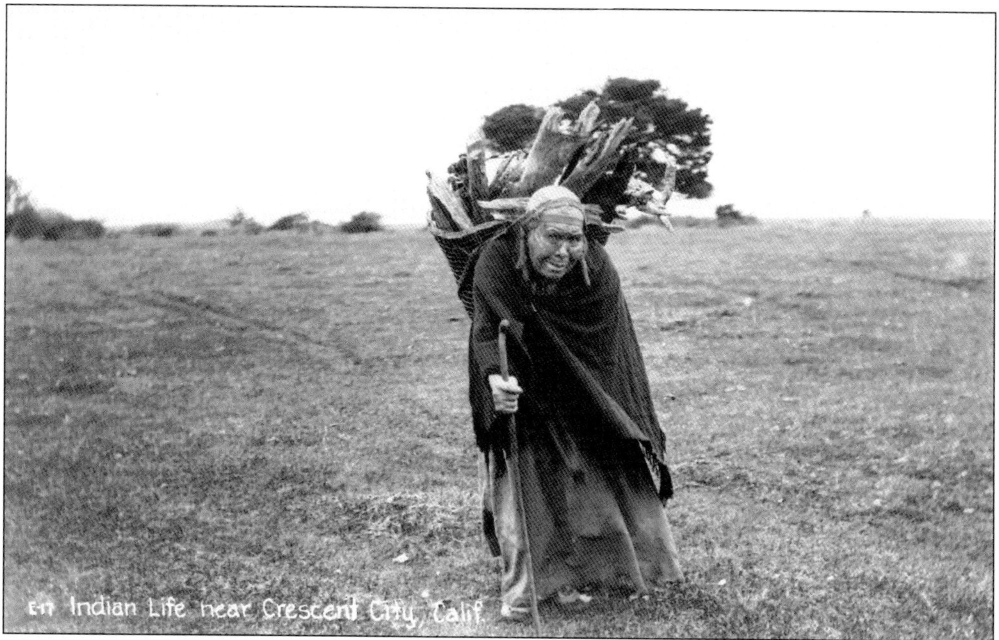

The Tolowa Indian women gathered driftwood and branches for firewood from beaches and along streams. They carried the wood in special baskets woven for firewood collection, and a strap attached to the basket was worn around the forehead. This picture was taken in the Lake Earl area.

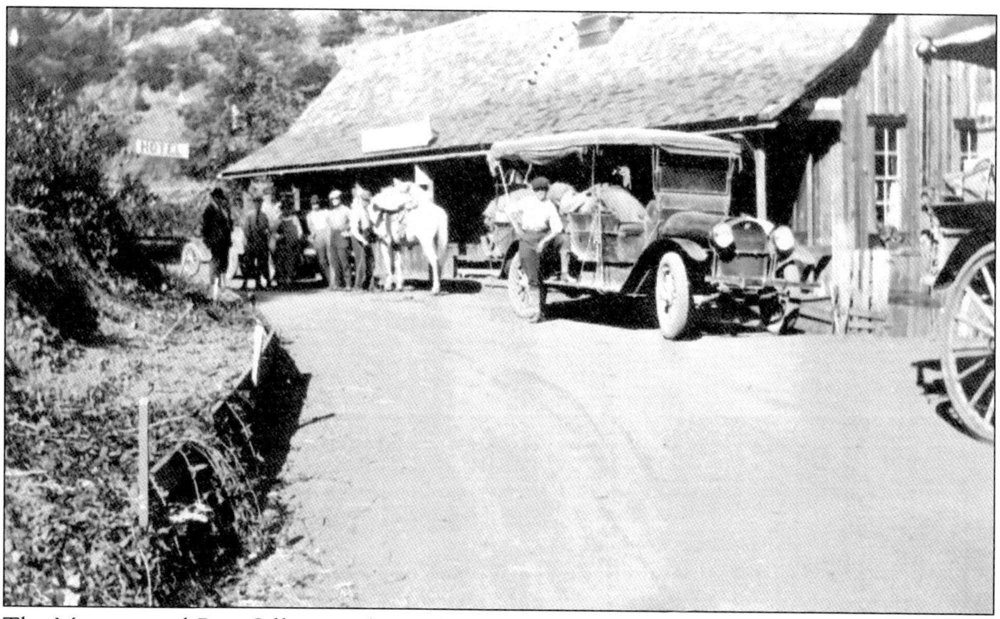

The Monumental Post Office was located in the Monumental Hotel. The mail from Crescent City was delivered on scheduled days, but the time of delivery varied due to weather conditions, accidents, and breakdowns. The hotel became a gathering place for local people waiting for the arrival of mail. Sometimes the wait extended into several hours.

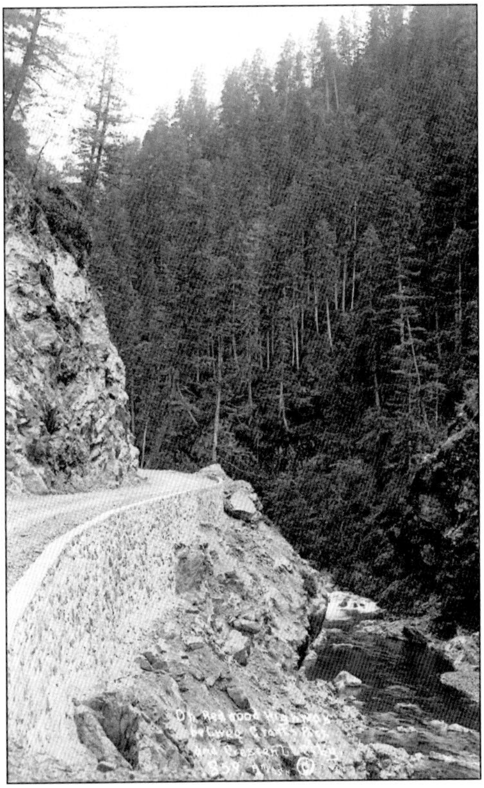

The Redwood Highway between Crescent City and Grants Pass is Highway 199. The present location of the highway opened in 1926 as a gravel-surfaced road that was narrow in many places. It required the construction of numerous retaining walls but was a vast improvement over the old roadway.

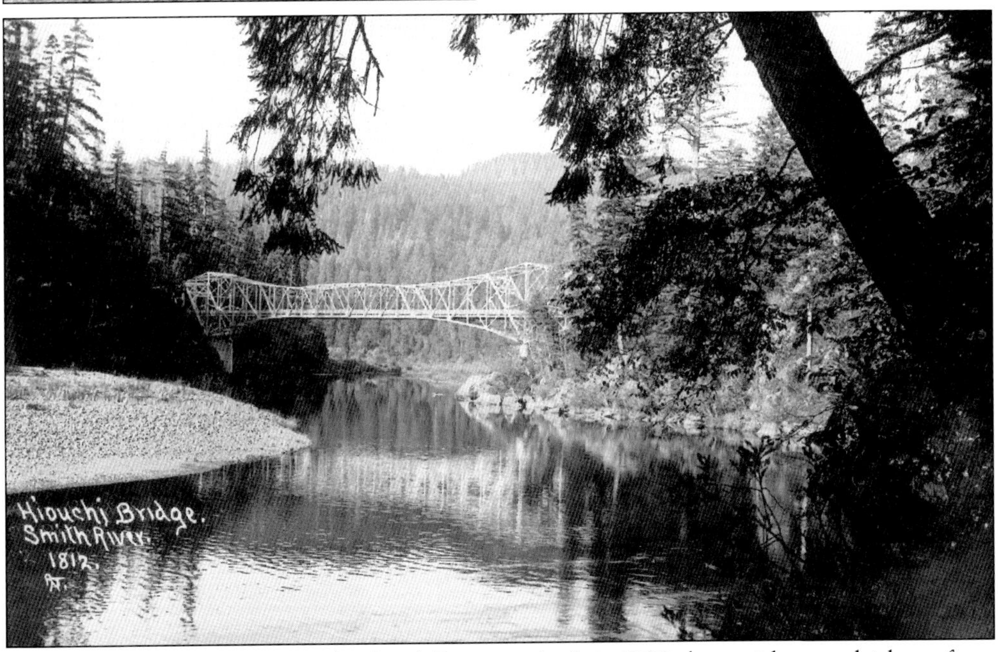

The first Hiouchi Bridge across the Smith River was built in 1929 along with a new highway from the Crescent City to the bridge. In 1924, the road from the bridge site to Gasquet was constructed with prison labor. In 1989, a truck ran into the bridge structure and knocked it off its foundation. The bridge had to be replaced.

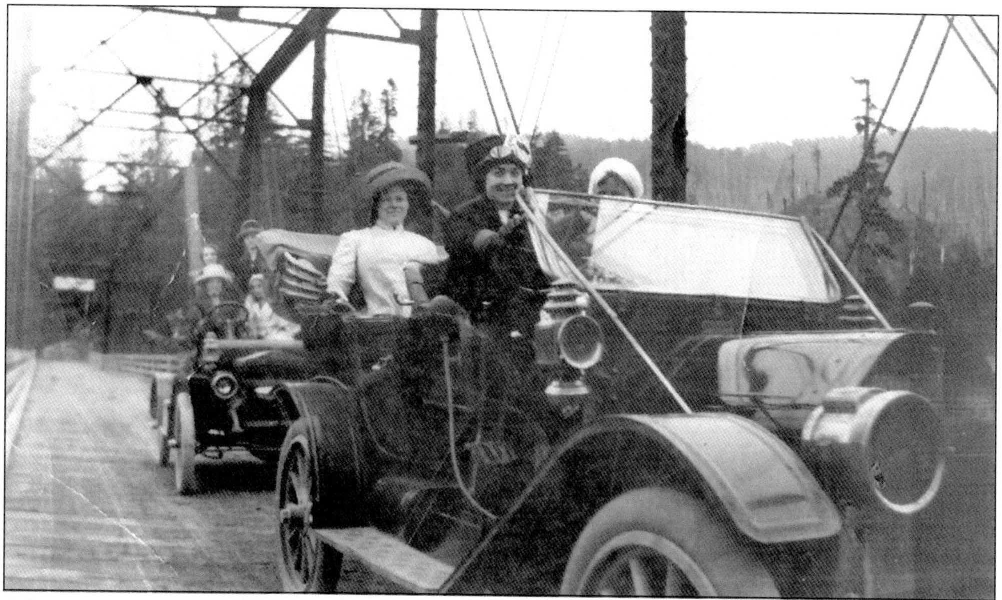

After construction of the Hiouchi Bridge, the Hiouchi area became the main travel route from Crescent City to Grants Pass, and buildings began springing up all over the area. The bridge made automobile travel possible and easy, especially between Gasquet and Crescent City.

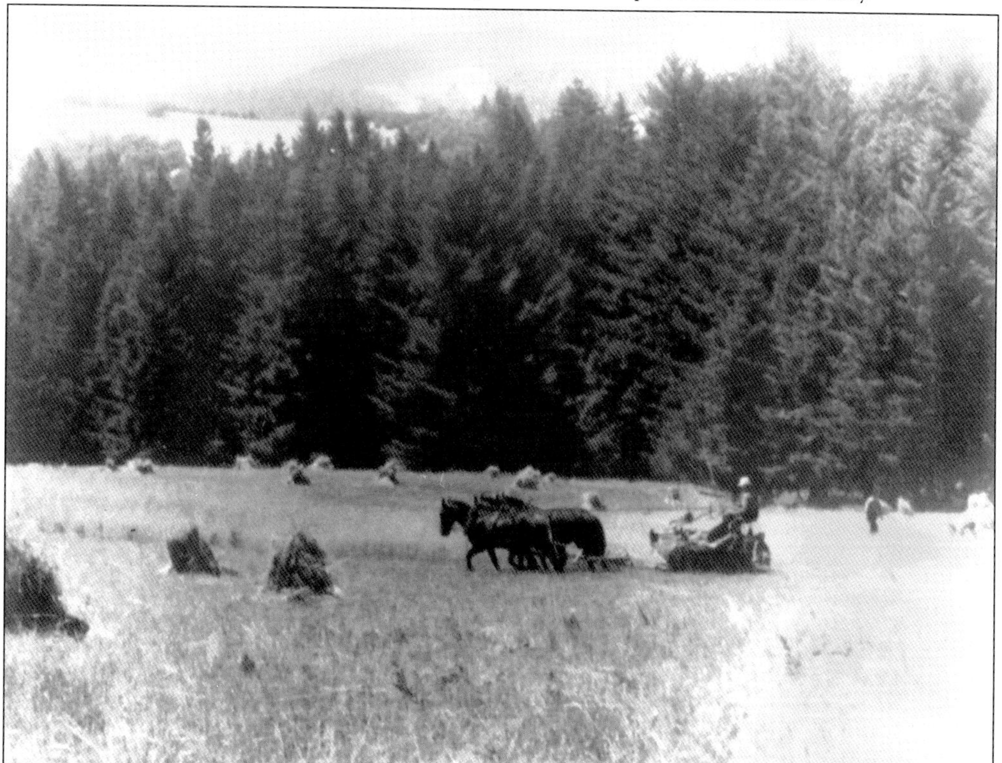

The Hussey Ranch was established by Frank Hussey and his family on North Bank Road along the Smith River. Eventually the family got out of the ranching business and sold the land. It was then developed into what is now the Del Norte Country Golf Course.

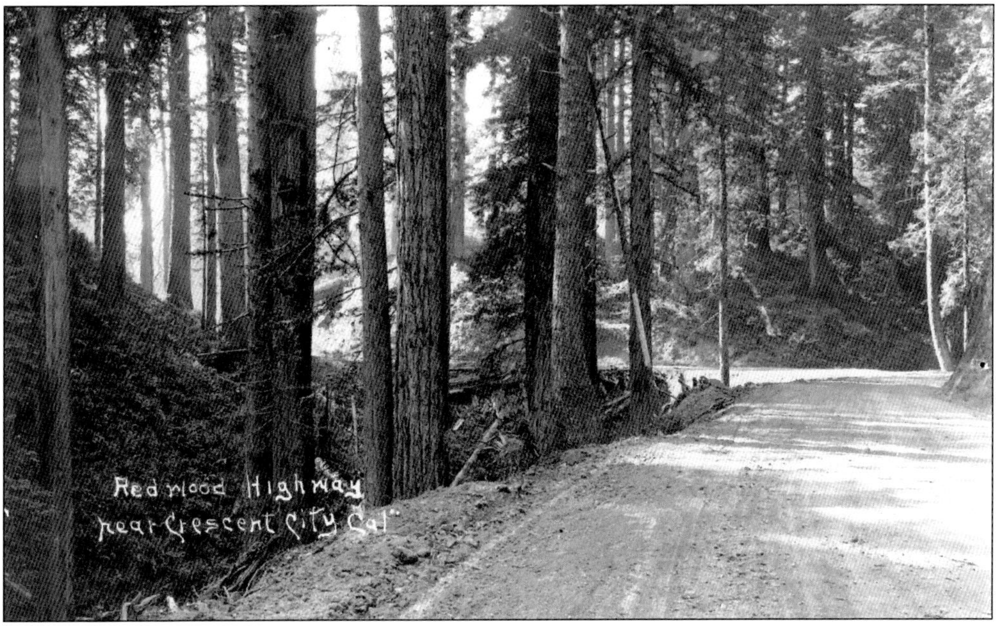

The Redwood Highway, just south of Crescent City, emerged from the redwoods to run along the bluff overlooking the ocean. It was a very scenic drive, but the highway experienced serious erosion problems. Portions of the bluff overlooking the ocean sloughed off frequently, a natural occurrence. The road had to be relocated back into the redwood forest.

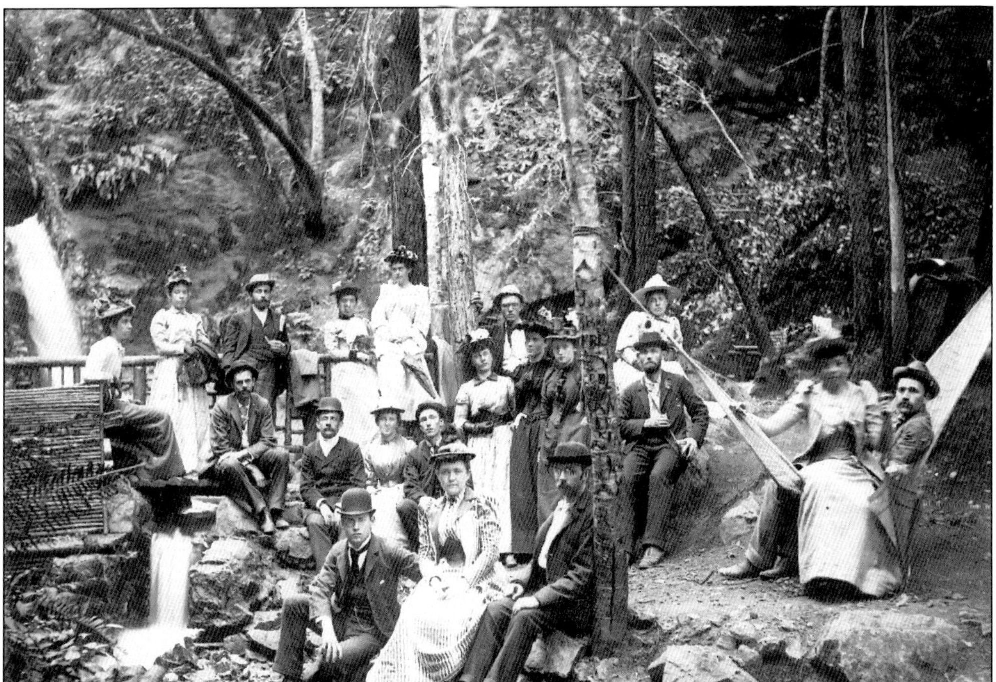

People used to dress up for the many picnics held at Cushing Creek south of Crescent City. The three people in front, from left to right, are James McNulty, a Crescent City attorney, his wife, Lillian, and Lillian's brother Milton McMurray, a dentist in Crescent City.

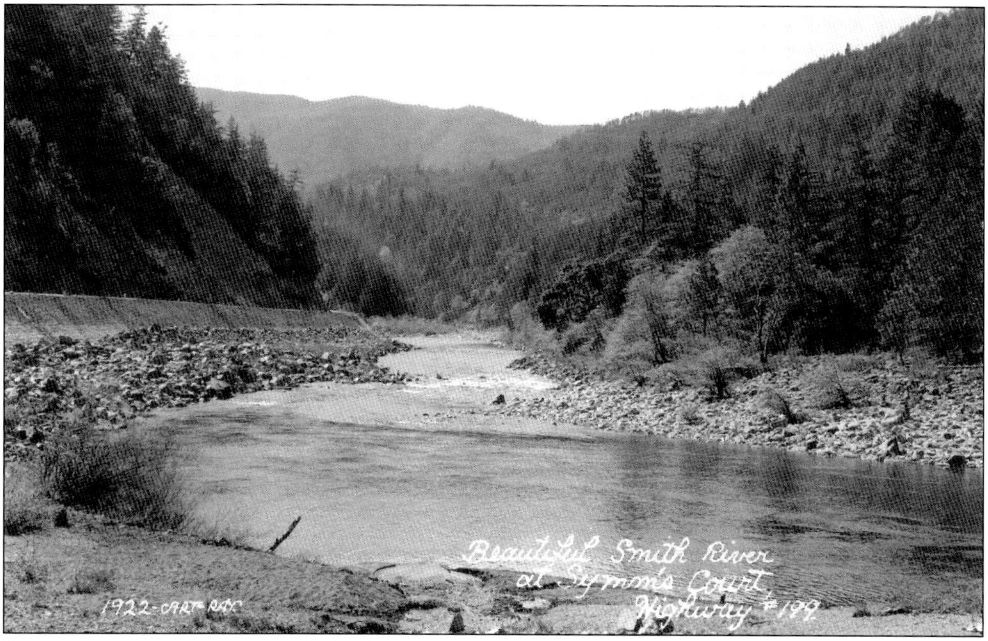

Symm's Court was an auto park built at this site along the Smith River. This area had originally been a part of the Gasquet Village. Highway 199 is visible on the left side of the picture.

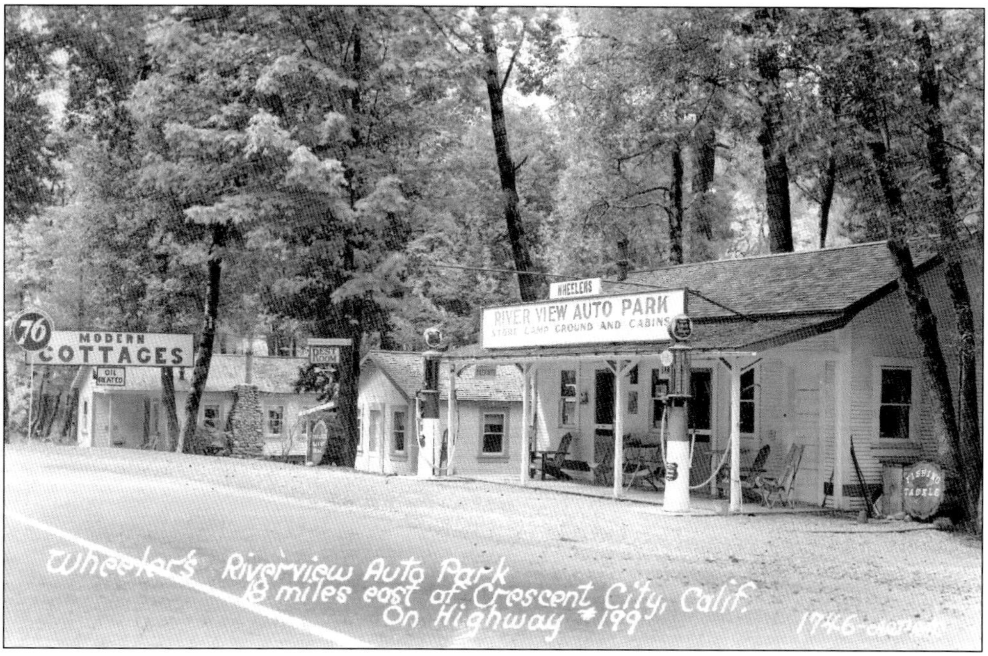

With the construction of Highway 199 (the Redwood Highway) from Crescent City to Grants Pass, tourism increased dramatically, and a number of auto parks were constructed along its length to accommodate the tourists. One of those auto parks was the River View Auto Park.

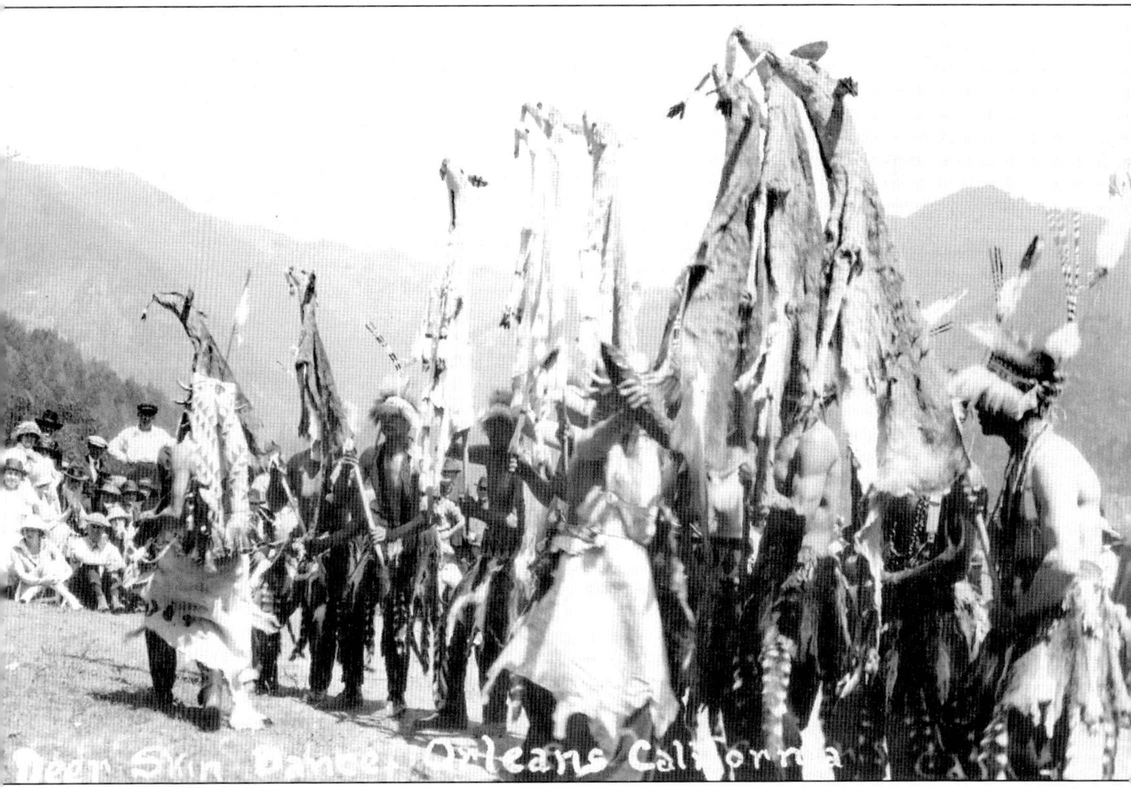

Yurok Indians perform the Deerskin Dance, a renewal ceremony. The dancers wore aprons of deerskin or civet cat around their waists, masses of dentalium shell necklaces, and a forehead band of wool fur to shade their eyes. The dancers carried poles on which were white, light grey, black, or mottled deerskins. The heads were stuffed and decorated with woodpecker scalps. The hide of the body and the legs hung loose.

Four

LOGGING IS KING

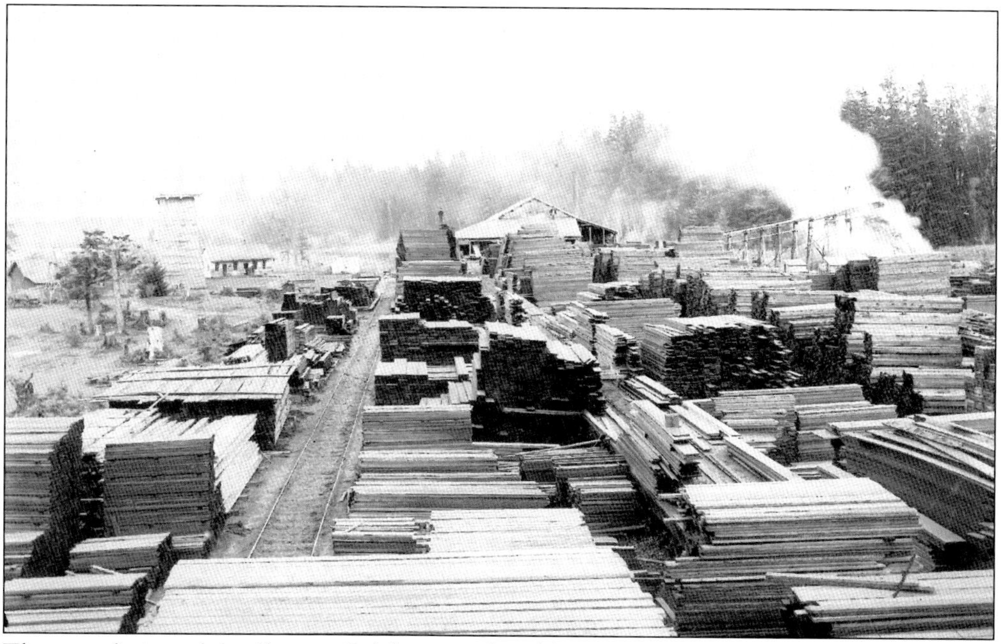

The completion of the Oregon-California railroad between Roseburg, Oregon, and Redding, California, was a stab in the heart of Crescent City. It was no longer a transportation hub for goods and materials to the Illinois Valley, and thus the economy suffered. Jacob Wenger Sr. called a meeting in 1869 to initiate steps to improve the economy. The vast timber resources of the county were virtually untouched when Wenger organized a joint stock company for the construction of a sawmill. It was a community venture, with stock certificates sold to the public under the name of Crescent City Mill and Transportation Company. A steam mill was also constructed on the south shore of Lake Earl named the Wenger Mill. This was the birth of the timber industry in Del Norte County, as finished lumber from the Wenger Mill was transported to the Crescent City harbor by mule-powered trains. The lumber was then loaded onto ships for transport to San Francisco.

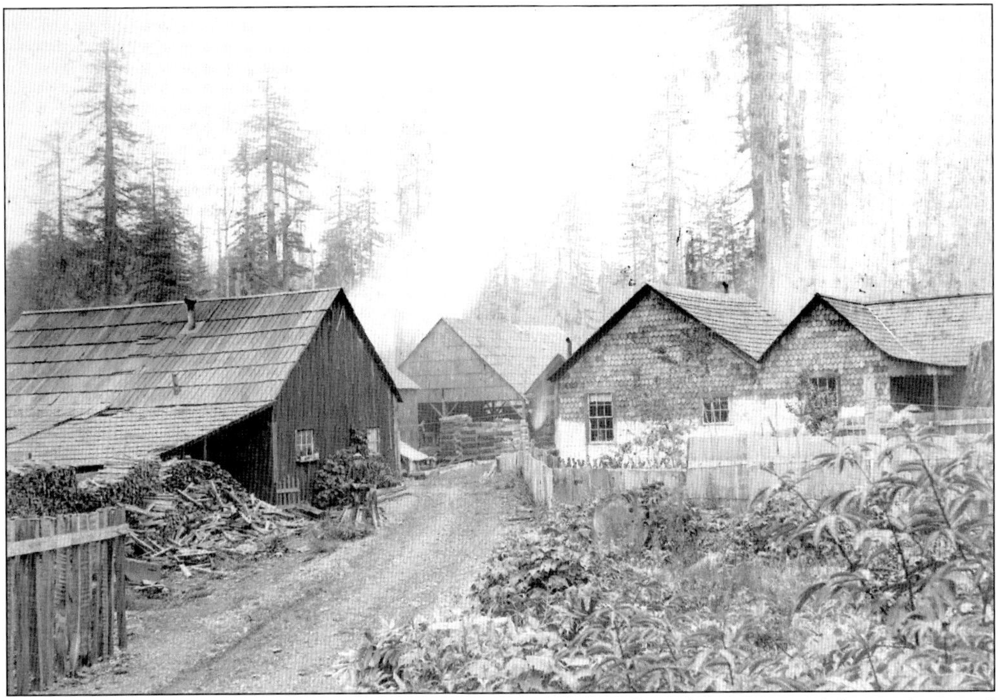

A mill camp was built at Lake Earl to house and feed the mill workers. Most of the workers and their families lived at the mill camp, but some lived in Crescent City. There was also a store at the camp to supply the needs of these people.

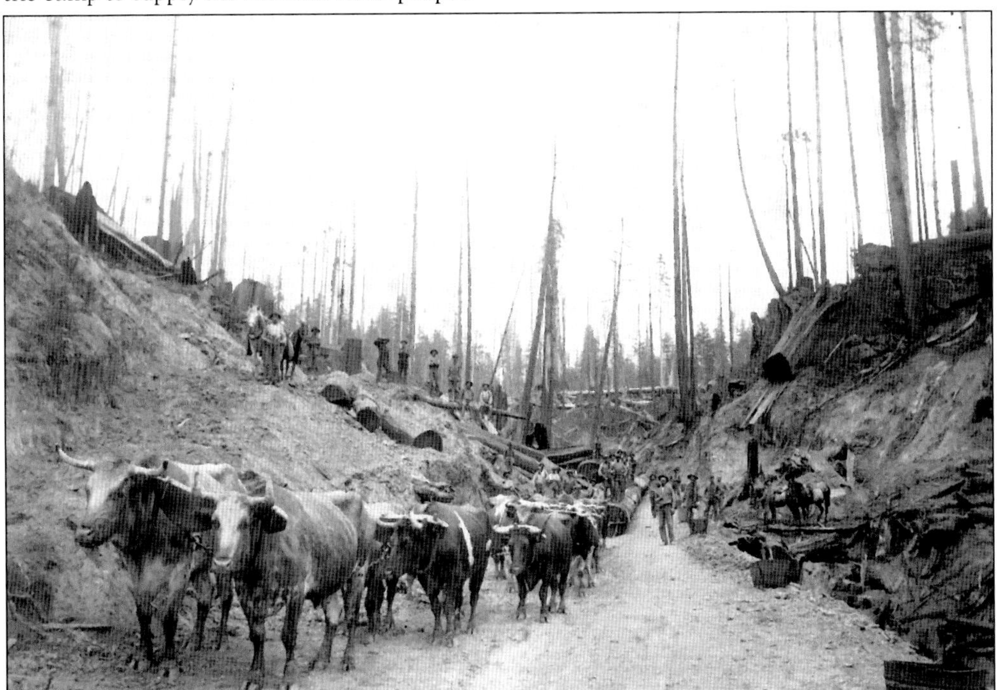

Oxen were used to drag logs out of the woods to rail sites or waterways for transport to the lumber mills in the early days of lumbering. Mules were not capable of performing the work.

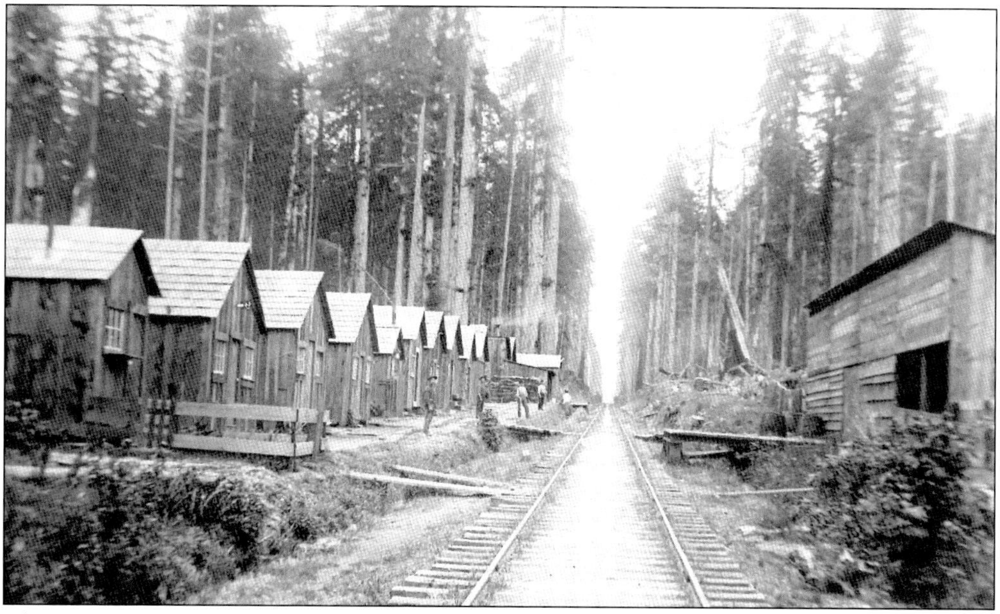

The Burns Camp was one of the many logging camps owned by Hobbs, Wall and Company. This one was located along the old Hobbs, Wall railroad about a mile from the Plaisted Ranch in Kings Valley. Camps were established to serve large tracts of timber land and were moved as the tracts were cut off.

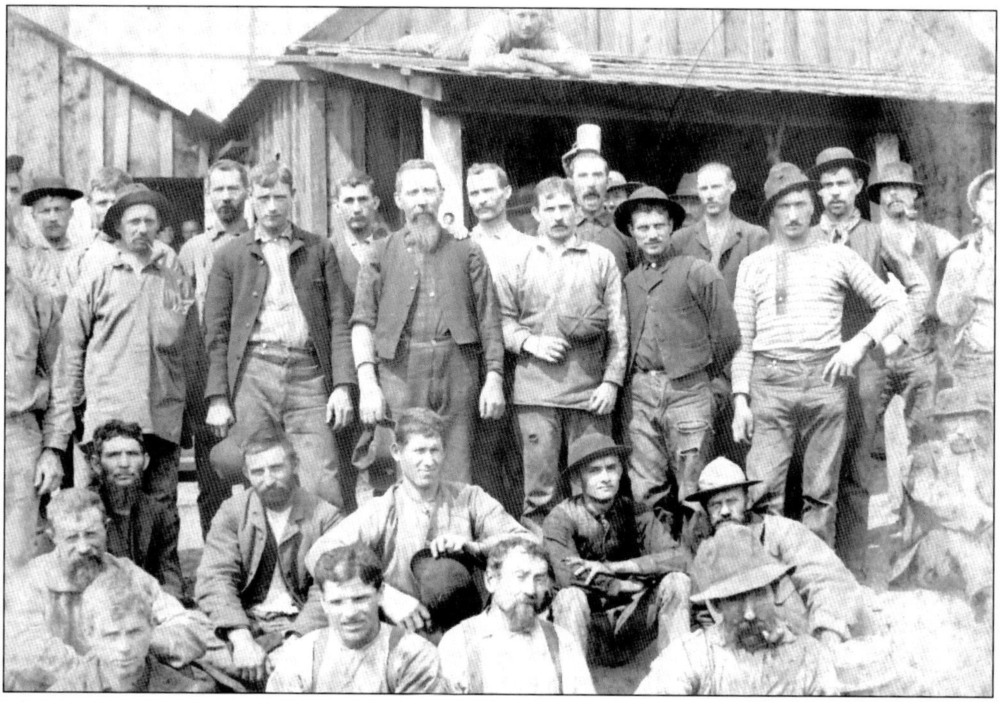

The man standing with the long whiskers is John Burns, the camp superintendent. Each camp consisted of housing for men and their families or bunkhouse facilities for single men. There was also a cookhouse and dining hall to feed the loggers. An expert cook could demand high wages as good food was important to attract good loggers.

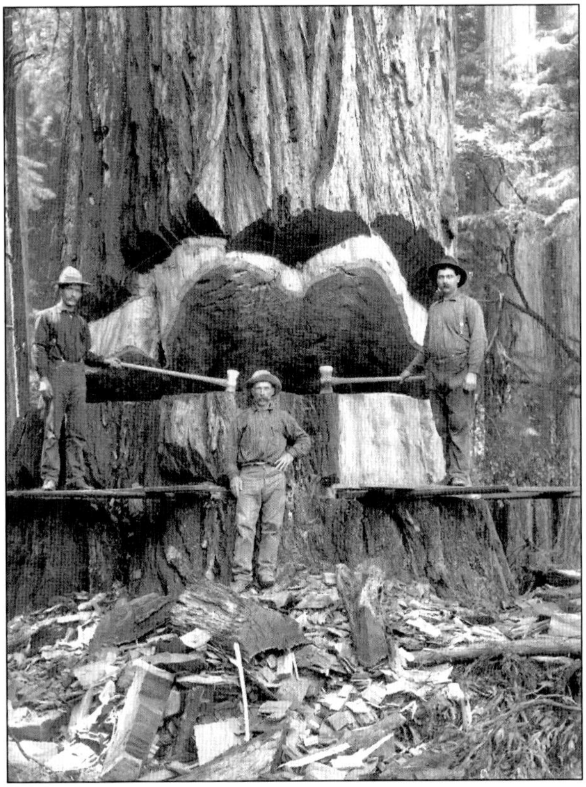

Felling a tree was a team effort. Platforms had to be attached to the trees for loggers to stand on while they used axes to notch the tree. Redwood trees have thick bark, which was very spongy and had to be removed before the trees were undercut.

After a tree was felled, the branches had to be cut off and discarded. The trees were then cut into lengths, and crews would remove all of the bark from the timber length.

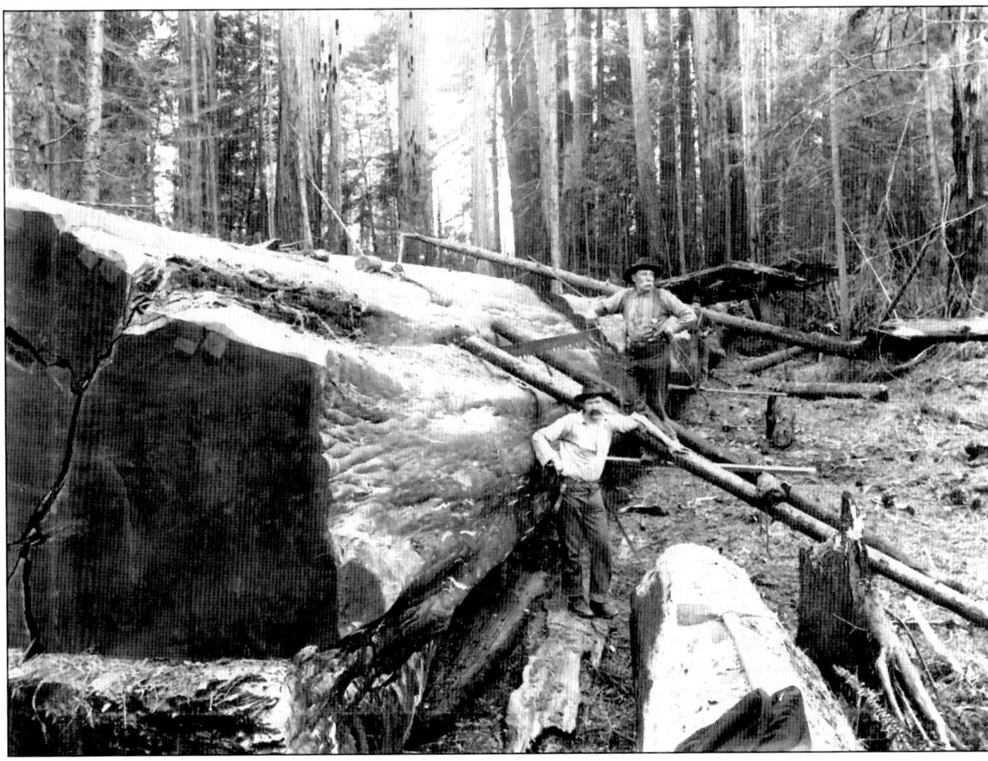

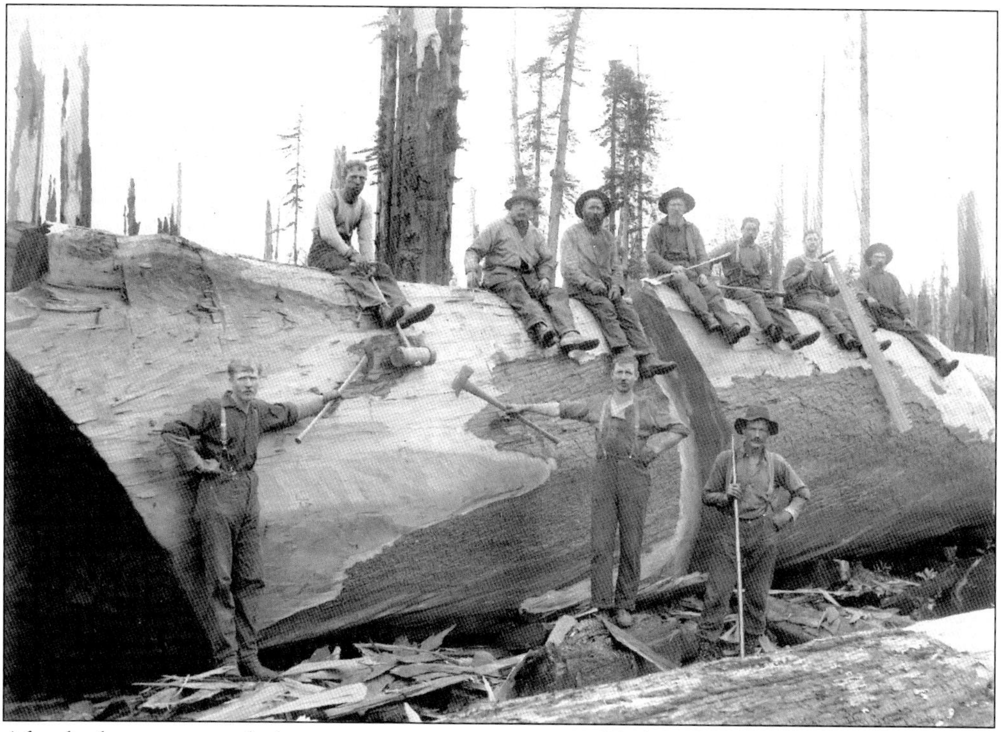

After bark was removed, the trees were cut into manageable lengths that could be dragged out of the woods to a rail head or a waterway to be transported to the sawmill.

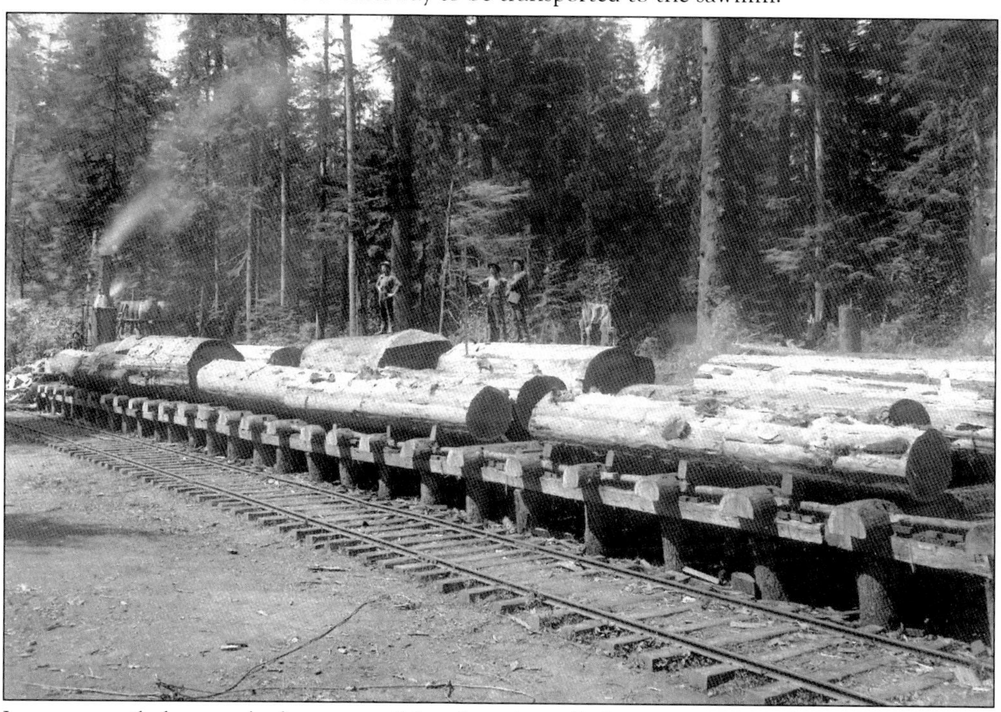

Logs were piled onto platforms at rail heads to be rolled onto train cars for transport to the sawmills. Once at the sawmill, the logs would be rolled off into the mill pond.

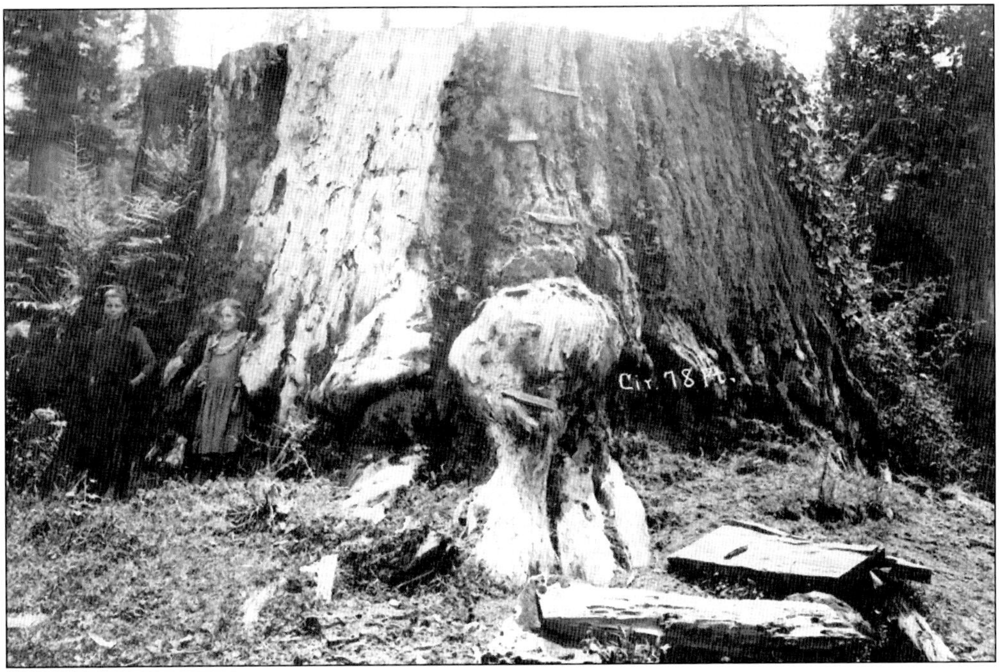

This stump had a circumference of 78 feet. It was hollowed out and a blacksmith shop was set up inside of it. Blacksmith shops were vital during logging operations to repair equipment, so the closer the blacksmith shop was to the work area, the better.

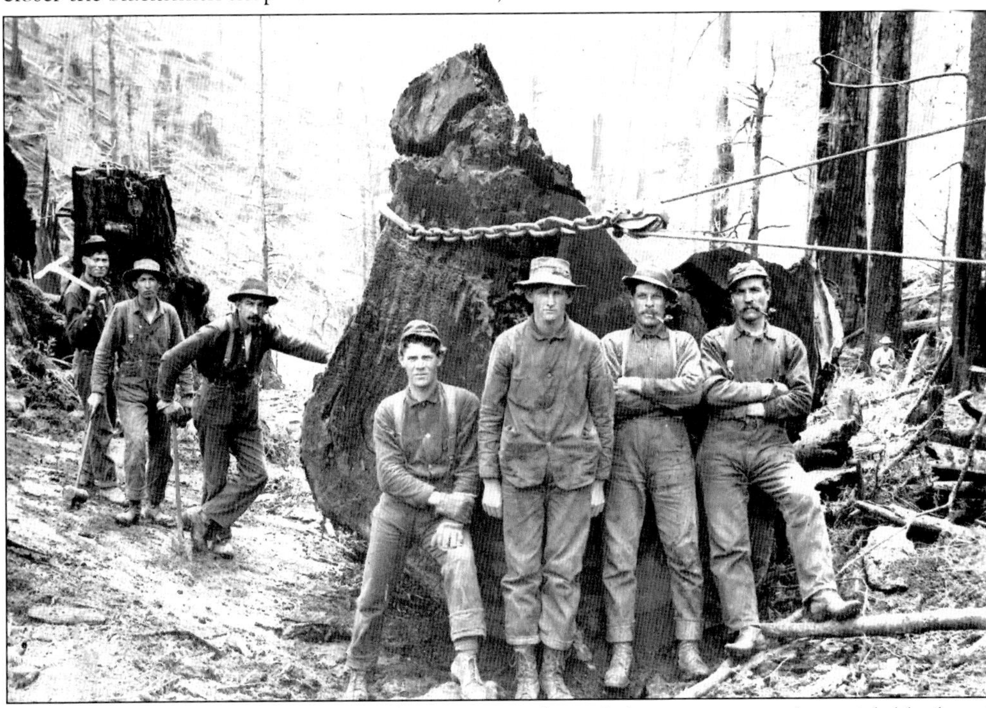

A logging crew takes a break to have their picture taken while moving some logs with block and tackle with the use of a steam donkey. Hobbs, Wall and Company took many photographs of the logging operations to document their methods and to identify loggers.

A man would select and mark one of the giant redwoods before the crew set out to fell it. In the early days of logging in the county, there were vast forests of old growth redwoods to be cut and milled.

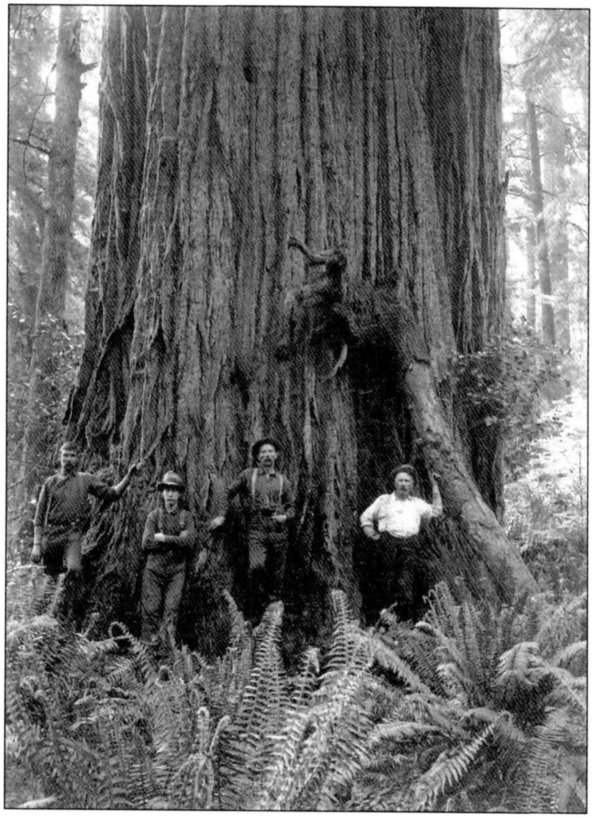

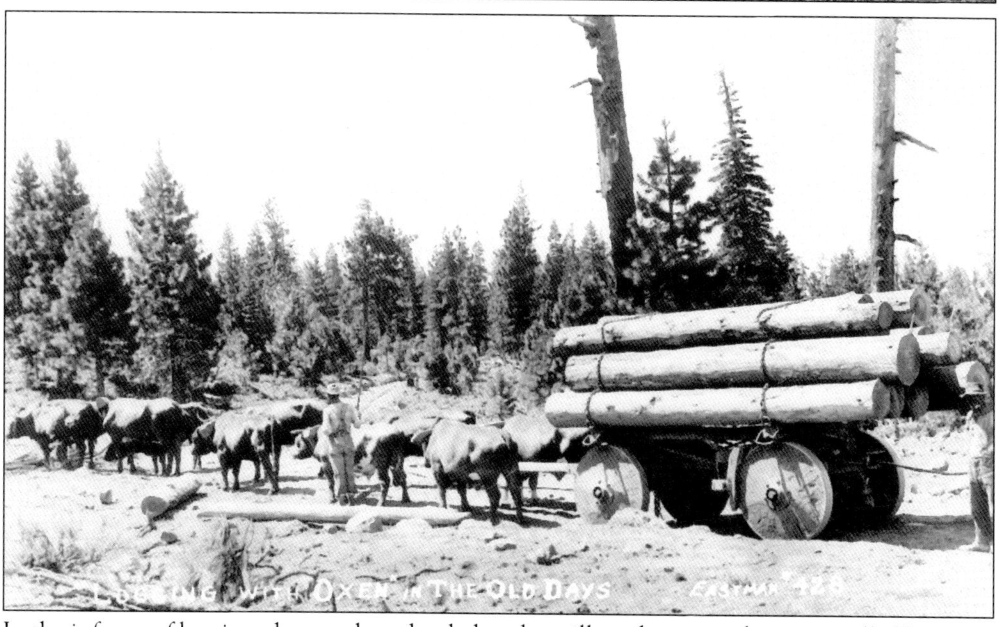

In the infancy of logging, the wood was hauled to the mills on huge wooden carts pulled by teams of oxen. When it began, the forests came almost down to the beaches and the edge of town, and as they were cut the timber moved farther from the mills and methods of transporting the logs had to be developed.

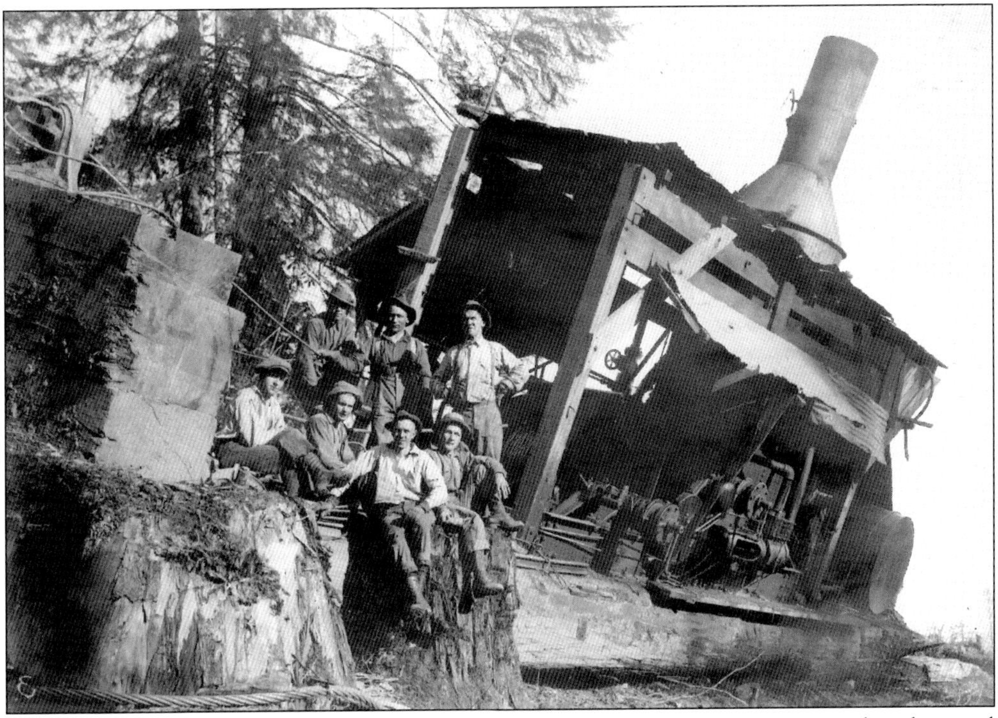

The steam donkey was invented by John Dolbeer, a Humboldt County logger. It replaced animal power in logging operations and they came in many different sizes. This photograph shows a huge steam donkey and the crew working with it to move the timber.

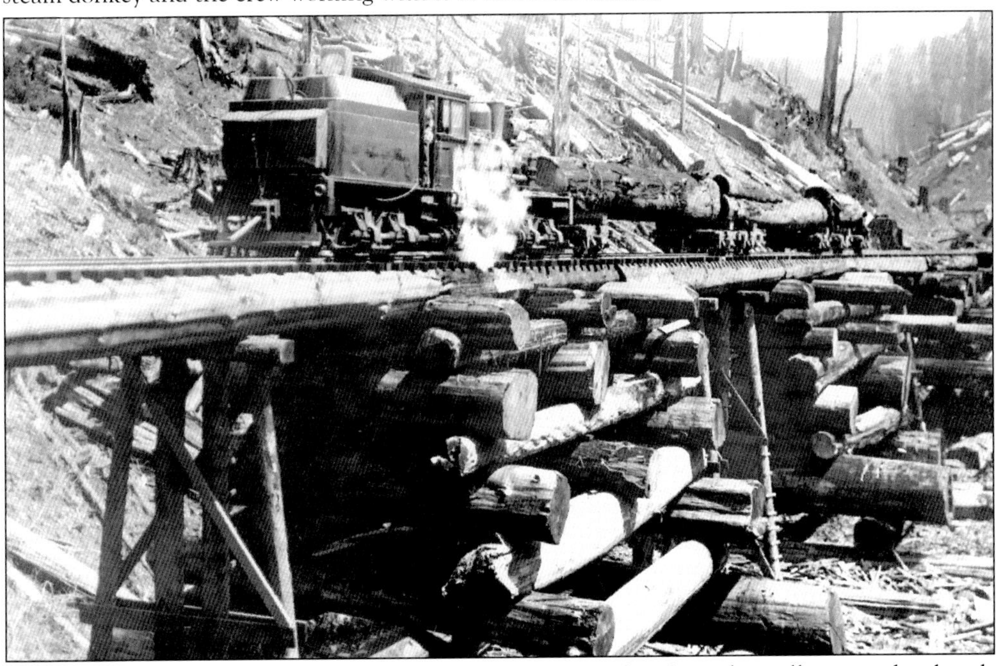

As more areas opened up for logging, operations moved farther from the mill sites and railroads had to be built to haul timber to the mills. Small redwood logs were used to construct trestles across the numerous drainage swales to provide gradual grades for the engines.

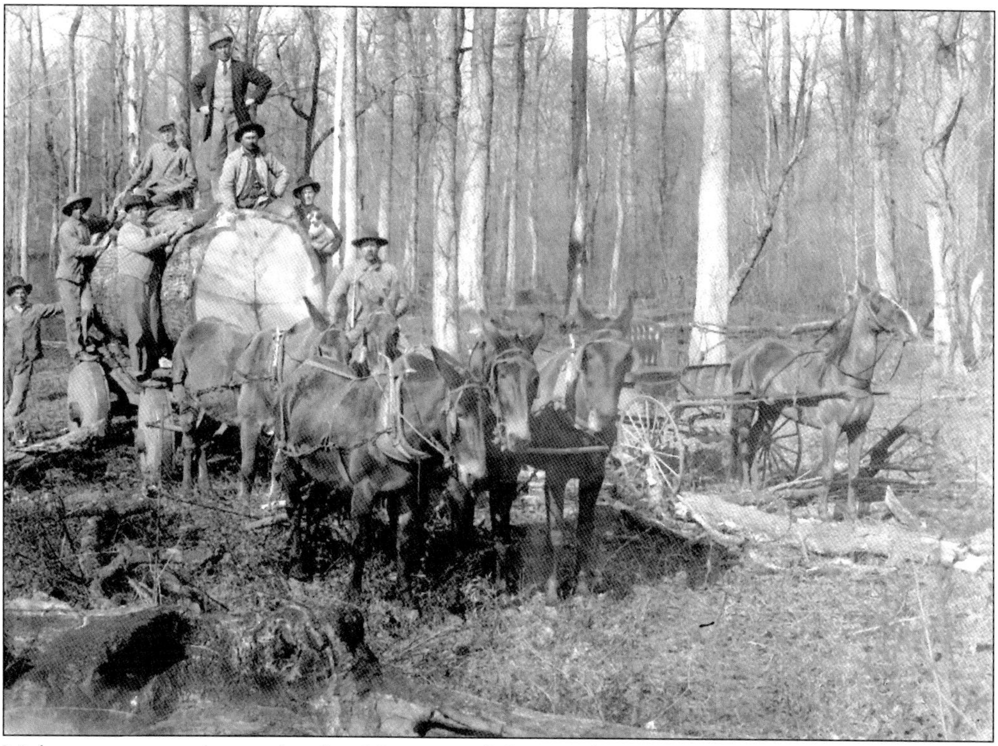

Mule teams were also used to haul logs out of the woods to train-loading platforms, although they were not able to move very large trees. Spruce and fir trees were also harvested along with the redwoods.

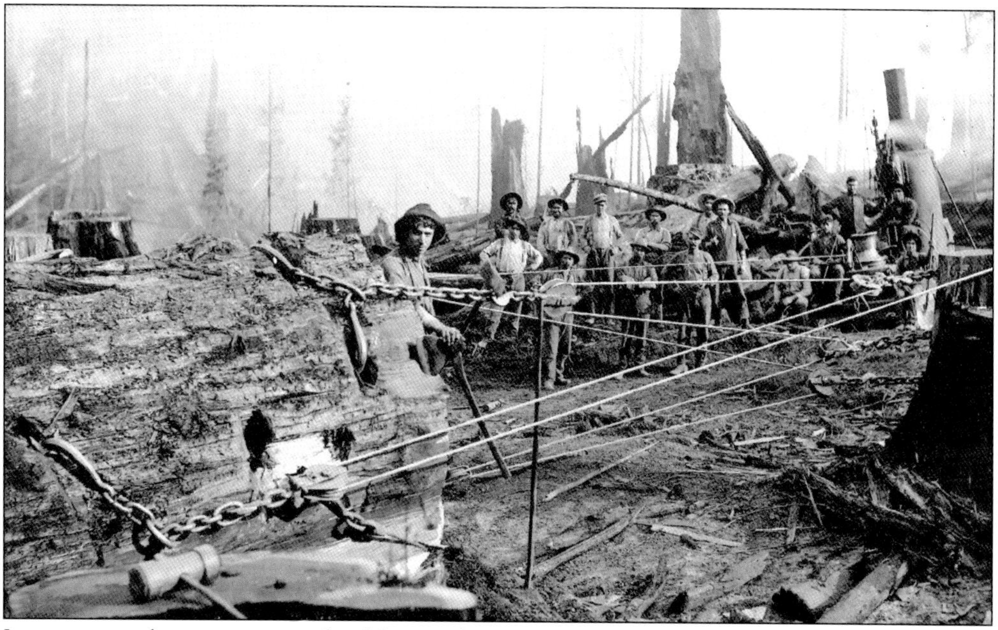

It was a complex operation to haul logs with a steam donkey. This shot was taken at Logging Camp Five, located near Fort Dick. The logs had to be moved in stages, being dragged from one steam donkey to the next.

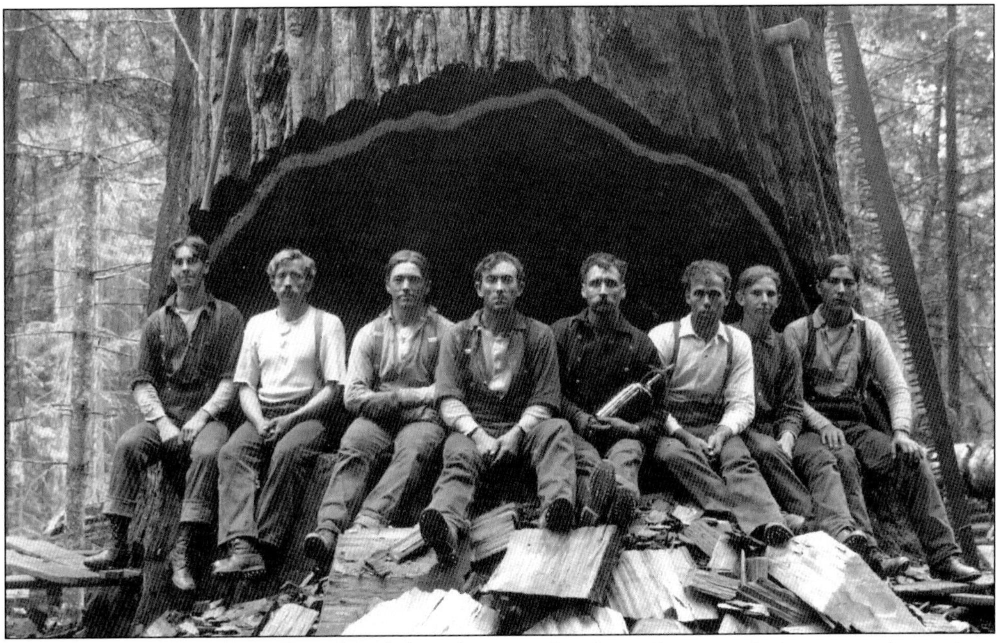

A logging crew took a break and had this photograph taken after completing an undercut in a giant redwood, which could take days. The undercut was very important, as it determined the direction the tree fell. An improperly felled tree could shatter, making the wood useless as lumber. This scene was at Newburg, later called Fort Dick.

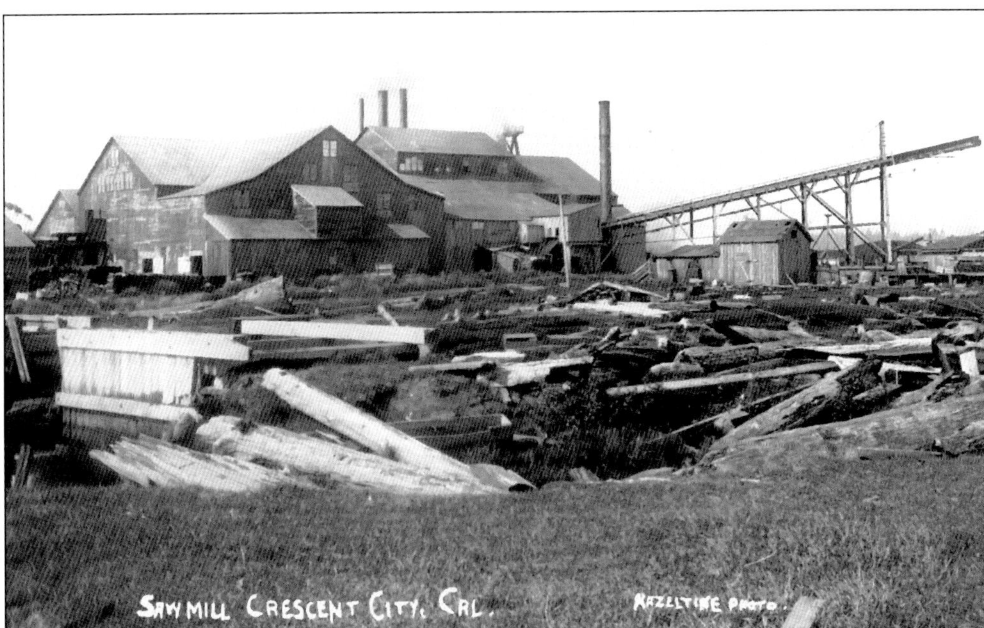

The Hobbs, Gilmore and Company sawmill and box factory was built on the east end of Third Street in 1870 by Caleb Hobbs and David Pomeroy of the company's San Francisco office. The mill was constructed next to Elk Creek, and a mill pond was created so logs could be floated to the pond. The mill closed in 1939.

Five

Klamath and Requa

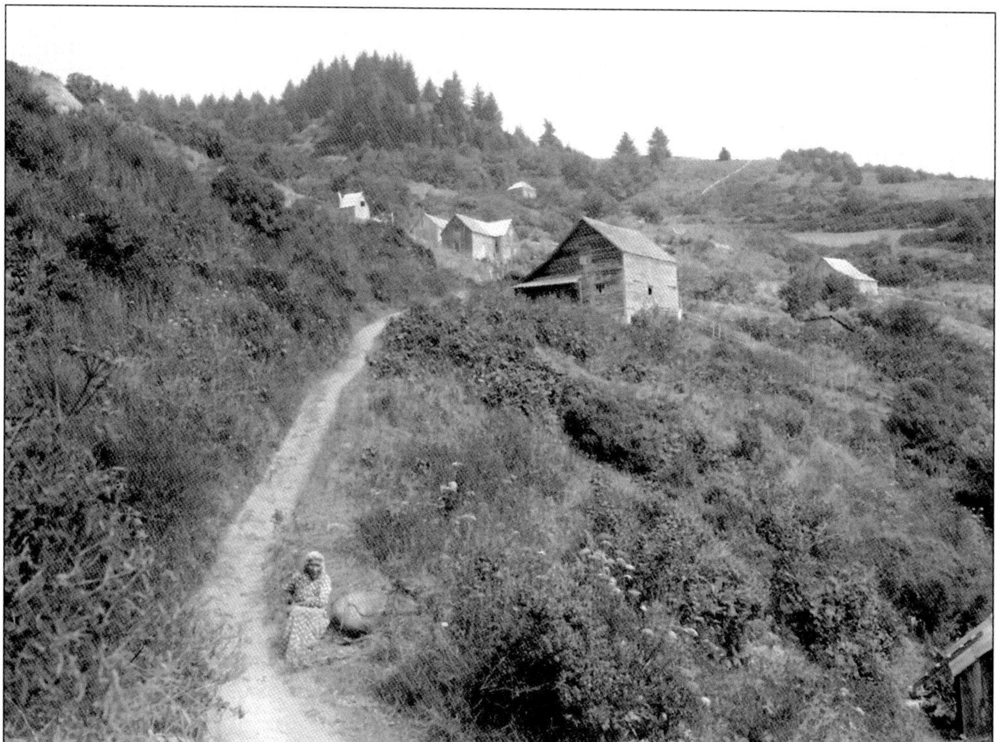

Mary Ann Frank rests with a basket of wood on Requa's first road. She was the mother of Alice and Robert Spott. In the right foreground is the first white man's house in Requa, and on the left is Captain Spott's house and smokehouse. Captain Spott, the father of Alice and Robert Spott, operated an ocean-going redwood canoe between Requa and Crescent City. He called himself "captain" because the masters of big ships were captains and he was master of his own canoe. The name stuck.

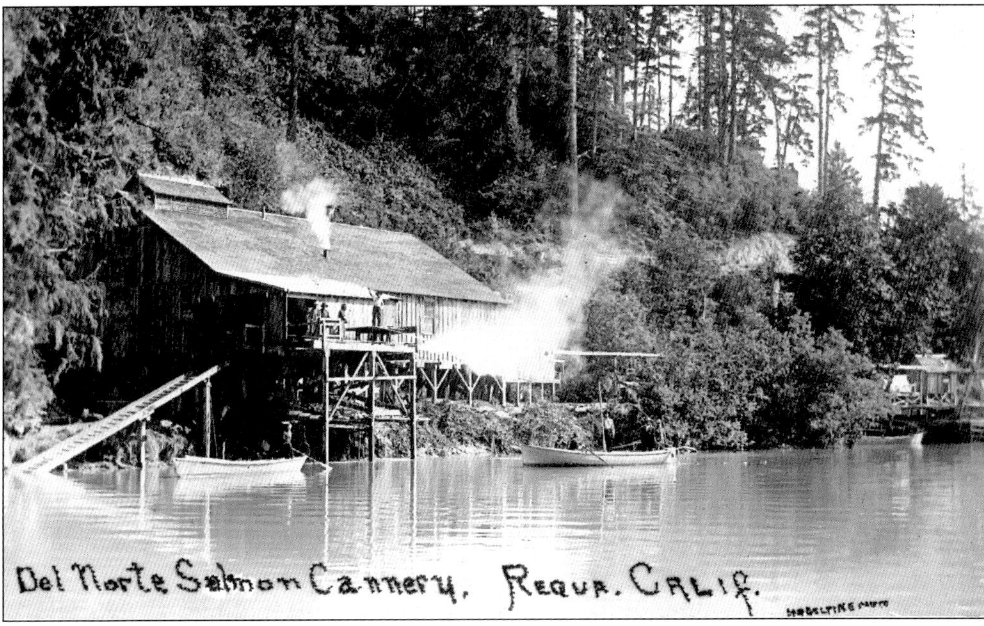

John Bomhoff obtained permission from the Indian agent on the Klamath River to build a cannery near the mouth of the Klamath River in 1886 called the Del Norte Salmon Cannery. Bomhoff employed many local Yurok Indians during the salmon-fishing season. The fish were preserved by salting.

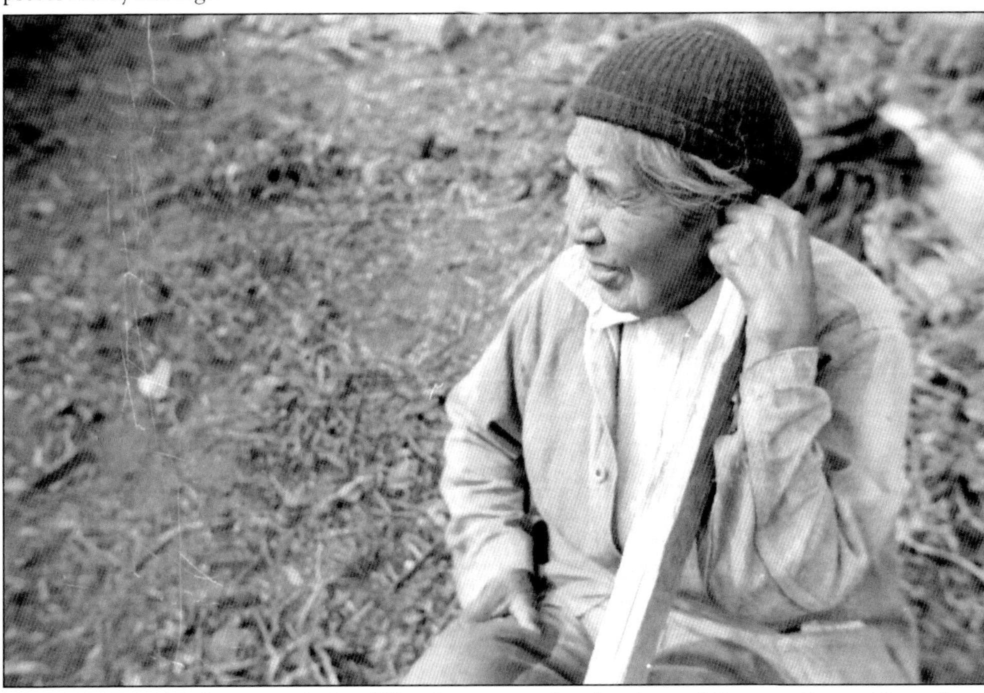

Alice Spott Taylor, born in 1864 in Weitchpec, was the daughter of Captain Spott. Considered to be higher class by the Yurok, she moved to Requa and worked in the canneries there for years. During World War II she worked at the Crescent Plywood plant on the lagoon near Wilson Creek. She died in December 1964.

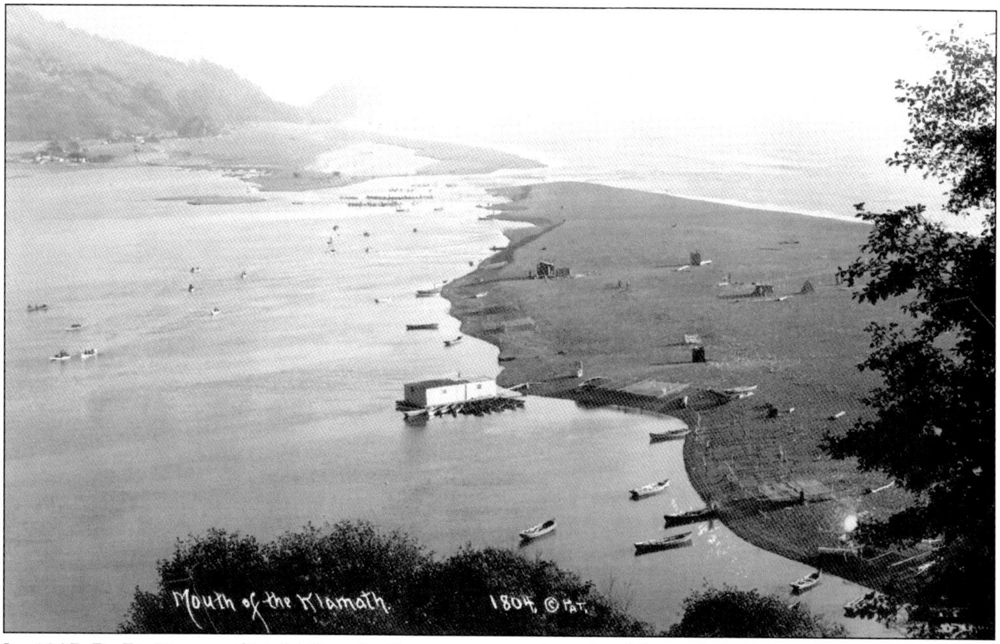

In 1887, R. D. Hume of Gold Beach, Oregon, moved to the Klamath River and set up a floating cannery during salmon runs. Then in 1889 Hume built a cannery about a mile upriver from the Bomhoff cannery. The floods of 1890 destroyed parts of the buildings and damaged the Bomhoff cannery. That spring the two companies consolidated and opened a new operation under the name of the Klamath Packing and Trading Company.

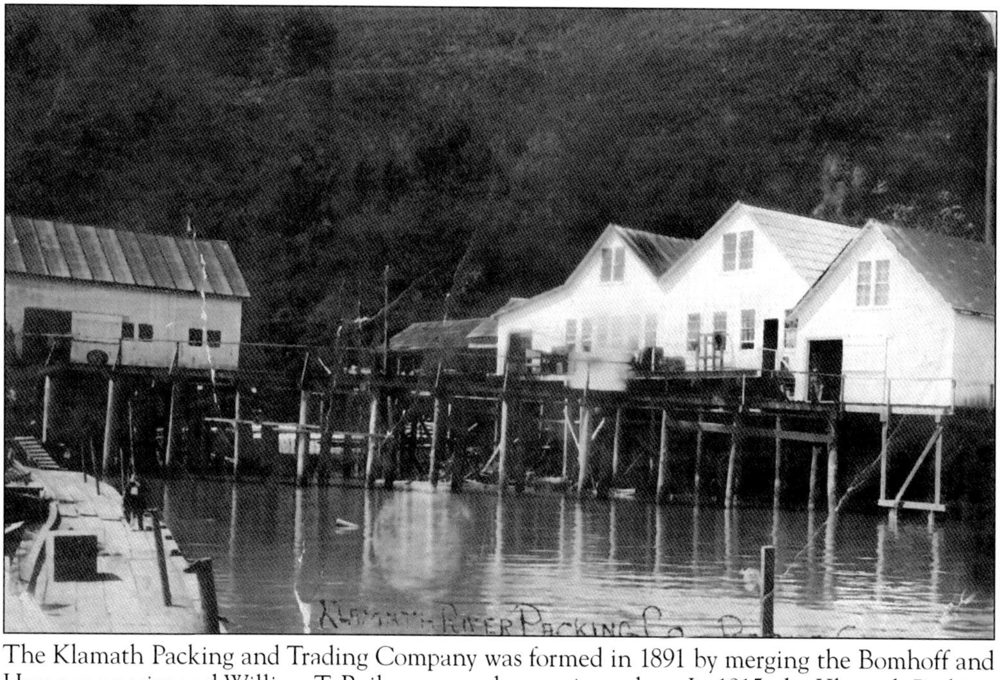

The Klamath Packing and Trading Company was formed in 1891 by merging the Bomhoff and Hume canneries and William T. Bailey was made superintendent. In 1915, the Klamath Packing and Trading Company purchased the other two canneries in Requa and merged the three to form the Klamath River Packing Association.

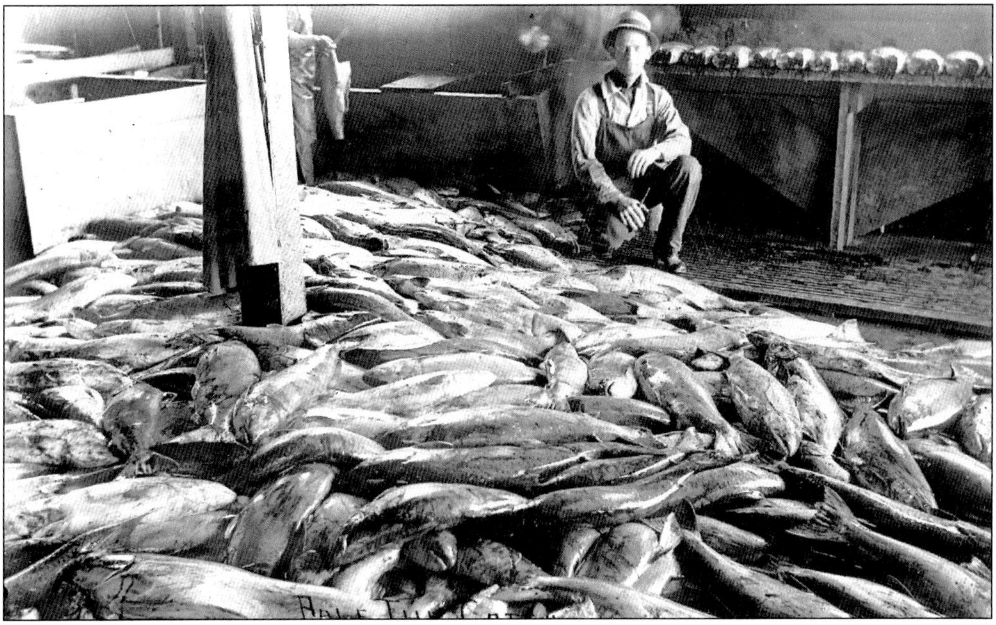

When the salmon were running, fish were delivered to the canneries in batches to keep the canning process running smoothly. This photograph shows a batch of salmon ready to be cleaned and prepared for canning.

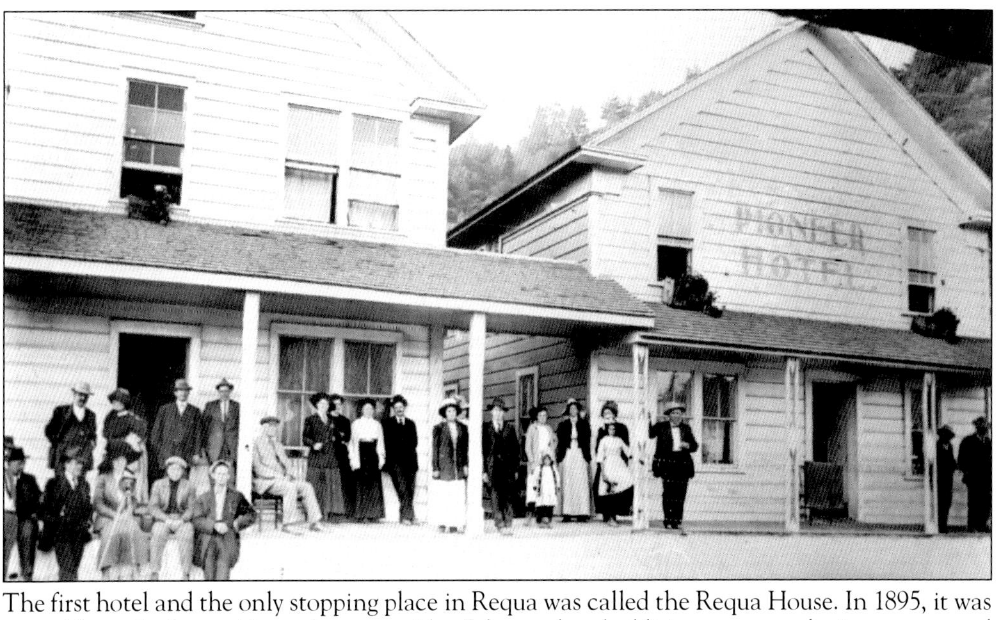

The first hotel and the only stopping place in Requa was called the Requa House. In 1895, it was moved from the lower side to the upper side of the road and additions were made. It was renamed the Pioneer Hotel and could accommodate 10 guests.

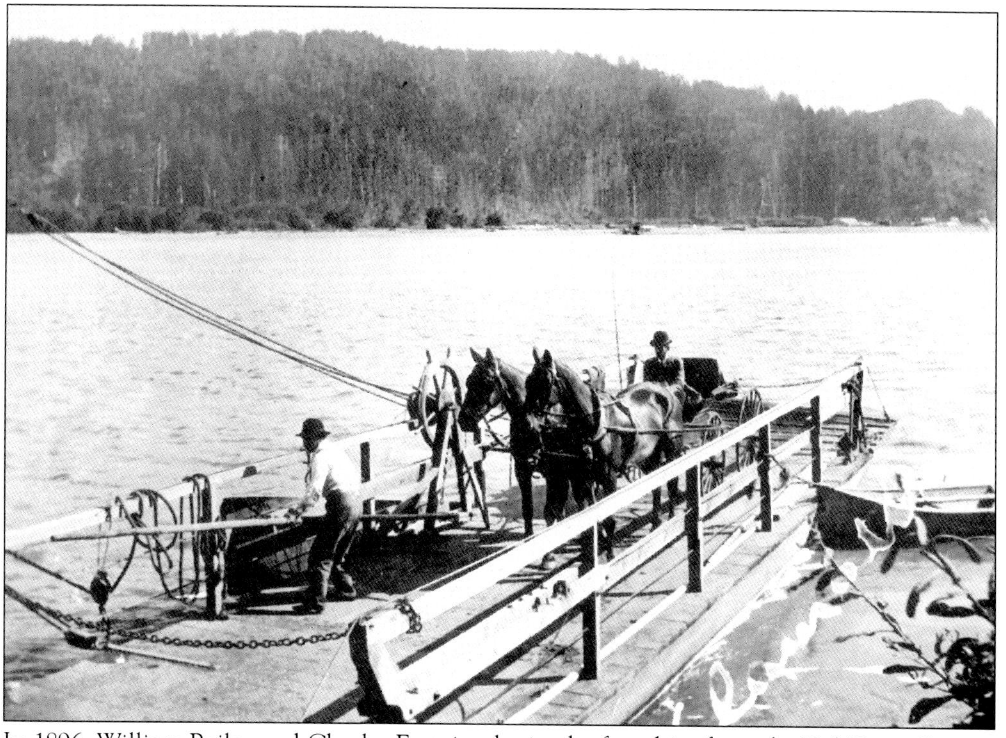

In 1896, William Bailey and Charles Fortain obtained a franchise from the Del Norte County Board of Supervisors to operate a ferry on the Klamath River. They stretched a 1,700-foot cable across the river and built the first real ferry boat. Before it was constructed people and supplies had to be transported across the river in redwood canoes.

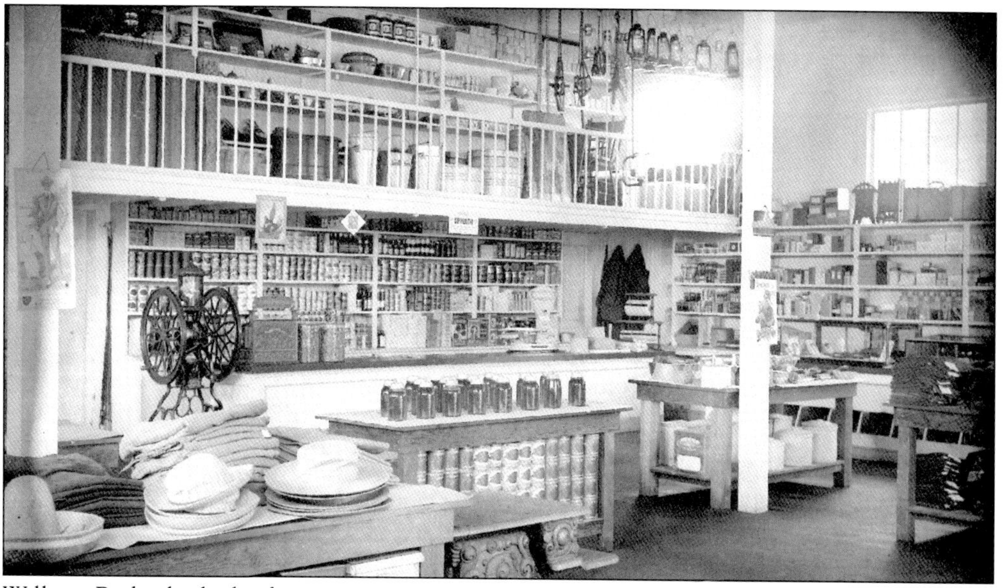

William Bailey built the first store in Requa in 1898 before selling it to the Samoa Mercantile Company in 1908. Two years later, it exchanged hands once again as it was sold to A. Brizard Company of Arcata. When the Douglas Memorial Bridge was opened to traffic in 1926, Requa was no longer a transportation hub, and a new Brizard's store was built in the new Klamath Town.

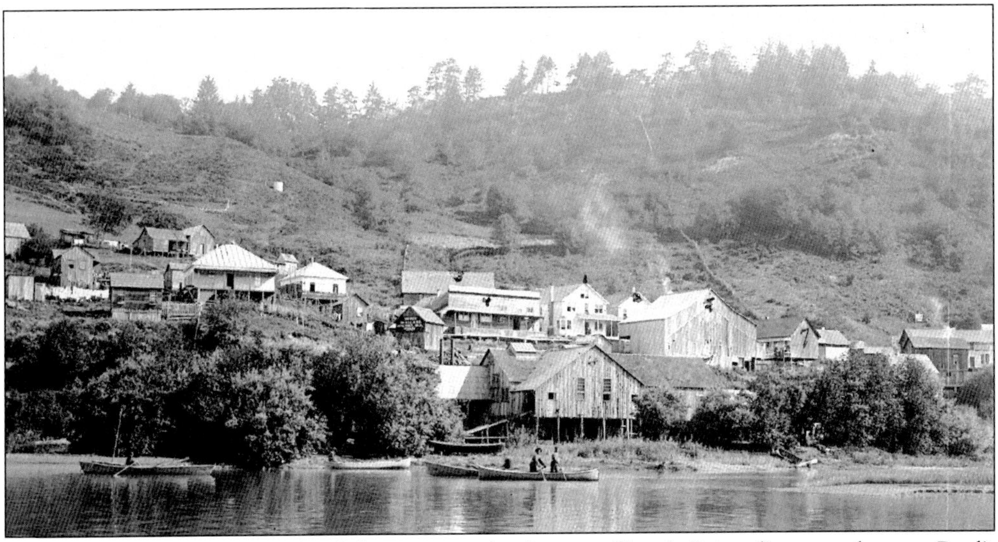

Buildings in Requa included a fish cannery, the Pioneer Hotel, Brizard's general store, Paul's general store, two saloons, a livery stable, and a dance hall. In 1914, a fire started in the Pioneer Hotel, quickly spread, and by morning every structure in town had burned to the ground. It was quickly rebuilt, thrived until 1926, and was active with the canning industry until 1933, when the rivers of northern California were closed to commercial fishing.

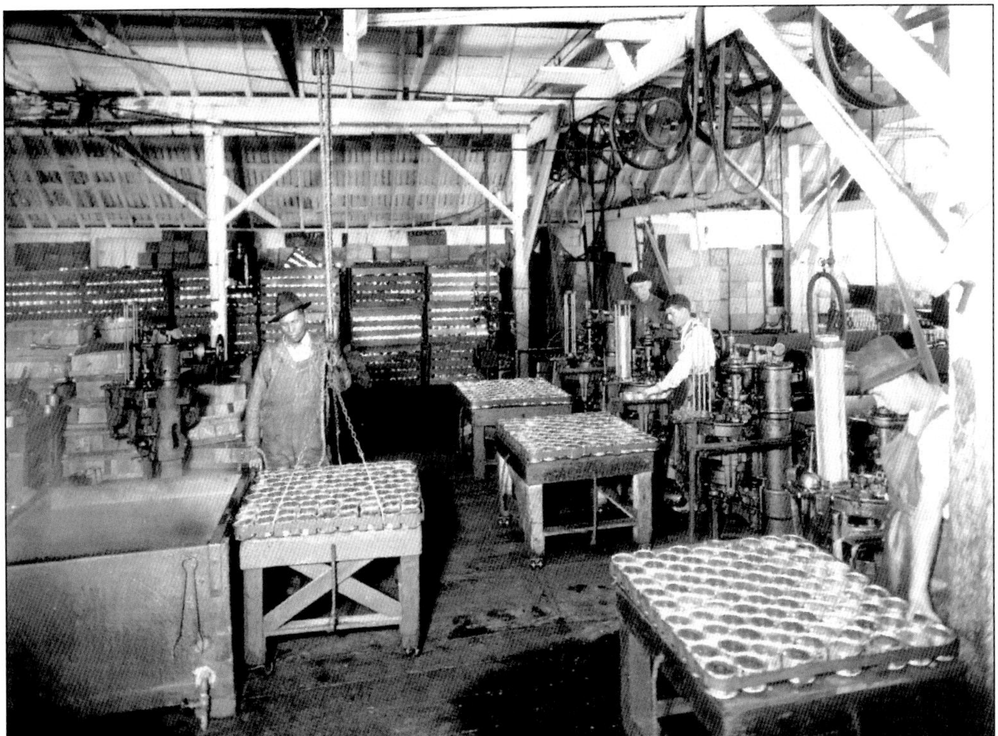

Pictured here is the interior of the Klamath River Packing Association cannery, which was formed by merging three canneries in 1915. The equipment inside was the newest technology in canning operations, as the original canneries didn't actually can fish but preserved them by salting the meat.

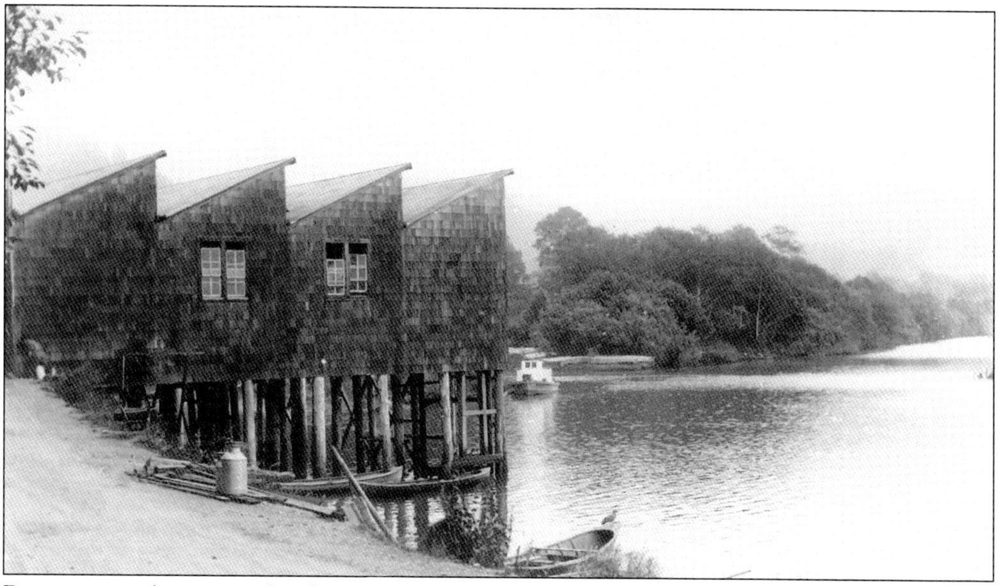

Dairying was the principal industry in the area, and in 1915 the Western Meat Company entered into an agreement with local ranchers to build a cheese factory and run the business there under a 10-year lease. Milk was delivered to the front of the building by truck and to the rear by boat.

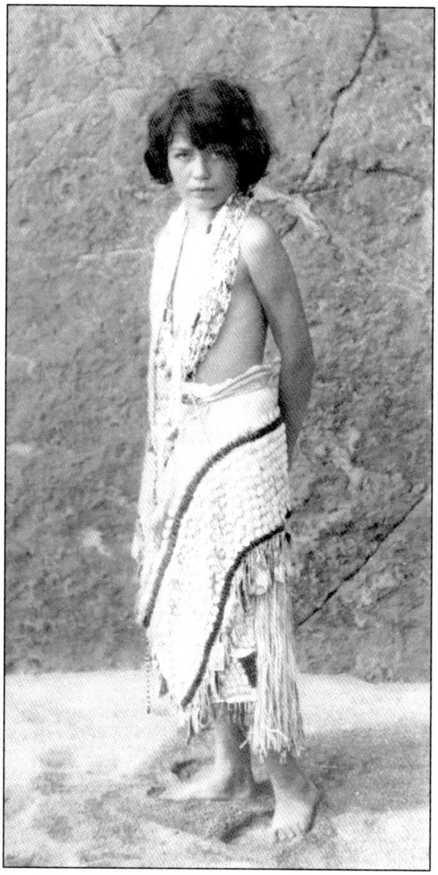

Tede Spott, the youngest daughter of Alice Spott Taylor in 1922, is dressed in a long deerskin skirt decorated with shells and wearing several dentalium necklaces. Dentalium shells were items of wealth and formed the basis of the Yurok monetary system.

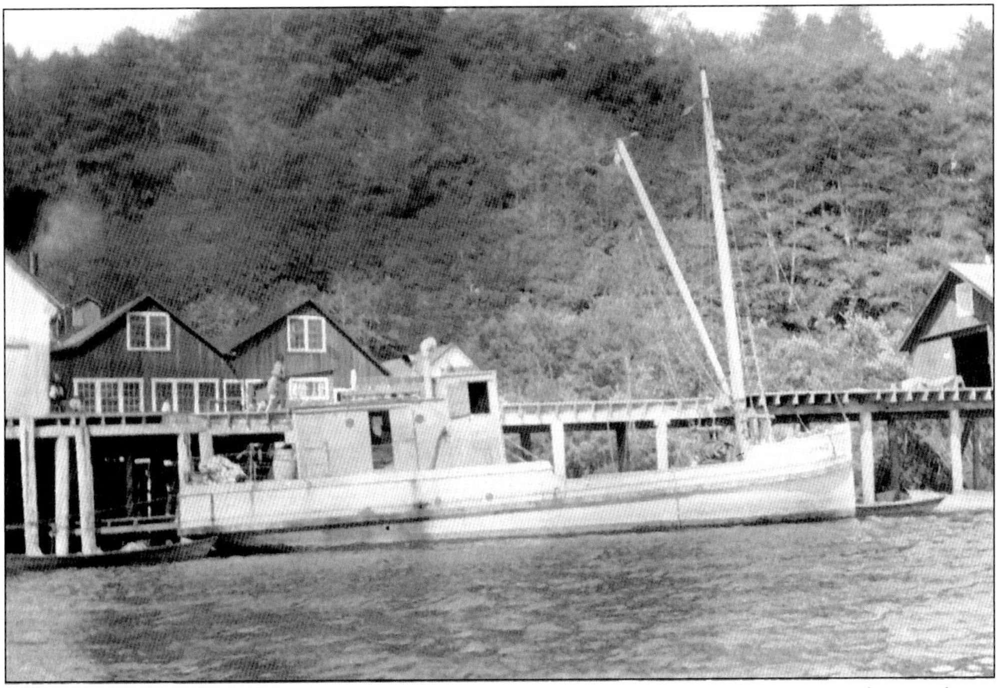

The freighter *Golden West* was often tied up at the Klamath River Packing Association wharf. It was one of steamers that brought supplies to Requa and picked up cheese and canned salmon destined for San Francisco. On the left is the fish house, the cannery is in the middle, and the warehouse is off to the right.

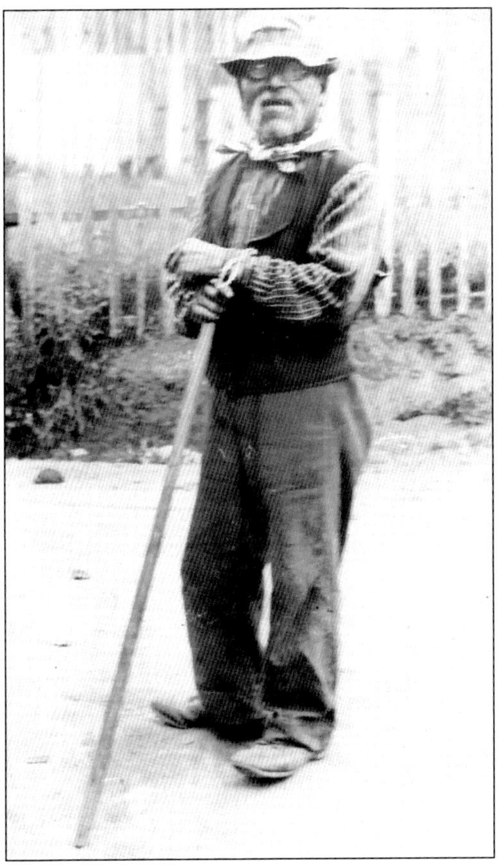

Captain Jack was born on the upper Klamath River in 1860 and as a young man he moved to Requa. He was a fisherman and owned his own redwood dugout canoe that he used to ferry people and goods across and upriver. Because the men who were in charge of the freighters that came to Requa were called "captain," he decided to call himself captain also, and was known as Captain Jack from then on.

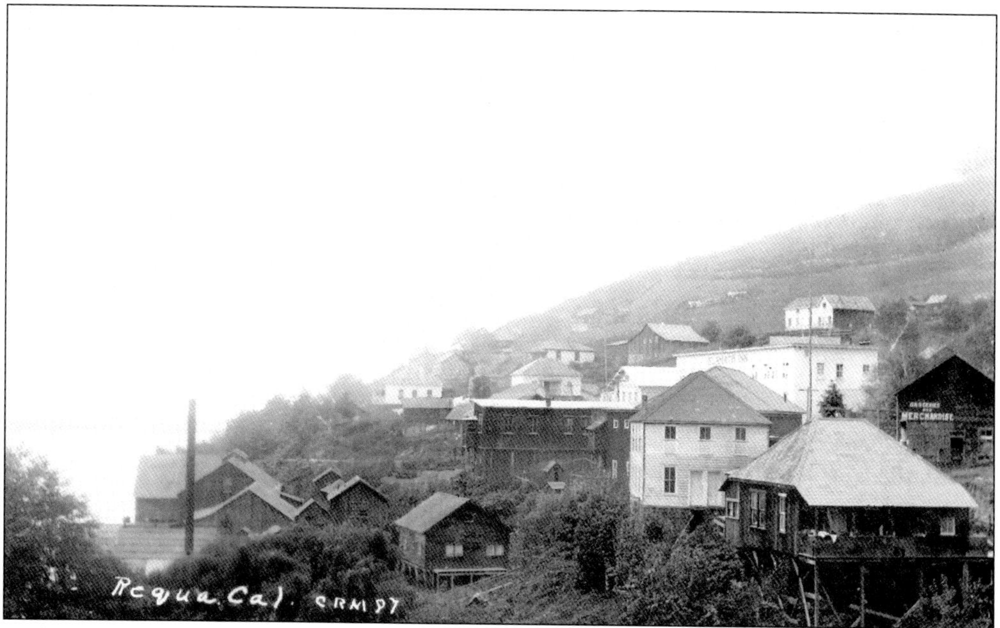

In the middle of the night in August 1914, a fire started in the Pioneer Hotel. By morning, every wooden structure in the town of Requa had burned to the ground. Almost before the ashes were cool, the work of rebuilding the town began. New and larger structures were built. A new hotel called the Klamath Inn was constructed on the site of the old Pioneer Hotel.

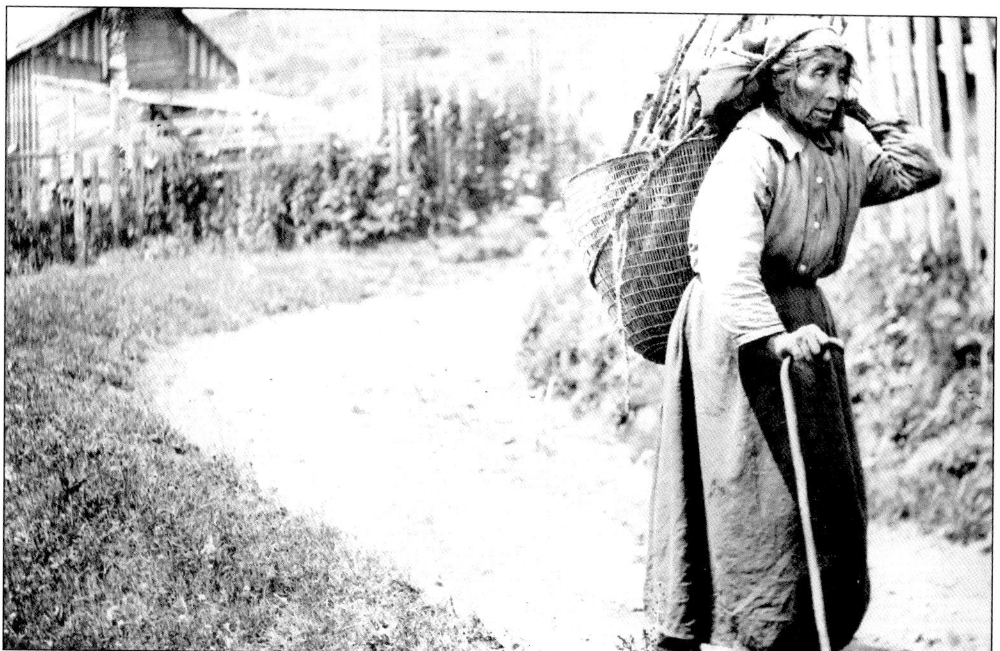

Nellie Big Fire was a Yurok Indian living at Requa. She was very old but still very active and performed her daily tasks. She gathered driftwood for cooking fires using a carrying basket she had woven herself. The Yurok basket was very similar to the carrying baskets of the Tolowa Indians.

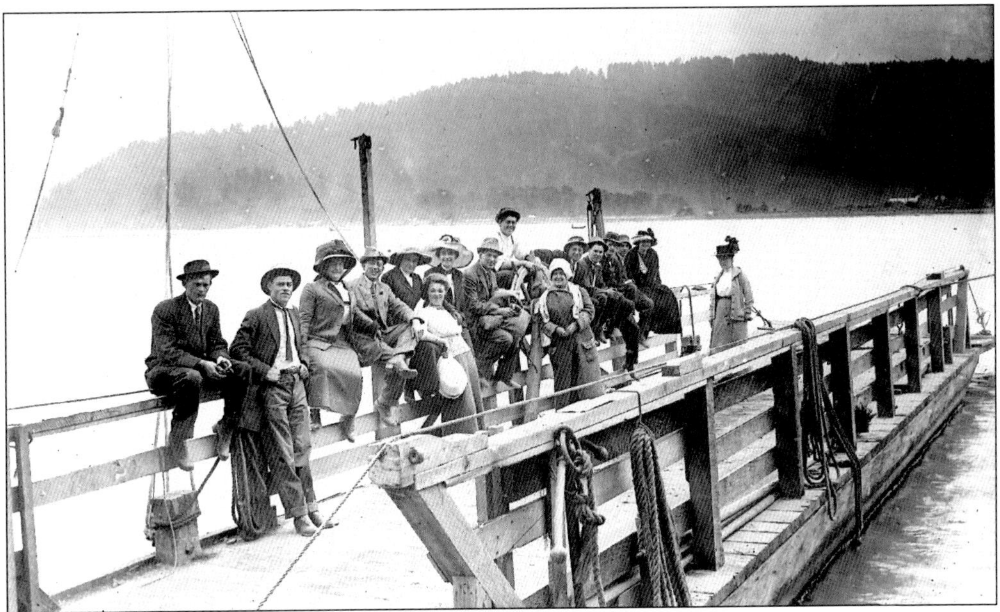

David Ball and Ralph Cara were contracted by the Del Norte County Board of Supervisors to build a new ferry in 1919, as traffic was increasing and a new one was needed to handle the demand. The new ferry was longer and wider and could accommodate three automobiles, and it operated until the summer of 1926, when the Douglas Memorial Bridge was opened to traffic.

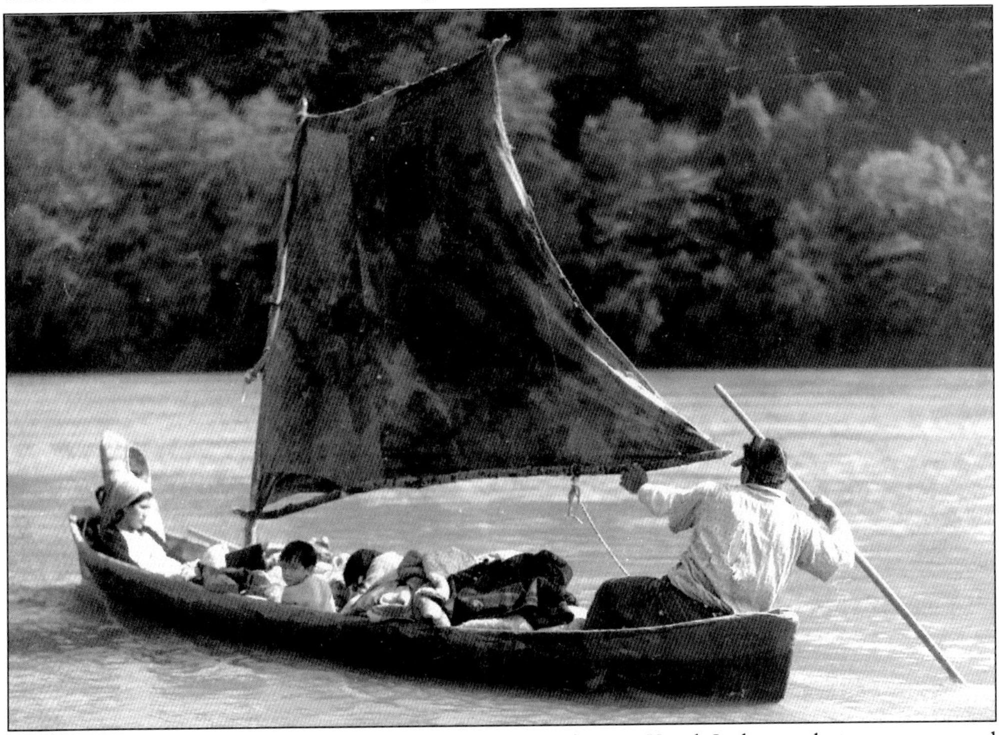

Pictured here with 4 of her 17 children, Lillian Ames Salazar, a Yurok Indian, is being transported up the Klamath River in a redwood dugout canoe with a sail. Lewis Oscar, the children's uncle, is steering the canoe. This was the only means to reach areas upriver from Requa.

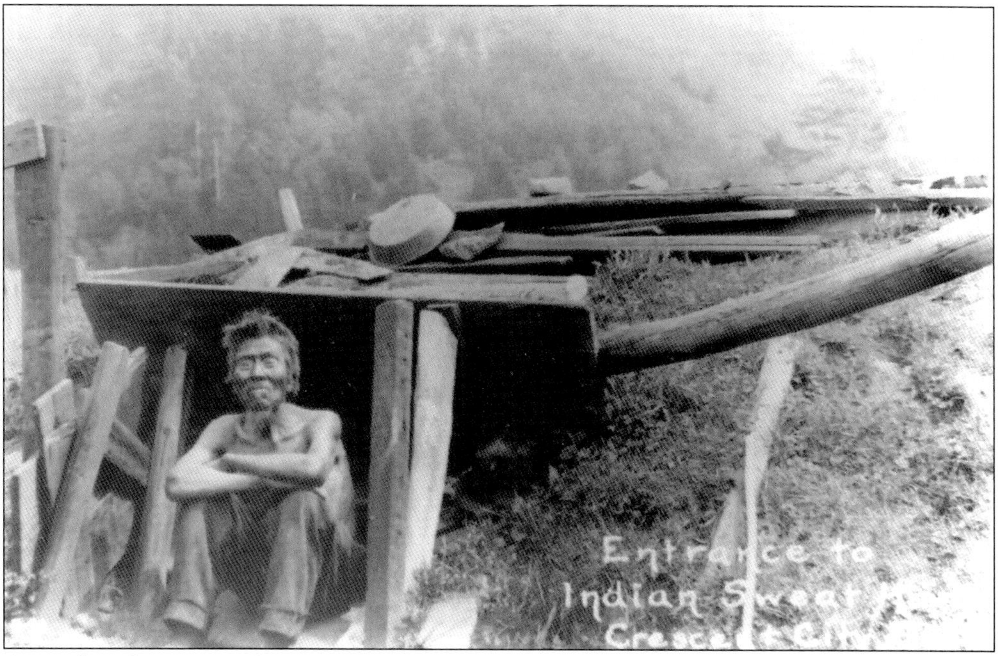

A Yurok Indian sits at the entrance to a sweat house where men and boys lived after puberty; women and girls lived together in redwood slab houses. The sweat house was smaller than the main house, about 12 feet by 11 feet, with the greatest interior height between 6 and 7 feet. The entire area was excavated to a depth of at least 4 feet and lined with redwood puncheons, and there were basically no walls above ground.

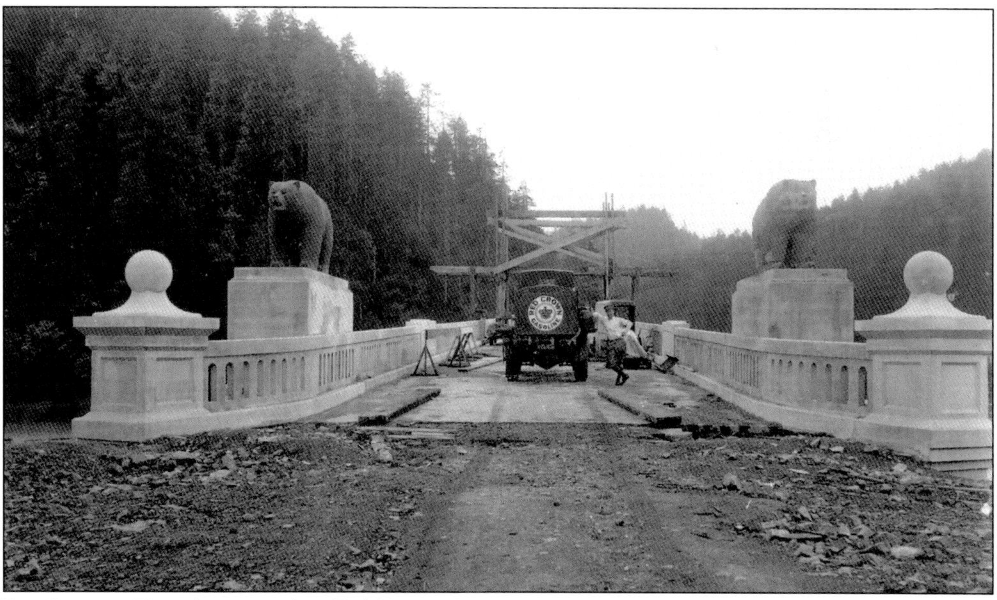

Dr. Gustave Douglas retired to Del Norte County in 1920. He was elected state representative from Siskiyou and Del Norte Counties in 1922. His first priority was authorization for a bridge across the Klamath, and in early 1923 he introduced a bill to fund its construction. On March 23, 1923, Douglas suffered a fatal heart attack. His bill was later passed. The bridge was designated the G. H. Douglas Memorial Bridge and dedicated on May 17, 1926.

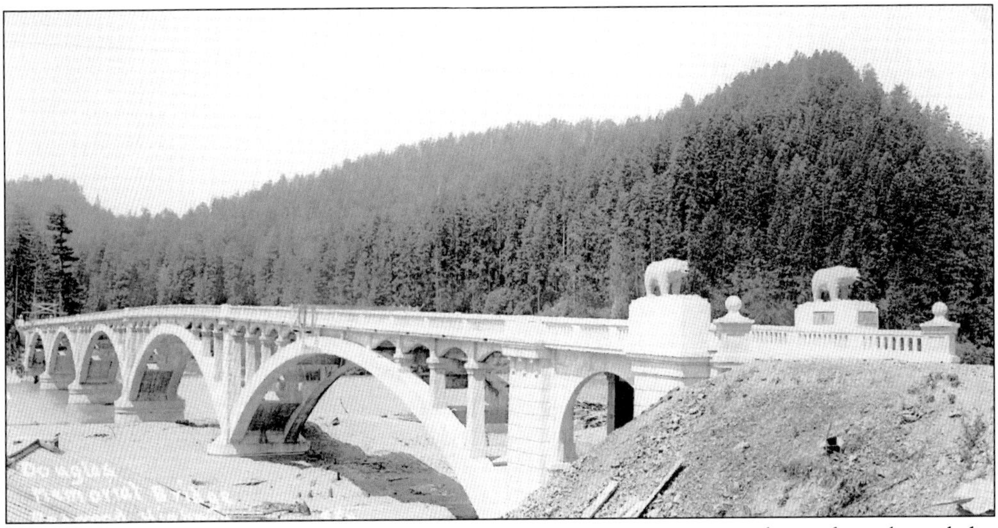

With the completion of the Douglas Memorial Bridge, tourism increased significantly and the Klamath grew rapidly into a prosperous town. The Redwood Highway was now complete from Eureka, California, to Grants Pass, Oregon and Highway 101 was also complete to Brookings, Oregon, and points north.

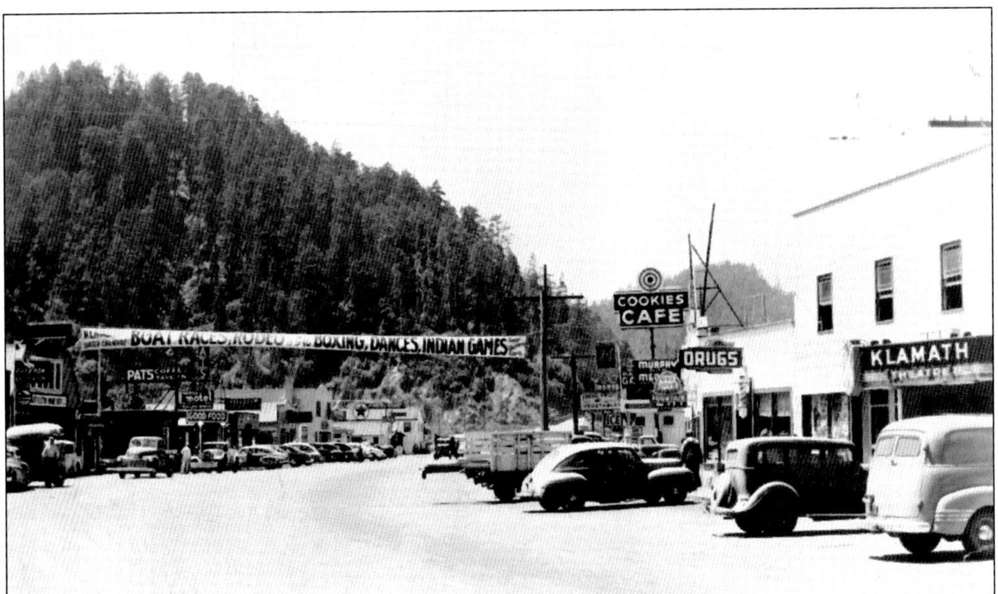

In 1939, downtown Klamath was growing and adding new stores. Requa had been bypassed by Highway 101, and most of the commercial development shut down and moved to the new Klamath town site. The new highway traffic needed more services and Klamath was doing its best to provide them.

Waukell Harry was born up the Klamath River, above Klamath Glen and moved to Requa as a young man. Here he displays Yurok Indian headdresses and other artifacts used in ceremonial dances. The redheaded woodpecker scalps in the headdresses were a sign of wealth.

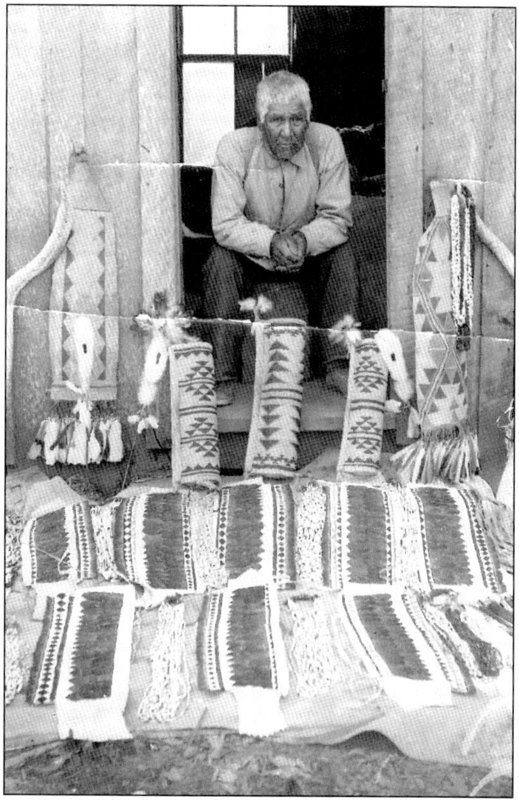

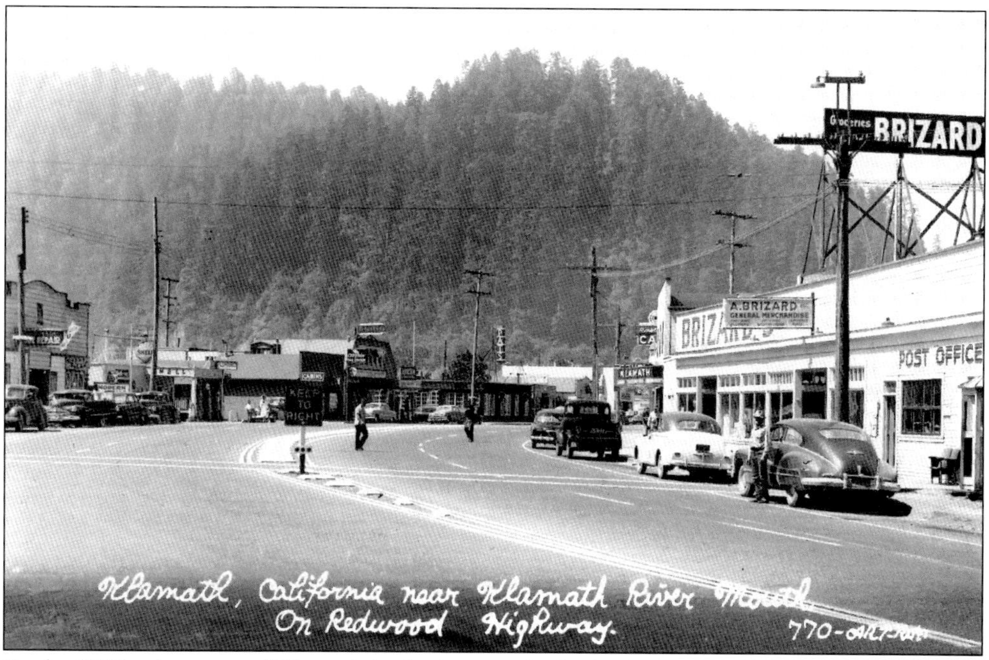

By the 1950s, the town of Klamath had taken on the look of a prosperous resort town and had grown considerably. There were motels, stores of all kinds, restaurants, a bakery, and several gas stations.

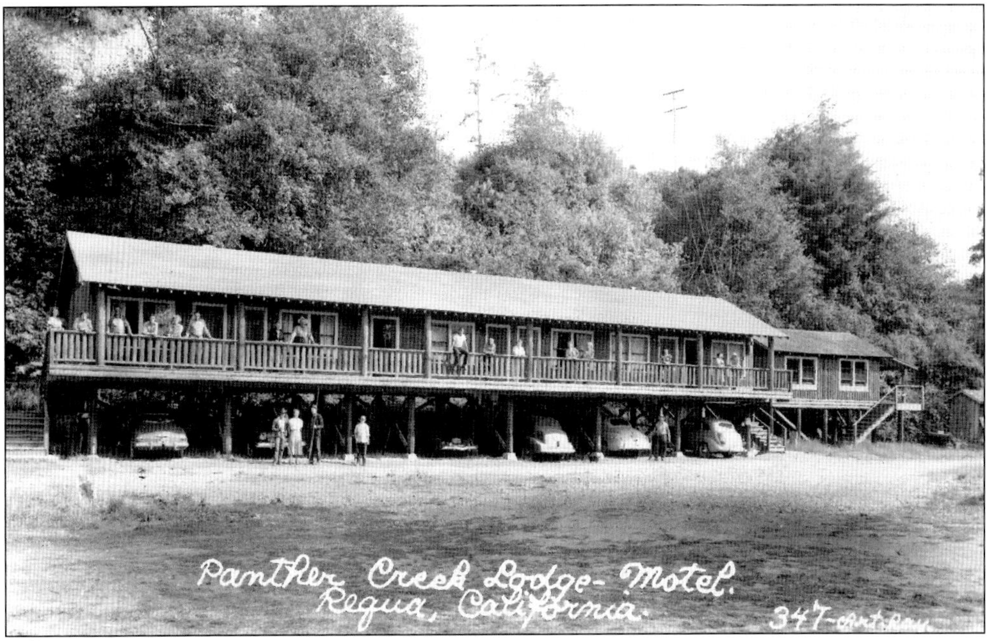

Many resort motels were developed in the Klamath area as it was a tourist area known for its beautiful scenery and magnificent salmon fishing available in the Klamath River. The Panther Creek Lodge and Resort was one of the destination resorts in the Klamath area.

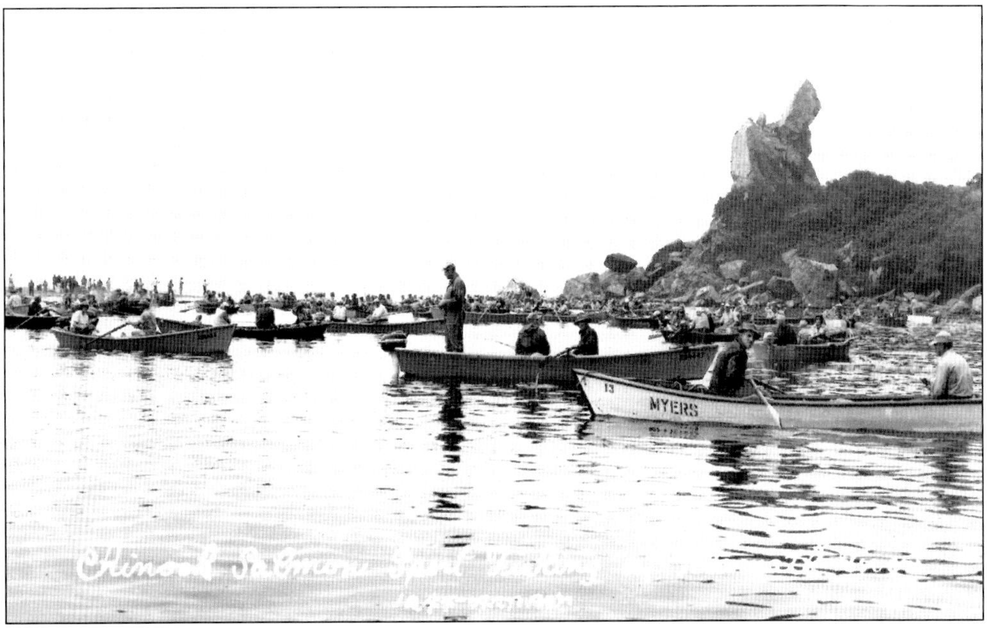

Chinook salmon fishing was wildly popular and drew fishermen from all over the country. When the salmon were running the river near the mouth was full of boats, and those boats were generally full of salmon.

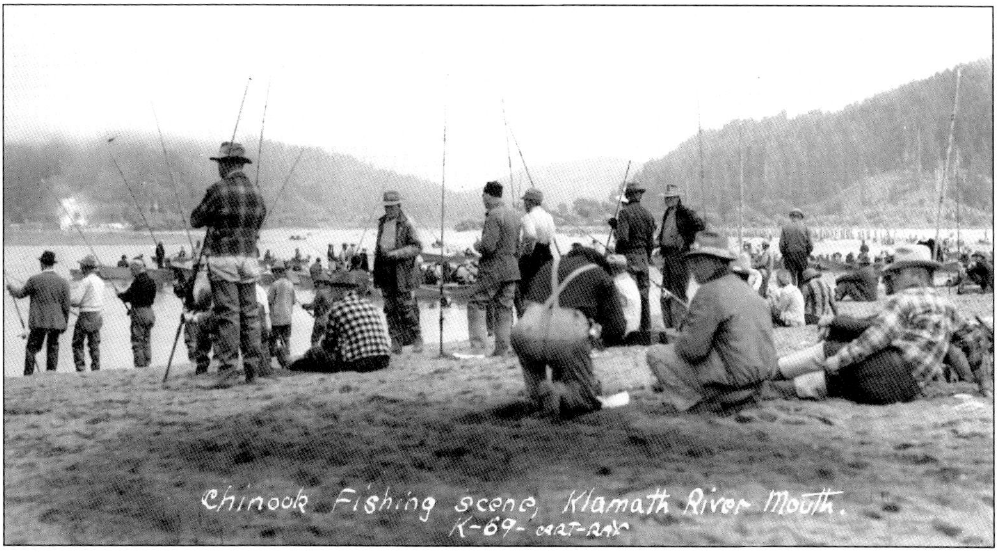

Fishing from shore was also very popular, and during salmon runs, the shore was crowded with fishermen. Several campsites and RV fishing parks were developed, and some fishermen camped out for the entire salmon run.

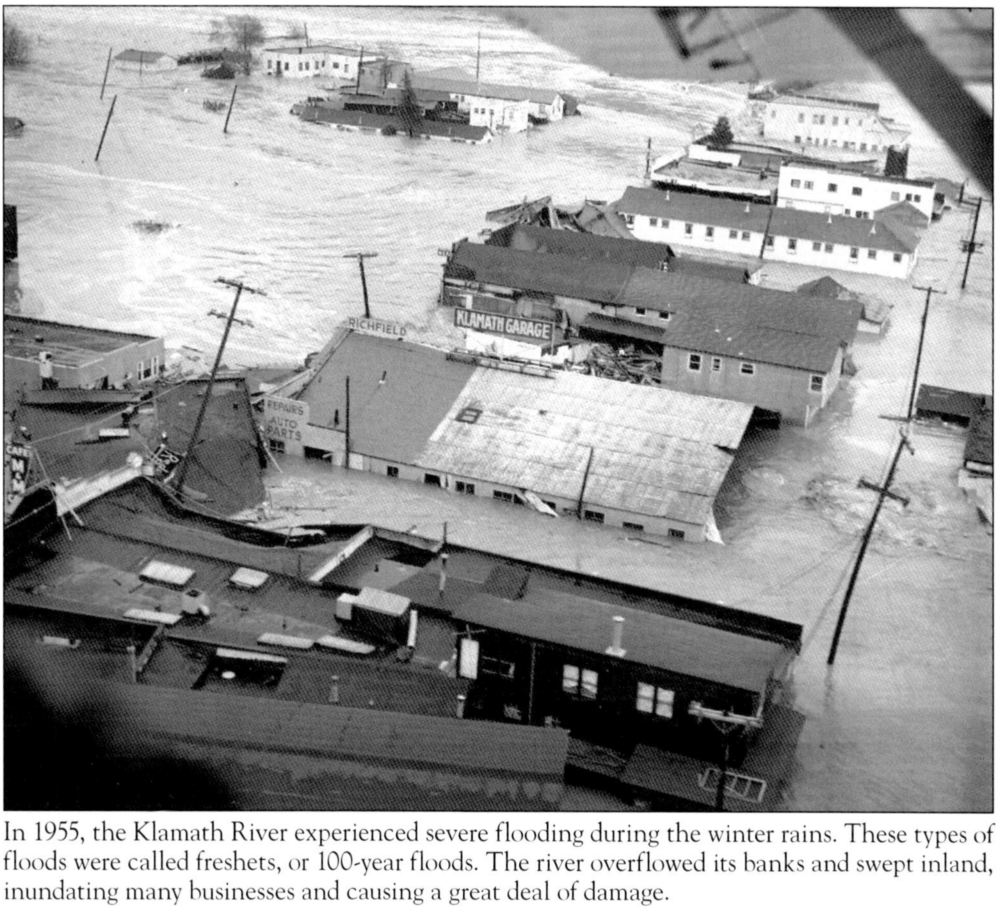

In 1955, the Klamath River experienced severe flooding during the winter rains. These types of floods were called freshets, or 100-year floods. The river overflowed its banks and swept inland, inundating many businesses and causing a great deal of damage.

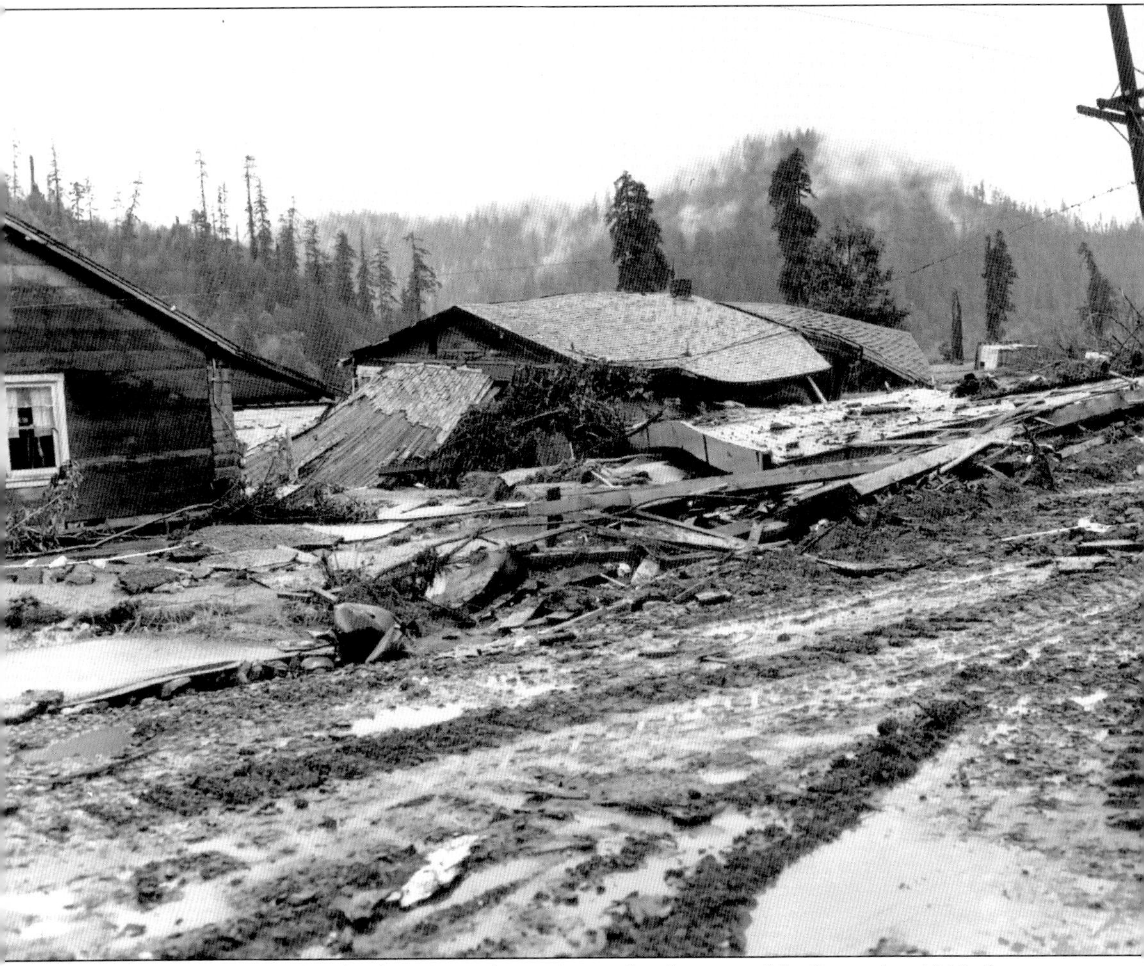

Nine years after the floods of 1955, another 100-year flood occurred. In December 1964, the storms came in off the Pacific one after another. The weather was also warm, which caused the snow in the mountains to melt and run off into the river. The Klamath River crested 10 feet above the 1955 flood level, sections of the Douglas Memorial Bridge were swept away, and the entire town of Klamath ceased to exist. Outlying homes were destroyed by the rushing river waters that tore them from their foundations, deposited silt in and on them, or demolished them with multiple collisions. The Klamath town site was consequently abandoned.

Six

Del Norte County
The Later Years

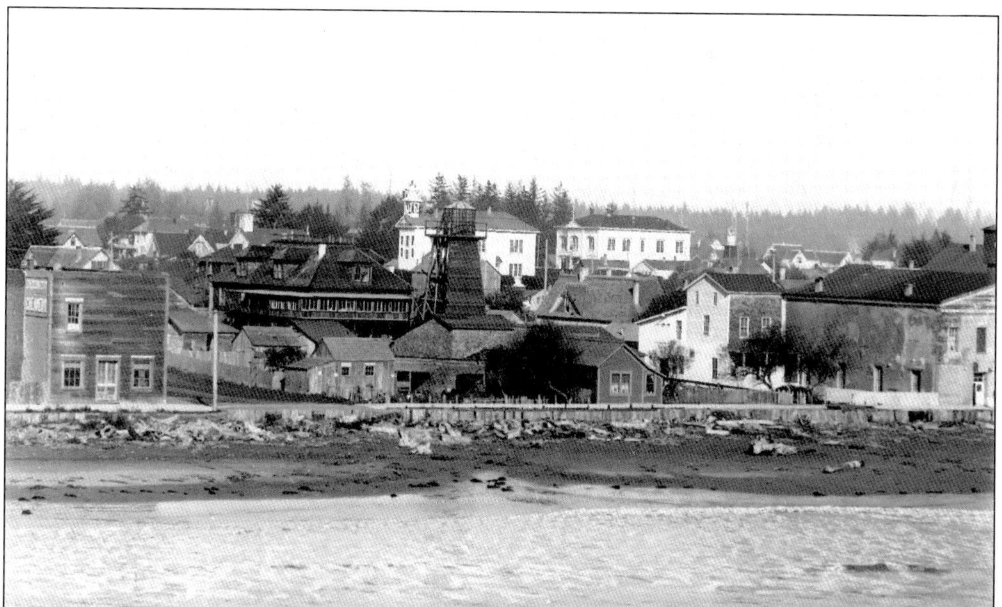

This is a shot of the western end of Front Street from the Hobbs, Wall wharf with a seawall that had been constructed to protect the buildings from waves and storm surges. The structure on the right is the Darby Building, the tall white building in the background on the left is the first grammar school, and the white building on the right is the courthouse.

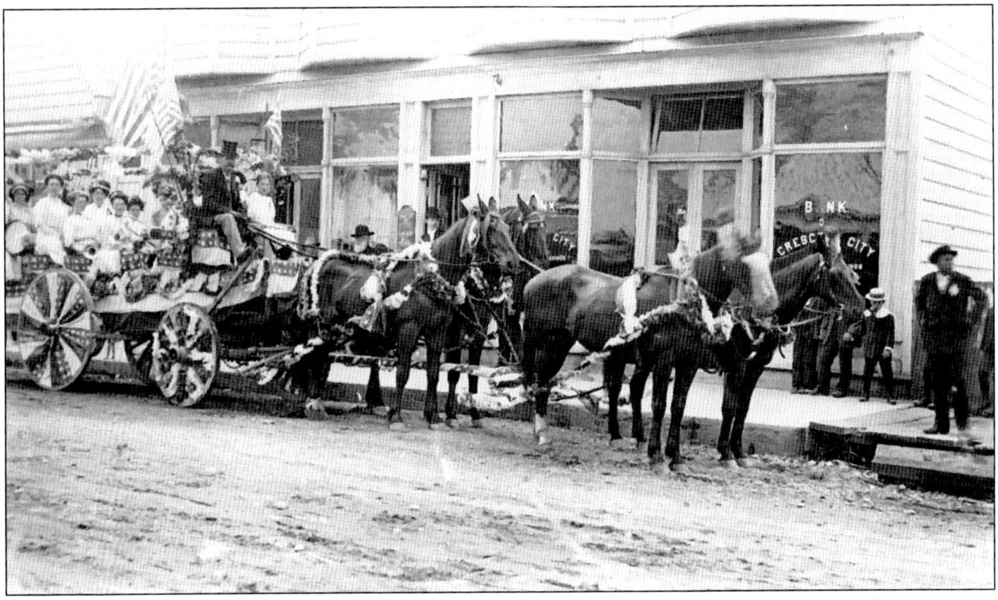

Frank Williams was an Iowa farmer when he came to Crescent City in 1892. He bought a grocery store from his brother Wesley and learned the candy-making business from his brother Milton. He also learned watch and clock repair and jewelry making. Later he bought a vacant lot across from his grocery store and constructed the two-story Williams Building. This float in the 1914 Fourth of July parade waits in front of that structure.

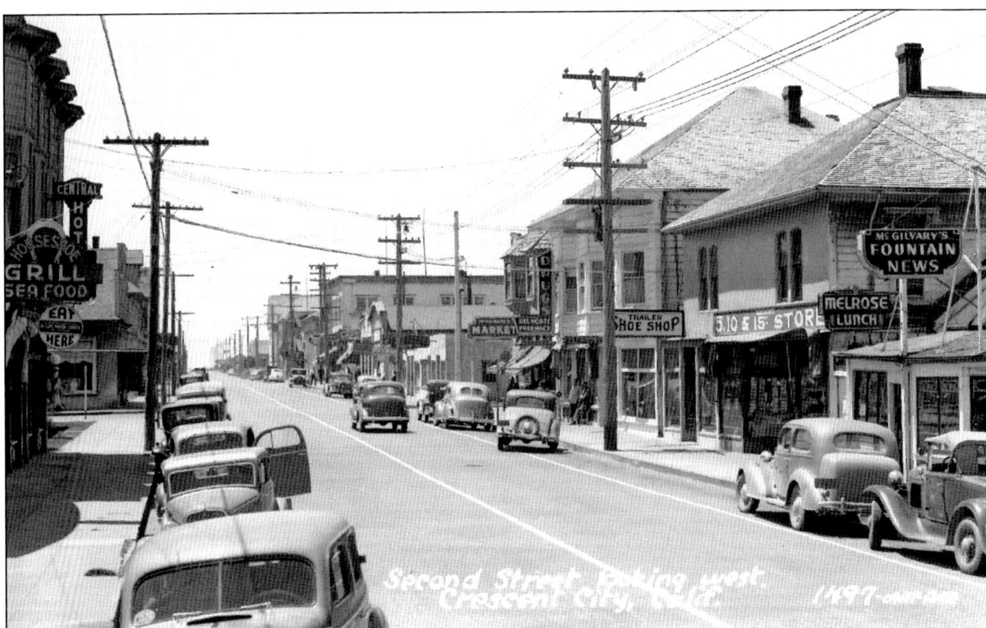

Second Street was the major commercial street in Crescent City and this photograph is of it looking west. The Williams Building, which later became the Central Hotel, is on the left.

In 1915, Martin Lund, a world-renowned diver, and J. C. Freese, a marine contractor, came to Crescent City to look for the wreck of the *Brother Jonathan*, which had been carrying the government payroll for the troops at Fort Vancouver. Army troops were always paid in gold coin so there would have been a great deal of the precious metal on board. It was also reported that there had been a large amount of jewelry on the ship.

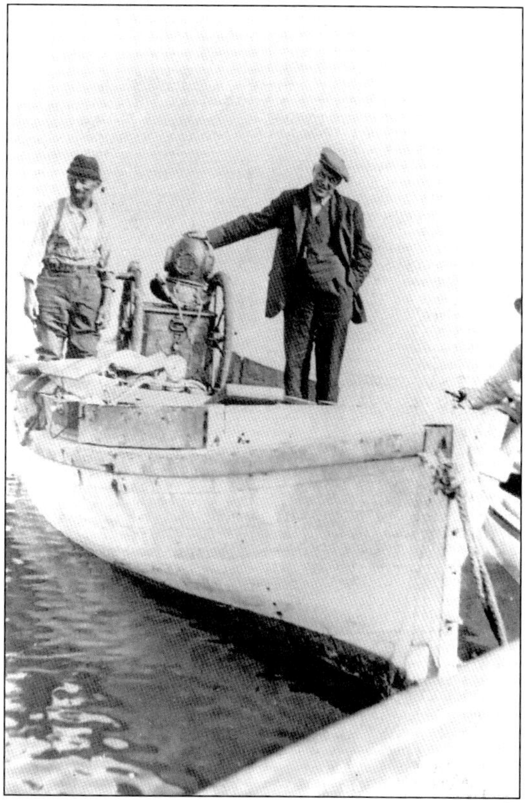

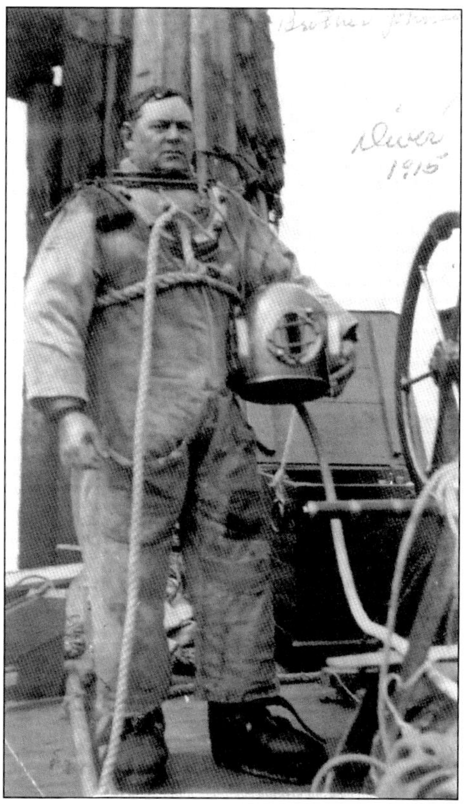

Tio Francisco was a local fisherman who pulled in a railroad tie in his fishing net from the *Brother Jonathan* and he gave the location to Lund. With this information, a hard-hat diver was able to locate the *Brother Jonathan* exactly 50 years to the day after she sank. It wasn't until 1993 that salvage operations on the *Brother Jonathan* began.

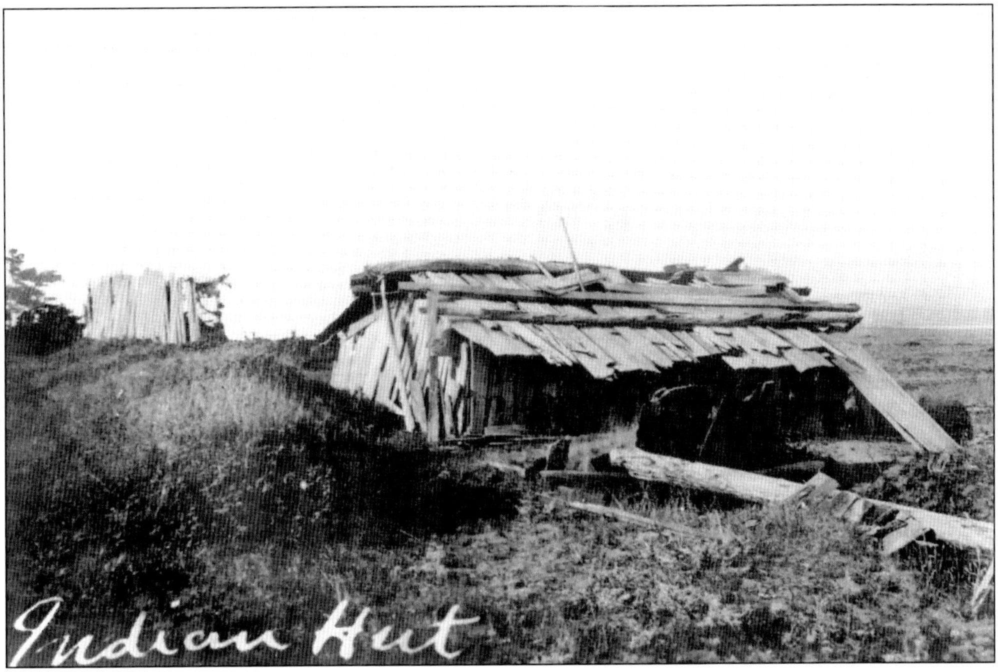

A typical Indian plank house was built of vertical redwood planks set into the ground and a roof using the same material with one side extending over the other and a space for the smoke to escape. The houses were about 15 square feet and had an interior pit about 10 feet square and 3 feet deep. The floor was either redwood plank or flat beach stone. The ledge around the interior pit was used to store food.

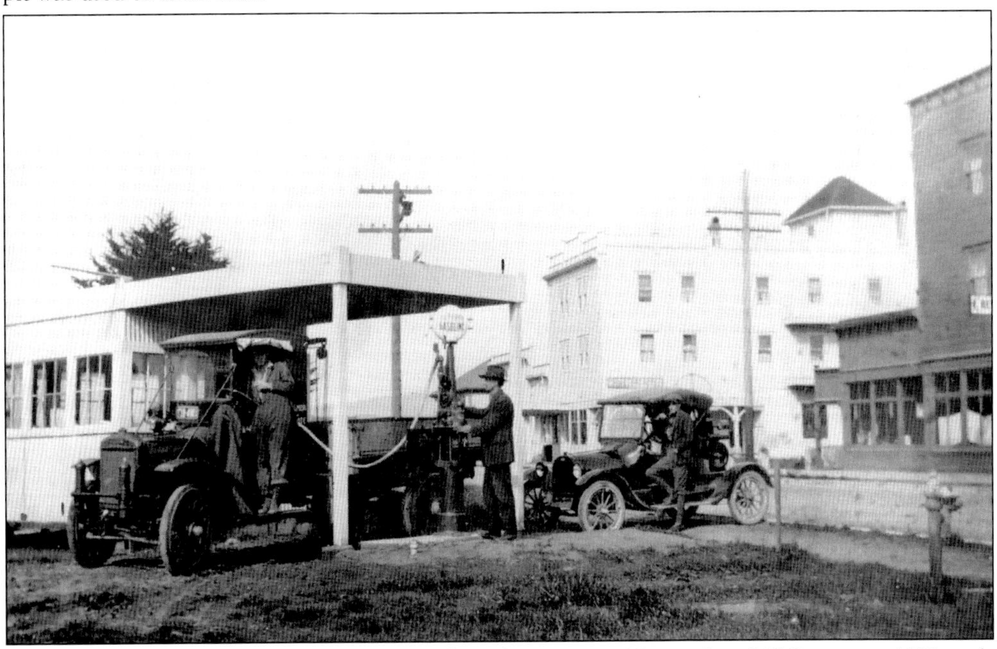

A gas station selling filtered gas was located on the corner of Second and K Streets in 1921 with the American Hotel in the background. There weren't many automobiles in Del Norte County until after the Redwood Highway was completed in 1926.

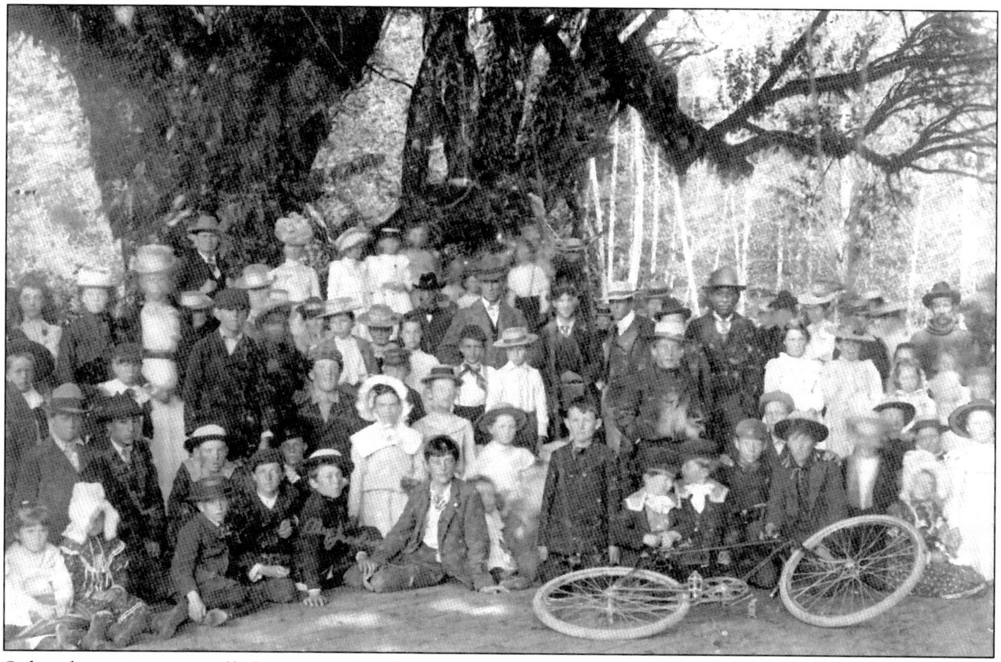

School picnics were all-day activities that were popular towards the end of the school year. Many mothers helped with food preparation and chaperoned the event as this served as an early form of the PTA. Myrtle Grove, located at the end of the Dr. Fine Bridge, was a popular picnic site.

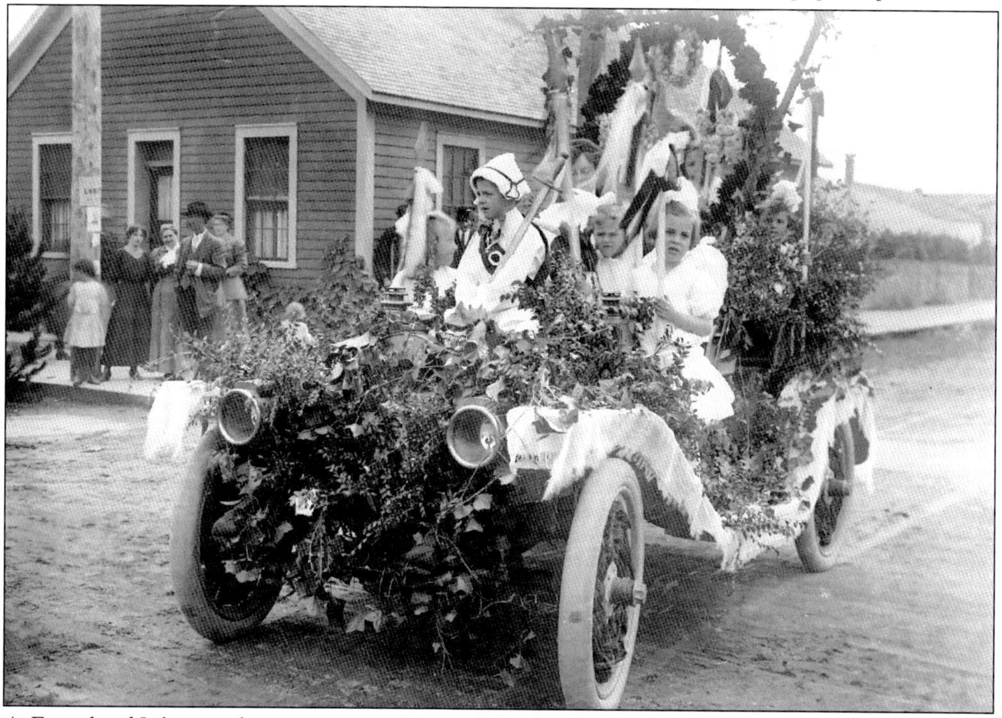

A Fourth of July parade entry sits in front of the home of Charles and Edith Frantz, who are seen here looking on. Edith Frantz owned a popular dress shop in Crescent City. As automobiles became more numerous, they replaced the horse-and-wagon as parade floats.

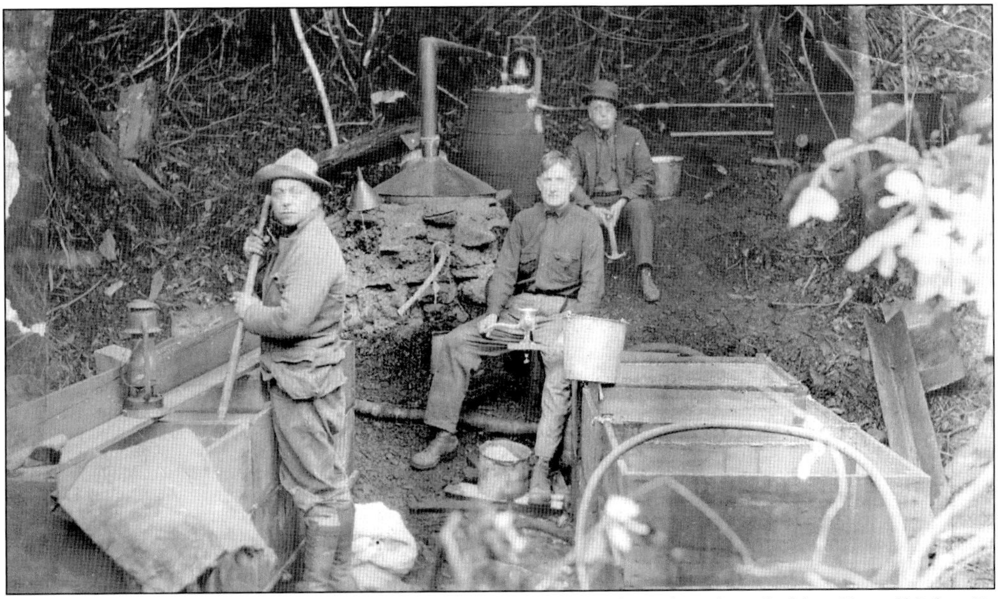

A still located about 10 miles north of Crescent City was found and raided by Sheriff John R. Breen in 1921. Del Norte County wasn't in favor of prohibition and prosecution of its laws was generally very lax. There were many home stills located in the county.

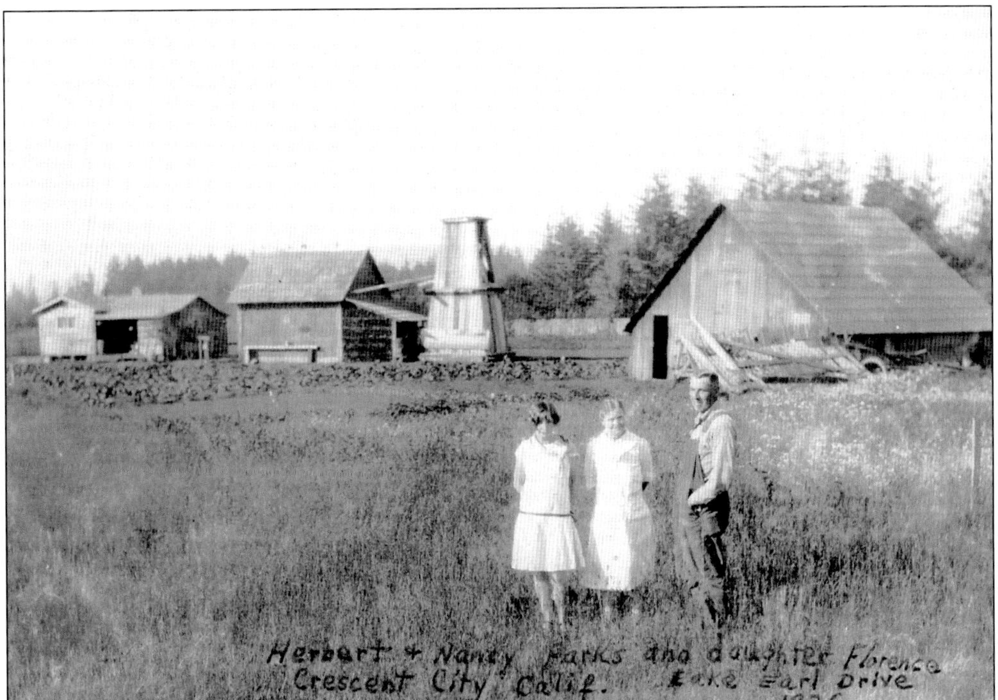

Herbert and Nancy Parks, with their daughter Florence, are pictured here on their farm on the road from Crescent City to Fort Dick, which is now Lake Earl Drive. Herbert Parks moved his family to Crescent City in 1920 and purchased the farm. Herbert worked on the construction of Highway 101 south of Crescent City and also the construction of Highway 199.

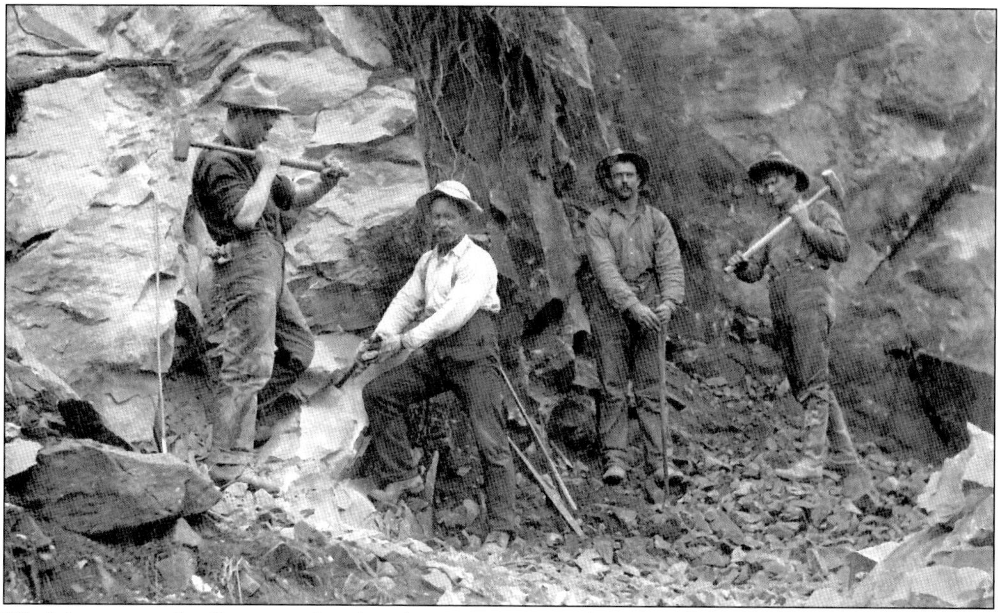

Work began on the Crescent City breakwater in 1920. This was the first quarry site at Hall Bluff (also called Lovers Rock by local Native Americans). The quarry provided rock for the breakwater until 1924. Kirby and Kern was the first contractor.

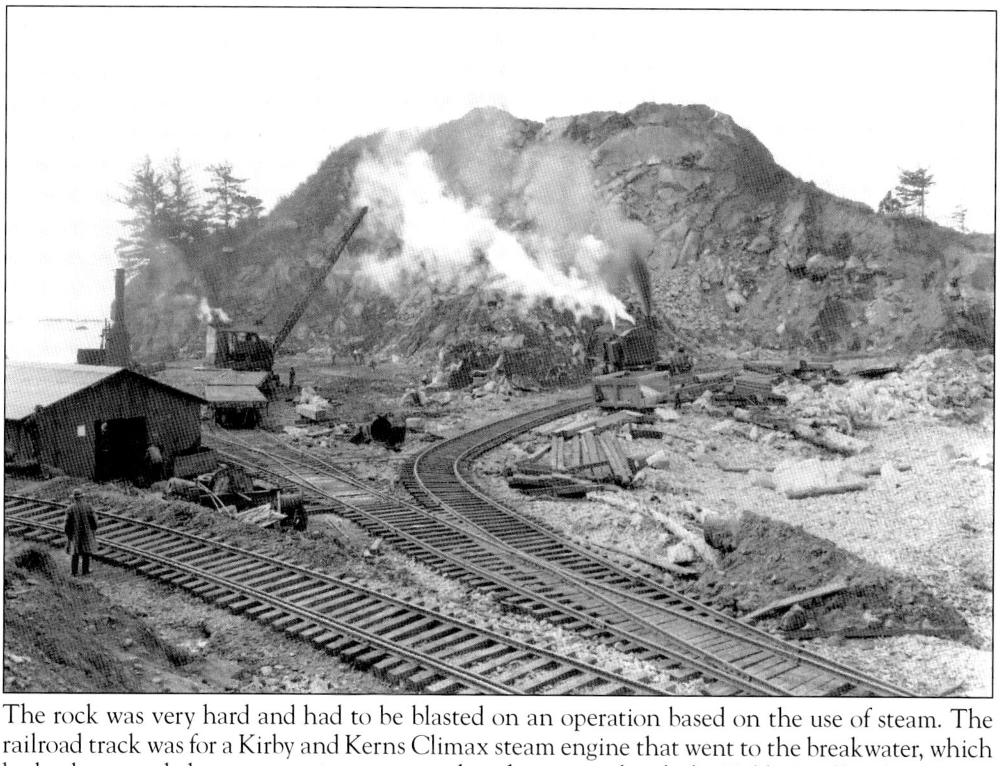

The rock was very hard and had to be blasted on an operation based on the use of steam. The railroad track was for a Kirby and Kerns Climax steam engine that went to the breakwater, which had to be extended as construction progressed, and connected with the Hobbs, Wall and Company railroad. A Hobbs, Wall and Company engine was used coming out of the quarry site.

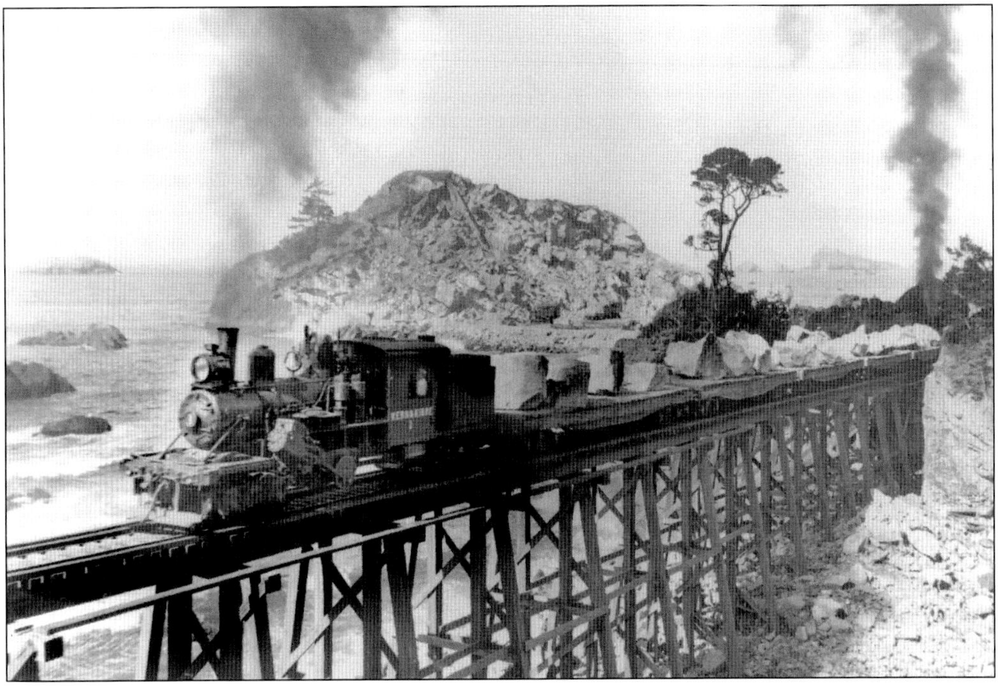

This photograph was taken from the Brother Jonathan parking area at the end of Ninth Street. The Climax steam engine is hauling the rock and a Hobbs, Wall engine is pushing from behind. The breakwater was 3,000 feet in length and was completed in 1930. Several other contracts were awarded to extend and raise its level, which was completed by 1952.

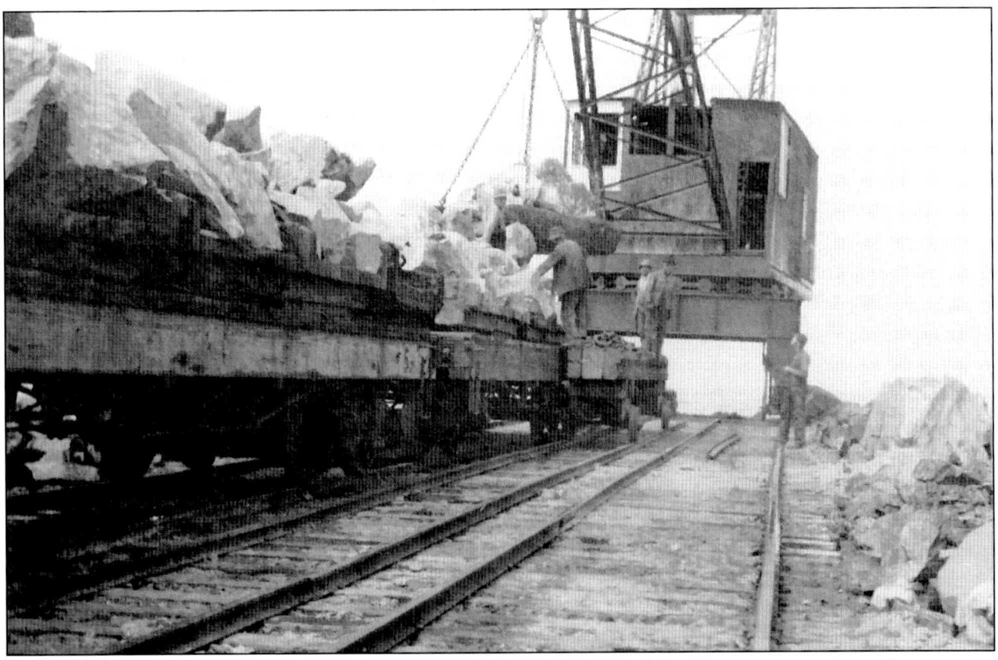

Rock for the breakwater was unloaded from the trains and placed by a crane that also ran on the railroad tracks. Along with extending the tracks as work progressed, they had to be repaired every year after the winter storms.

In 1848, George H. Washington was born in Ohio. In 1884 he acquired a mining claim near the Siskiyou fork of the Smith River where he built a cabin and mined for a number of years. In February 1927, he was killed in a landslide during a powerful storm while hiking from his cabin to the Patrick Creek Lodge. Washington Flat and Washington Peak are named after him. His land later became the home of the Bar-O Boys Ranch.

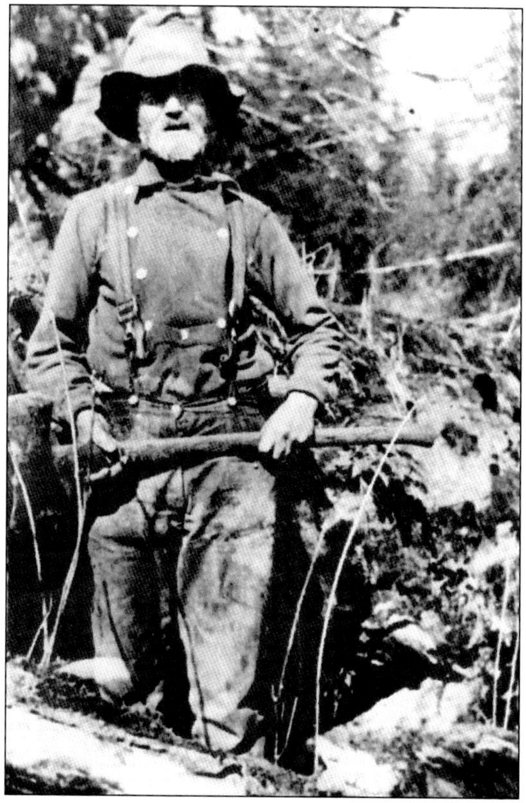

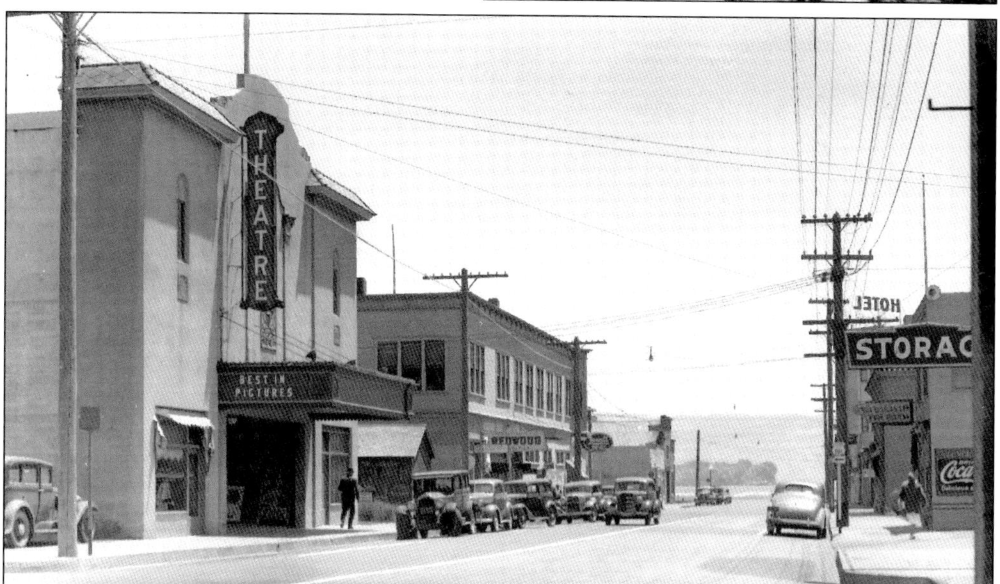

Joseph Endert and his son Chester built the first movie theater in Crescent City. This reinforced concrete structure, located on the southeast corner of H and Third Streets, was named the Mecca Theatre and opened in July 1928.

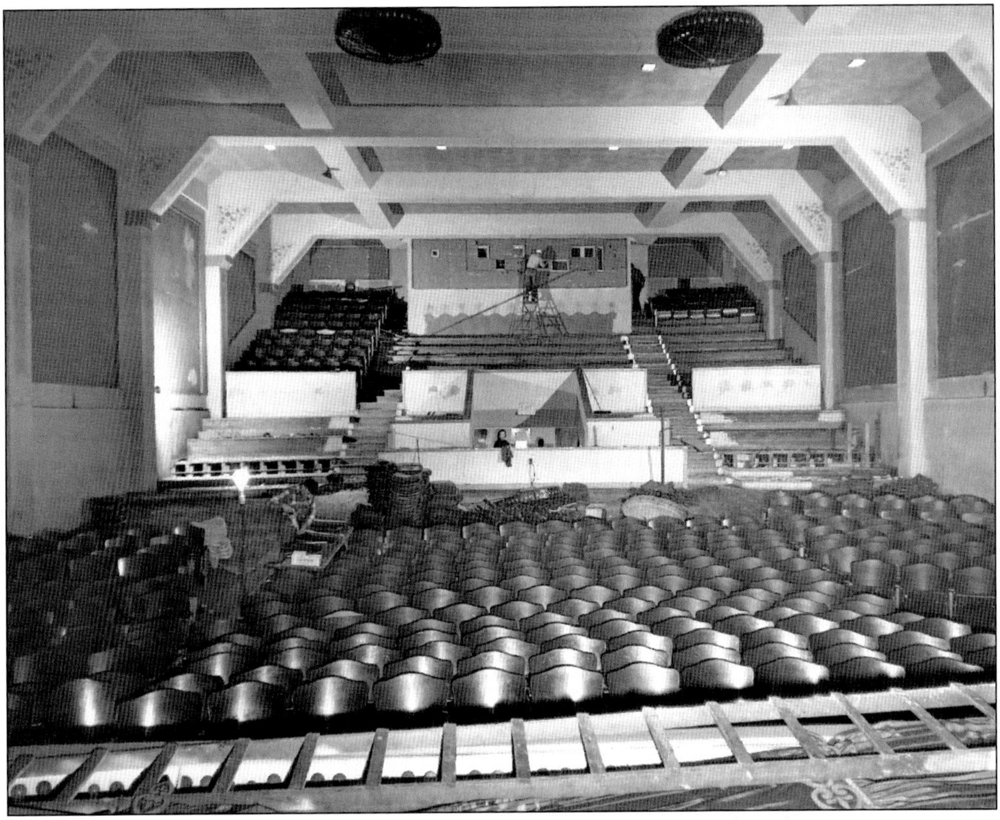

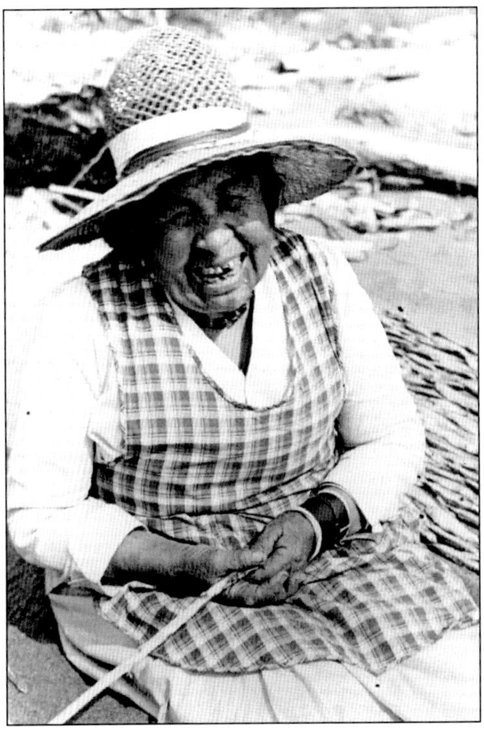

No money was spared in the construction of the Mecca Theatre as its balcony section rivaled theaters in much larger cities. In the early morning of September 15, 1963, fire broke out in the theater, causing extensive damage. On March 28, 1964, a series of tsunamis swept through Crescent City and the last, biggest wave delivered a fatal blow resulting in the theater being torn down.

Jennie Scott, a Tolowa Indian, was 63 years old when this picture was taken in 1930. She is sitting at the beach working on drying smelt to be stored for winter use. She recalled drying smelt every year since she was a young girl.

A Tolowa Indian is shown here wearing a deer-antler cap. Obviously made of deerskin, with antlers attached, the cap was tied underneath the chin for support. It was supposed to act as a decoy while hunting. The cap was also worn as a headdress in Tolowa ceremonies.

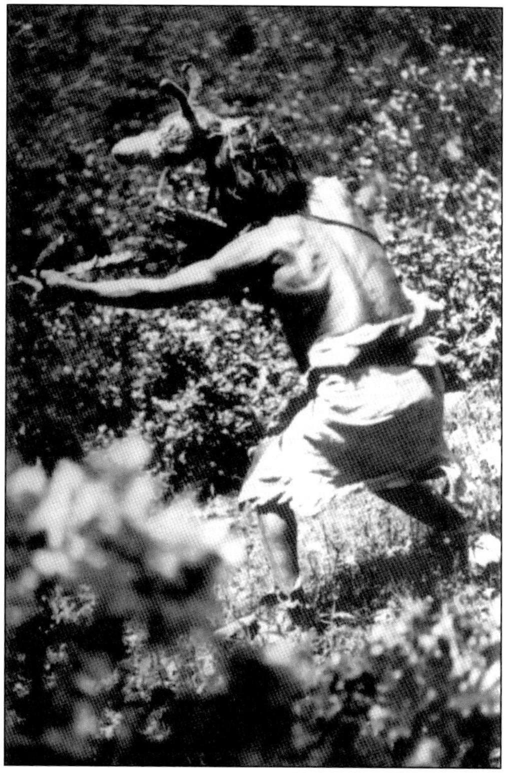

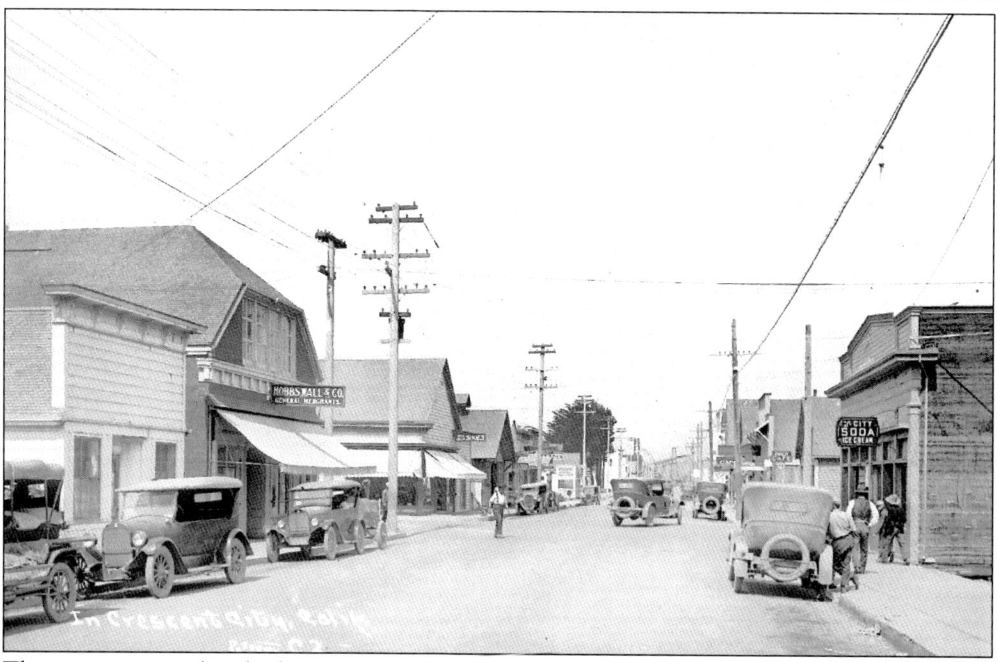

This picture was taken looking east on Second Street with the Hobbs, Wall and Company store on the left. Second Street was the main commercial street in Crescent City until 1964, when a tsunami destroyed or damaged most of these buildings. All of these structures were torn down when Crescent City was redeveloped after the tsunami.

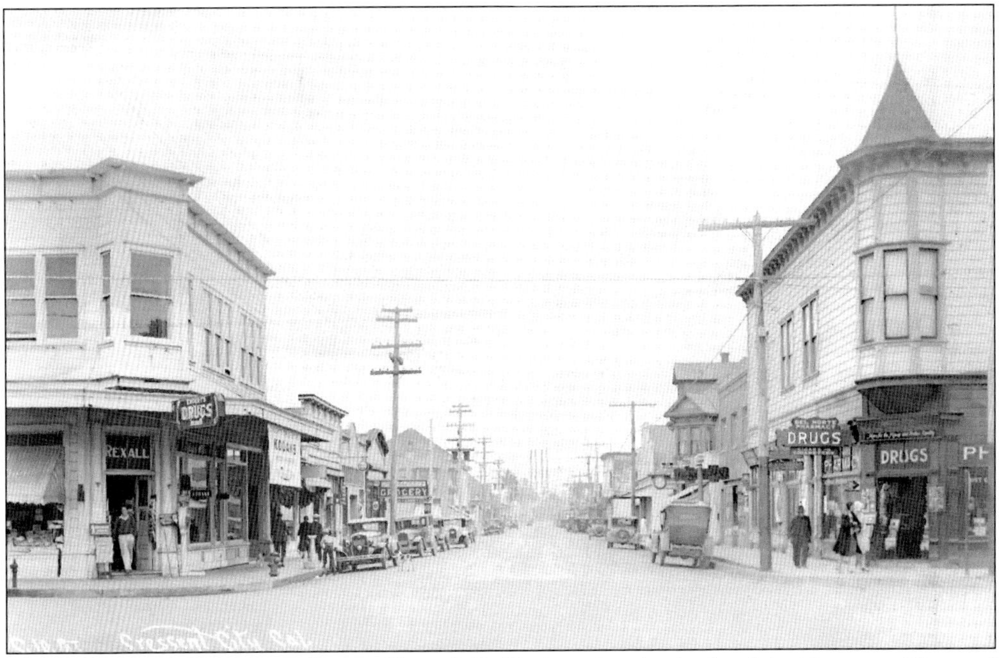

Frederick Endert, the second son of Joseph B. Endert, finished school in Crescent City and went on to college and became a pharmacist. His father helped him establish his business, the Rexall Drug Store, located on the northeast corner of Second and H Streets. The building was destroyed by the 1964 tsunami.

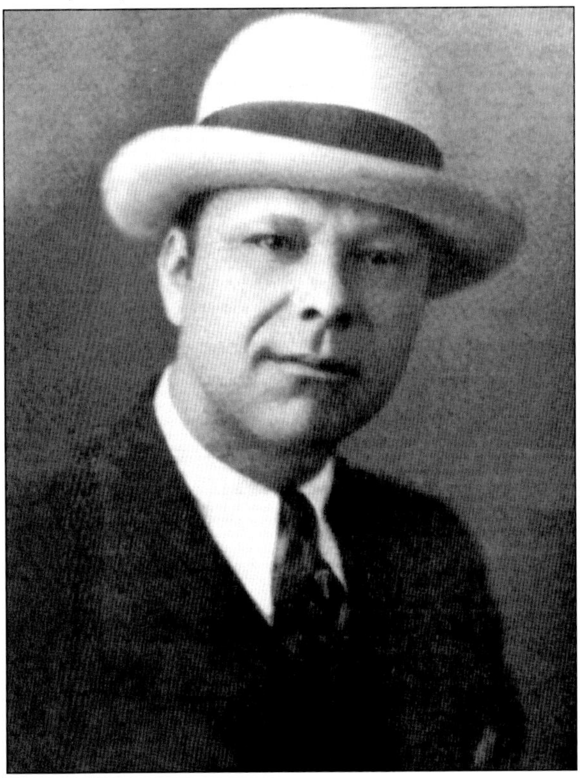

William "Billy" Boone was a building contractor, real estate agent, caterer, and dance band leader. A veteran of World War I, he moved to Crescent City with his wife in 1930 and became involved in just about every "good cause" that came along. He was called Mr. Fourth of July for his active participation in the annual celebration as he either directed or contributed time in 28 such celebrations. He was the unofficial Veterans Service Officer in Crescent City.

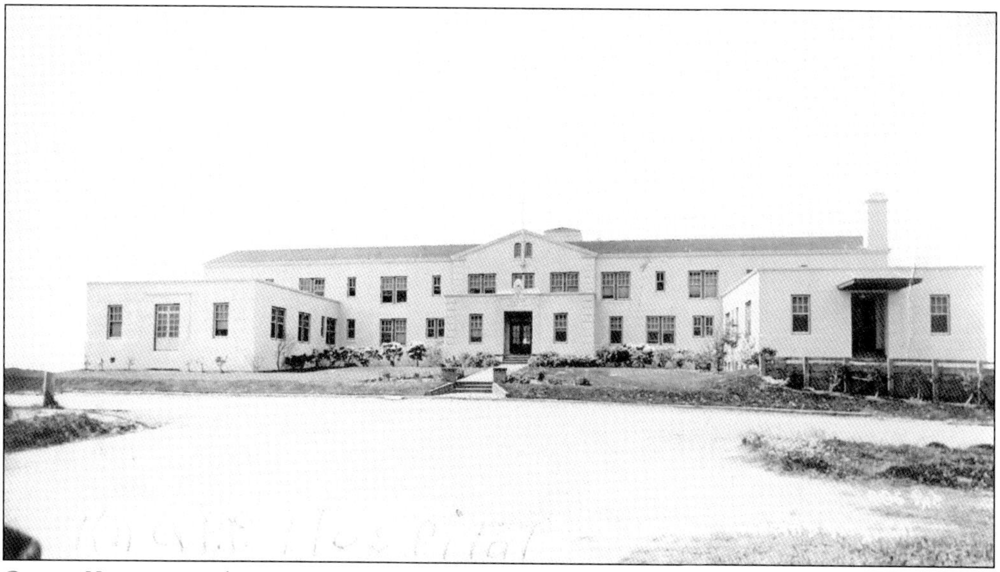

George Knapp retired to Santa Barbara and, as a member of the Save the Redwood League, he traveled the Redwood Highway to Crescent City. He built a summer home on the Klamath and visited Crescent City often. He was disturbed by the lack of medical facilities in the city, so in 1931 he built the Knapp Hospital. He helped fund the operation until his death in 1945 after raising funds for two additions to the hospital.

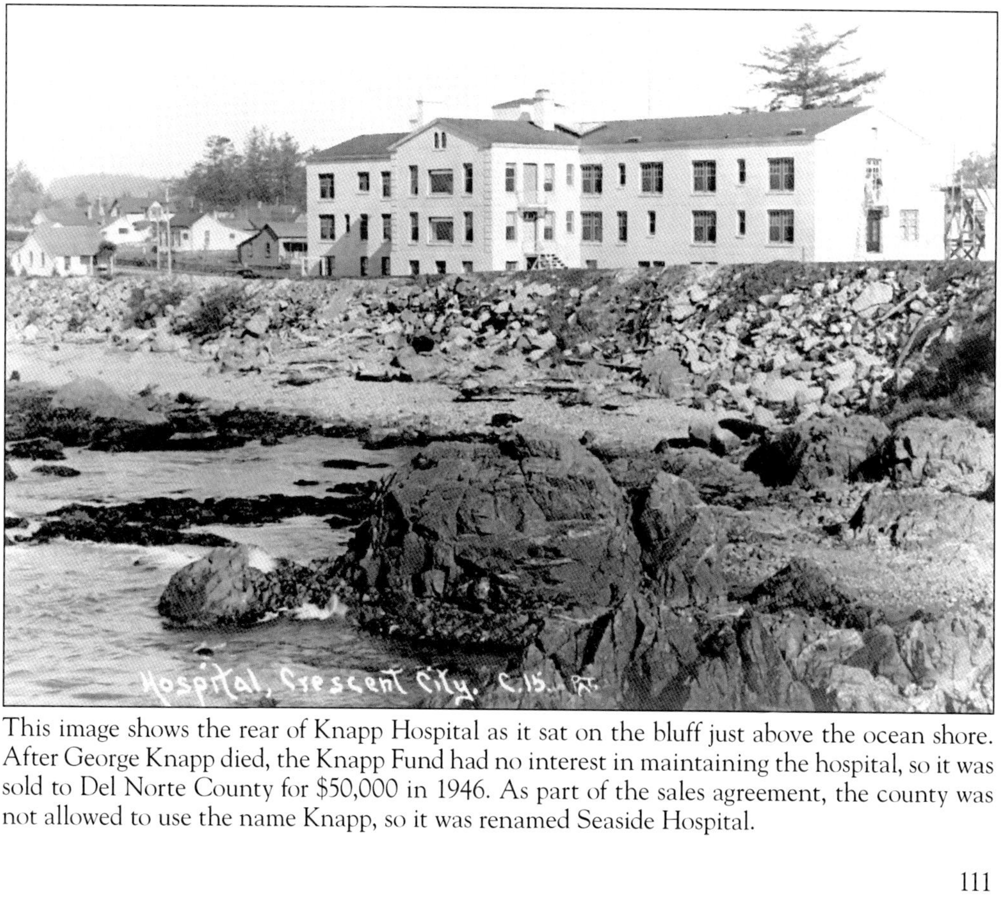

This image shows the rear of Knapp Hospital as it sat on the bluff just above the ocean shore. After George Knapp died, the Knapp Fund had no interest in maintaining the hospital, so it was sold to Del Norte County for $50,000 in 1946. As part of the sales agreement, the county was not allowed to use the name Knapp, so it was renamed Seaside Hospital.

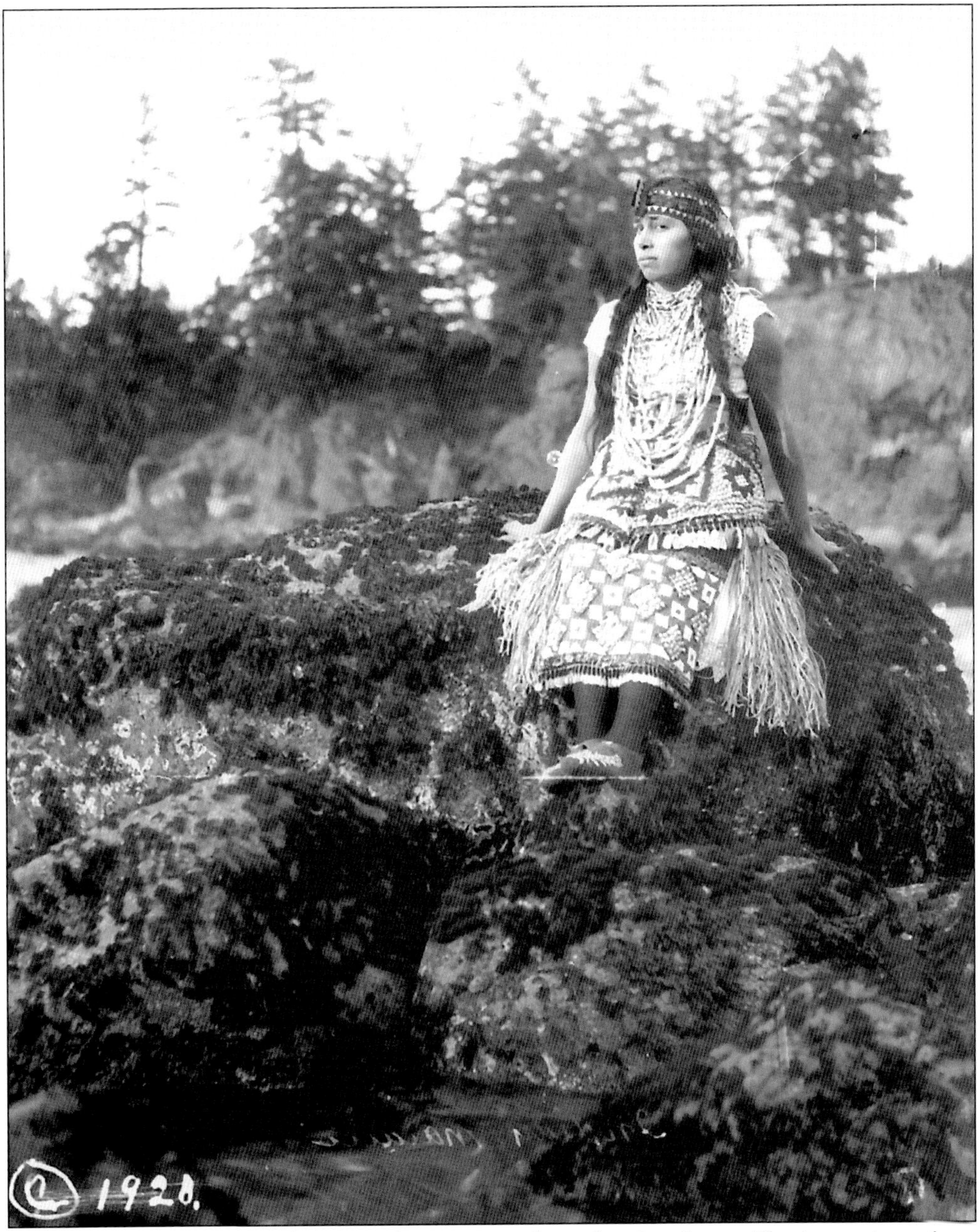

A young Yurok Indian maiden poses for a picture dressed in her finery. She is wearing a long wraparound deerskin skirt, fringed in the back, and a rectangular deerskin apron decorated with abalone shells, pine nuts, woven grasses, sea shells, and beads. She also wears strands of dentalium shell necklaces. The decoration on the skirt and apron was very intricate and took a long time to make. Woven caps were also worn by the Tolowa women. This attire was reserved for ceremonies and special functions and was a sign of family wealth.

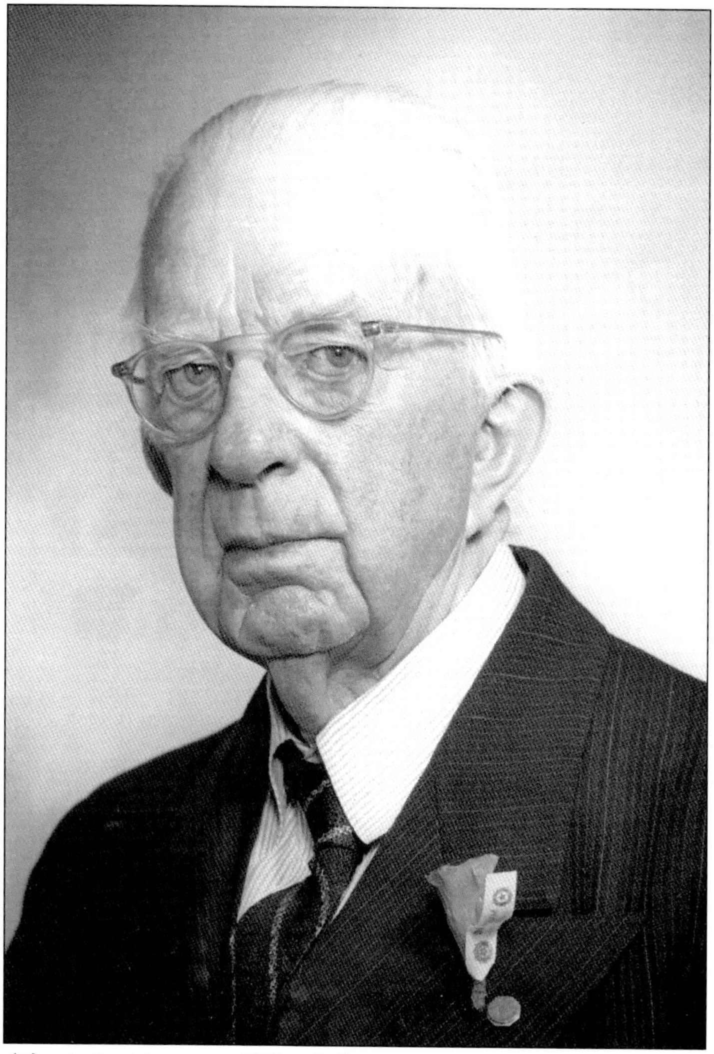

In the first California Legislature in 1852, a bill was introduced to separate northern California from the rest of the state and combine it with the southern part of the Oregon Territory. Several attempts were made in following years, but all of them failed until 1936, when Gilbert Gable moved to Curry County in Oregon and made substantial investments in docks, timber, real estate, and transportation to infuse the area. Still, southern Oregon and northern California desperately needed new road infrastructure, but were being ignored. A meeting was held in Yreka, and several counties decided to form their own state with California state senator Randolph Collier present and supporting the effort. On November 27, 1941, the State of Jefferson issued its "Proclamation of Independence." Yreka was designated as the temporary state capital, and Gilbert Gable was designated governor. Judge John Childs from Crescent City had been active in the whole process and was Gable's right-hand man. On December 2, Gable died from a heart attack. The leadership passed to Judge Childs, who was elected governor in a special election in Yreka and inaugurated governor of the State of Jefferson on December 4. At that time, the State of Jefferson was comprised of Oregon's Curry County and Del Norte, Siskiyou, and Trinity Counties in California. Three days later, on December 7, the Japanese attacked Pearl Harbor. On December 8, Governor Childs announced that, because of the national emergency, the provisional State of Jefferson had discontinued any and all activities.

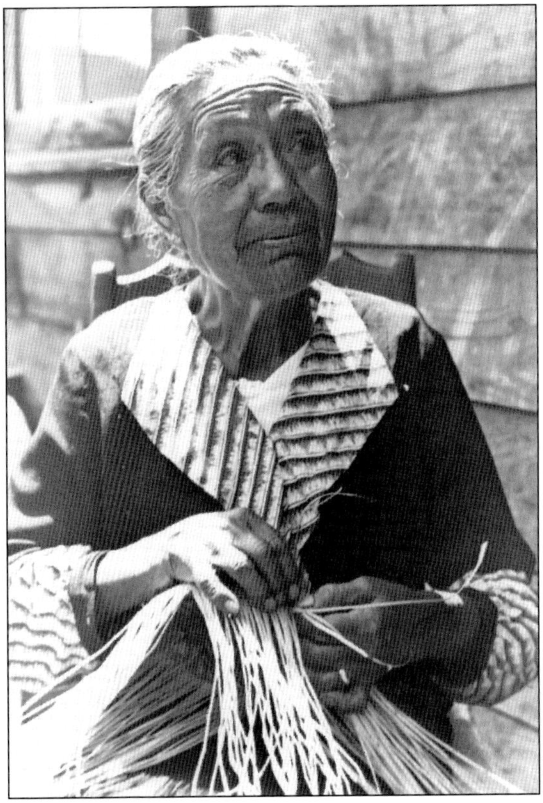

Nellie Medon Flounder was one of the last Tolowa shaman. A shaman was the Indian equivalent of a doctor, priest, and pharmacist who had a thorough knowledge of plants and herbs used in healing. They were also believed to be able to cast spells on people as well as remove spells cast by others.

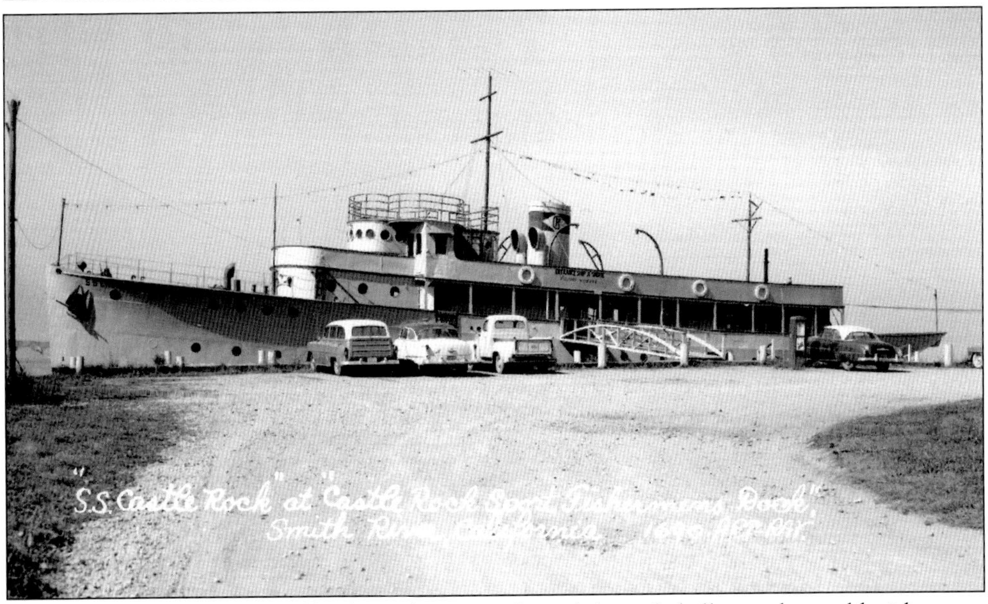

The *Caritas* was designed and built as a luxury yacht and she sailed all over the world with guests both rich and famous. In 1941 the U.S. Navy purchased her and turned her into a patrol boat for the Pacific. After the war, the vessel was purchased by Joe Sierka and brought to Smith River. Later, she was moved to a location on Highway 101 and is now a museum, gift shop, and well-known landmark called the *Ship Ashore*.

A Tolowa Indian girl displays some woven baskets made by members of her tribe. The knowledge and skill of basket-making and the many decorative designs have been handed down from generation to generation, but the number of skilled weavers is dwindling.

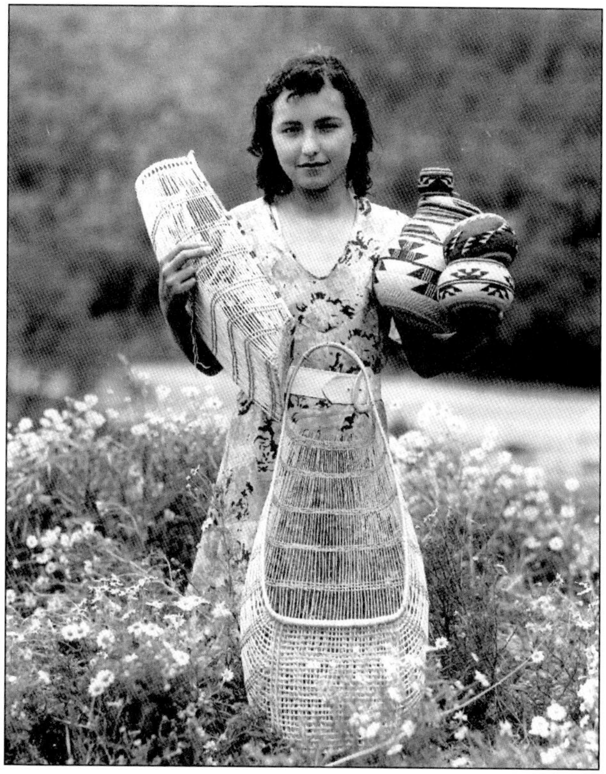

The Del Norte County Courthouse burned to the ground on the night of January 18, 1948, and many county land records were destroyed. There were many rumors as to the cause of the blaze, but the official verdict was of "undetermined" origin.

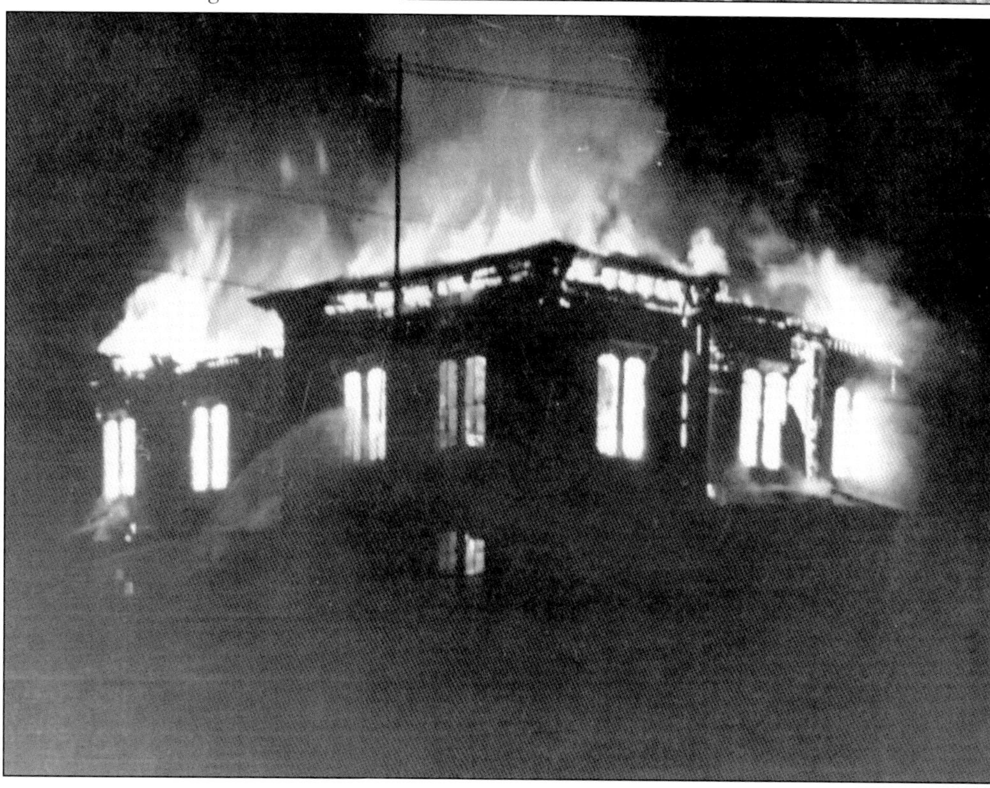

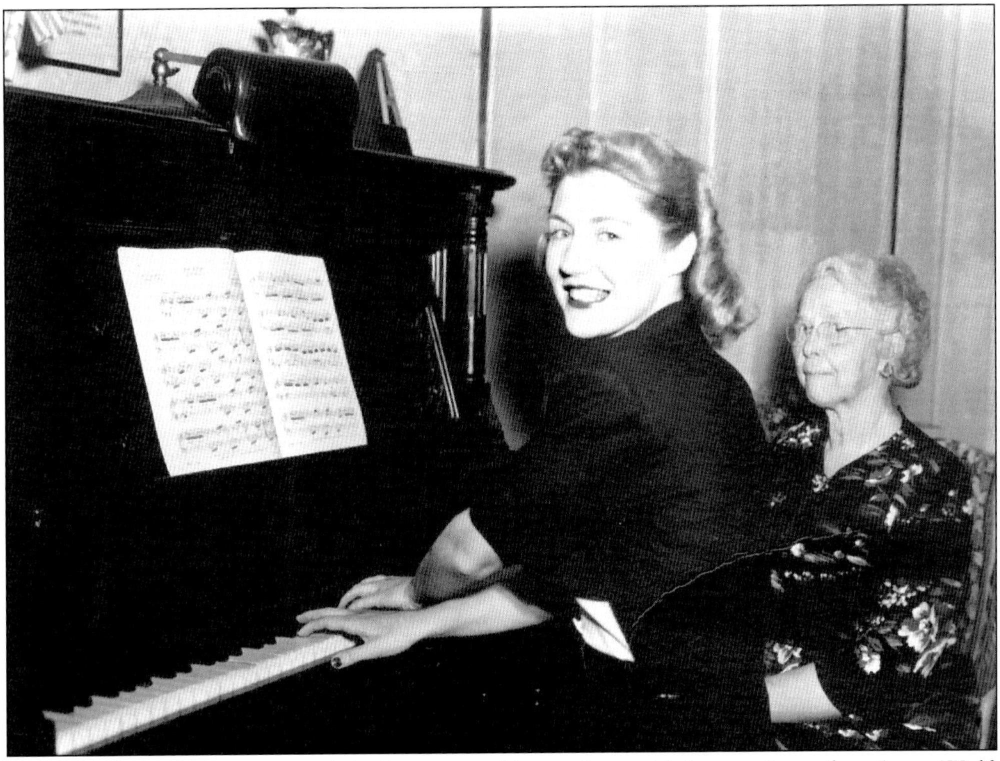

Patricia Lehman was an accomplished pianist and is seen here with her music teacher, Anna Wulf. After graduating from Crescent City High School, Patricia obtained her degree and teaching certificate. In 1951 she was teaching in Sacramento when she was selected as Miss California for the Miss America Pageant—her piano talent was a factor in her selection. Patricia was the daughter of Allen Lehman, a noted Del Norte County historian and successful businessman.

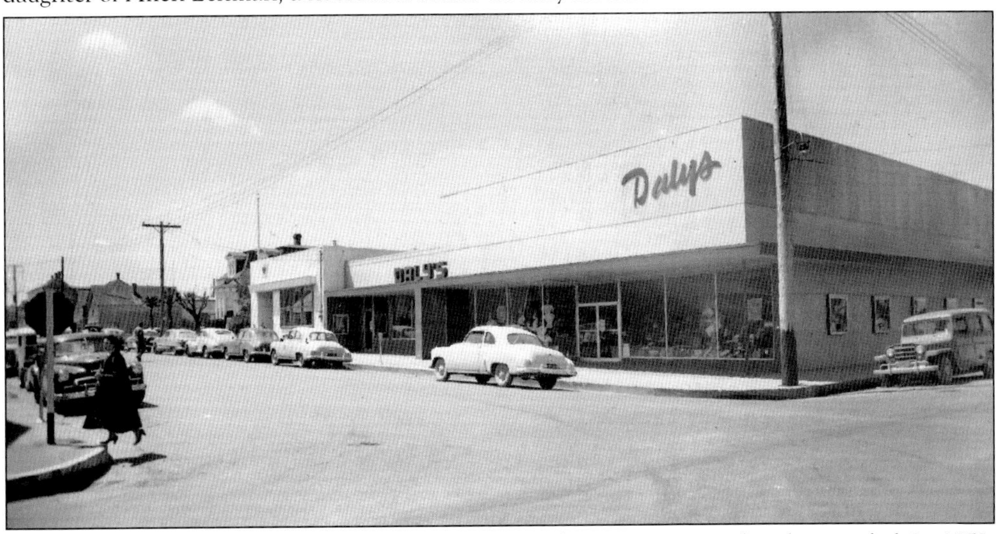

Daly's Department Store opened in Eureka in 1895. The store prospered and expanded. In 1952, the Daly brothers opened the first chain store in Crescent City. Located on the northwest corner of Third and I Streets, it was very successful. Unfortunately, the 1964 tsunami caused extensive damage to it.

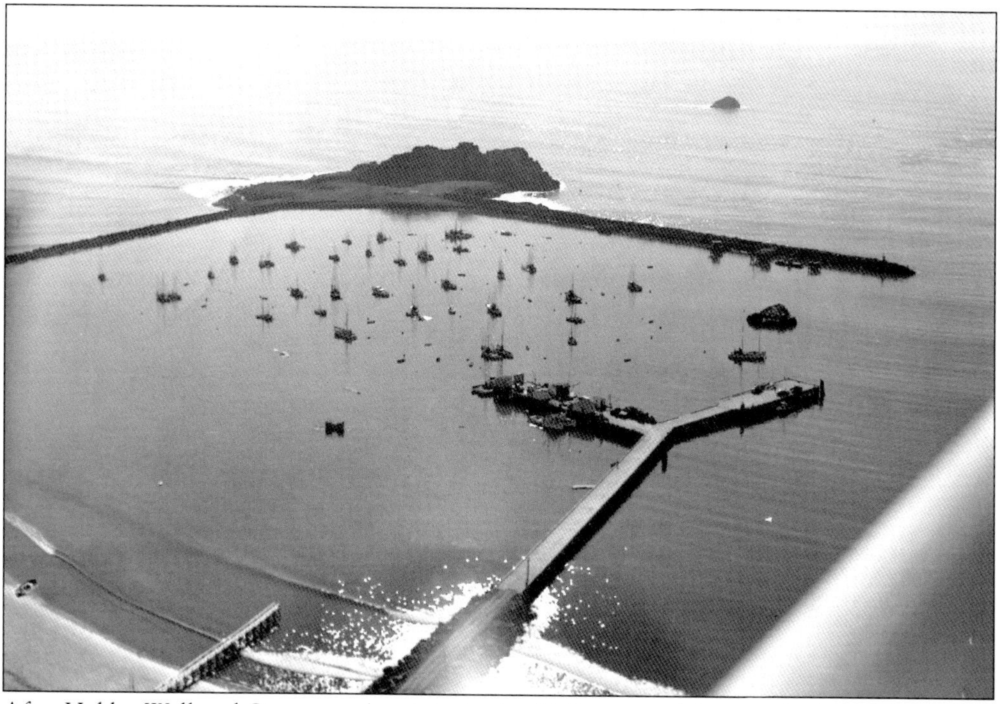

After Hobbs, Wall and Company closed their wharf fell apart as fishermen had no place unload their catch. After World War II, the county tried to get federal funding for a wharf, but no funds were available. The citizens of Crescent City worked together and were able to get donations of time, money, and materials to build the dock, which was completed in March 1950 and named Citizens Dock. It was the greatest community effort ever put forth by local residents.

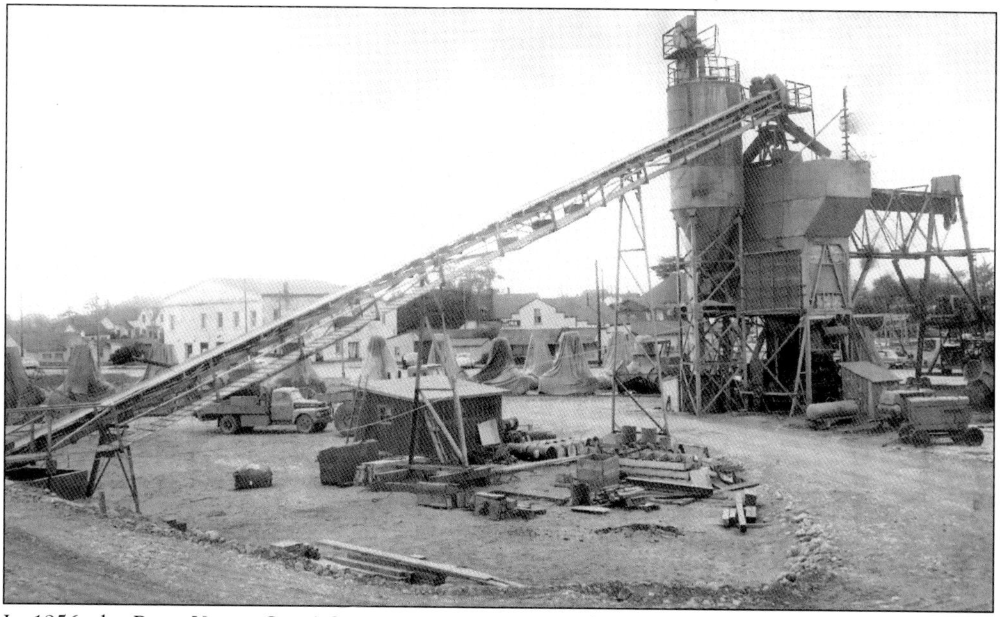

In 1956, the Peter Kiewit Sons' Company was awarded a $1.3 million contract to make and place tetrapods on the breakwater—a first in the western hemisphere. A fabrication plant was set up on the beach side of Front Street near the Surf Hotel, and the first tetrapod was cast on June 14, 1956.

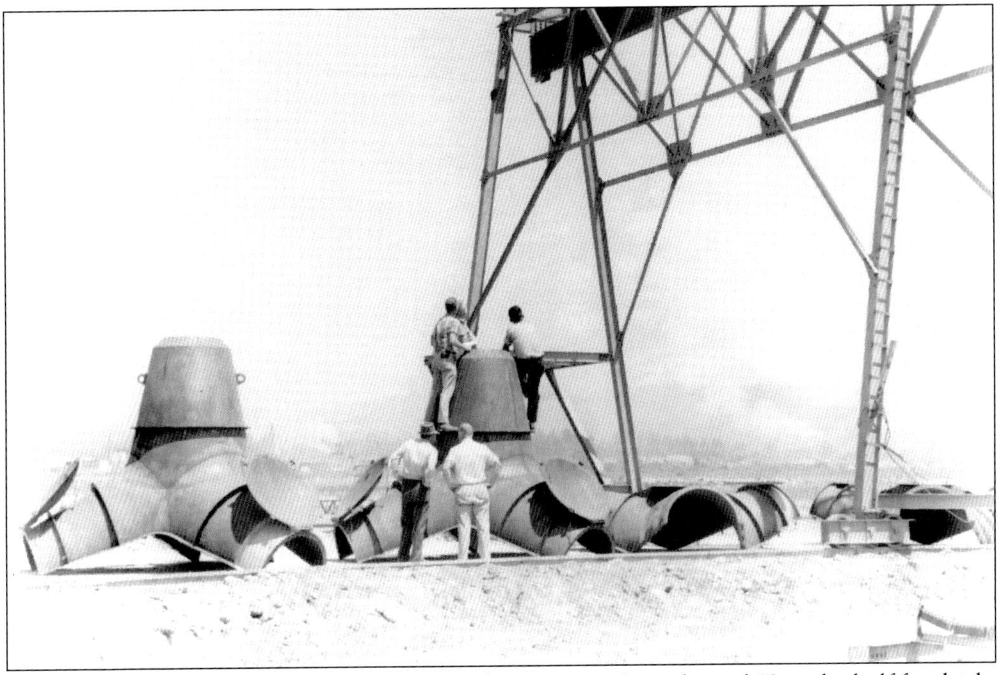

Tetrapods are shaped like children's jacks, weigh 25 tons each, and stand 10-and-a-half feet high. The molds are made of four pieces and held together with steel bands.

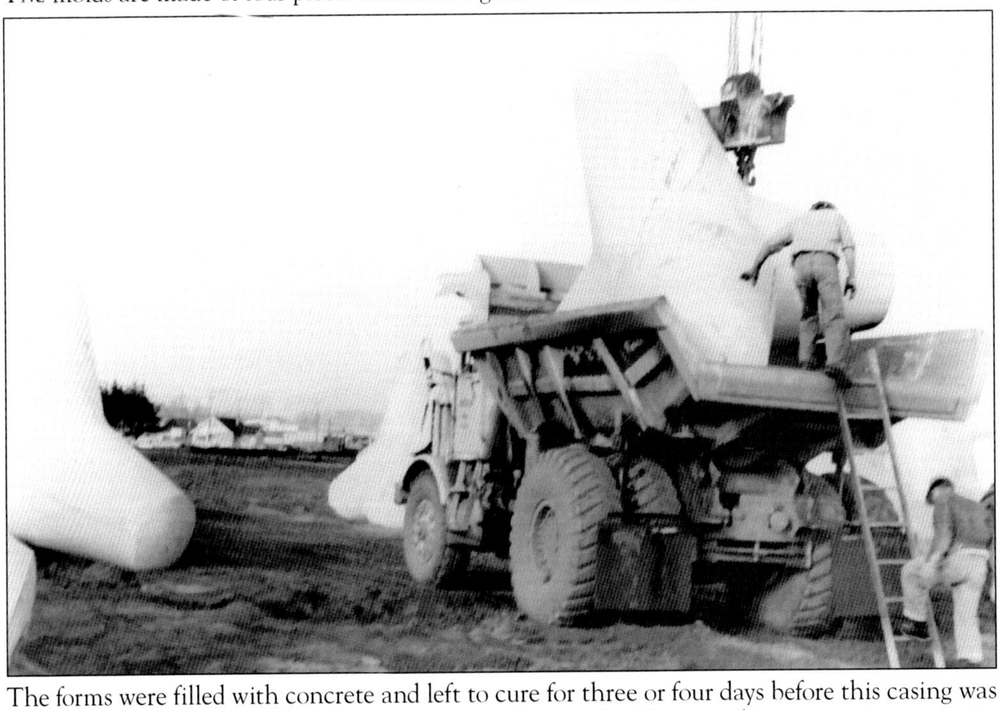

The forms were filled with concrete and left to cure for three or four days before this casing was removed. They were moved to a storage area and painted with a membrane covering to retain moisture and then cured for an additional 21 days. When the tetrapods were fully cured, they were loaded on trucks and hauled to the breakwater for placement by crane. On October 8, 1957, the last tetrapod was placed.

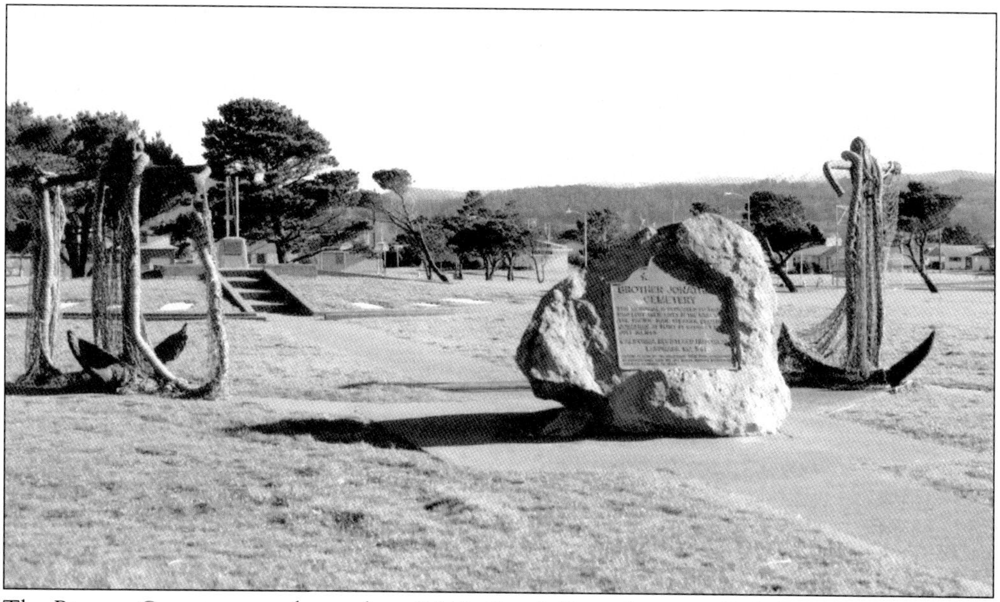

The Pioneer Cemetery was located on Pebble Beach Drive between Eighth and Ninth Streets. When the *Brother Jonathan* sank, many of the bodies were buried in Pioneer Cemetery and it became known as the Brother Jonathan Cemetery. The area was subject to erosion, and many of the graves started to fall into the ocean. Many of the bodies were moved to a new cemetery. The city acquired the old cemetery in 1958 and developed the Brother Jonathan Memorial Park.

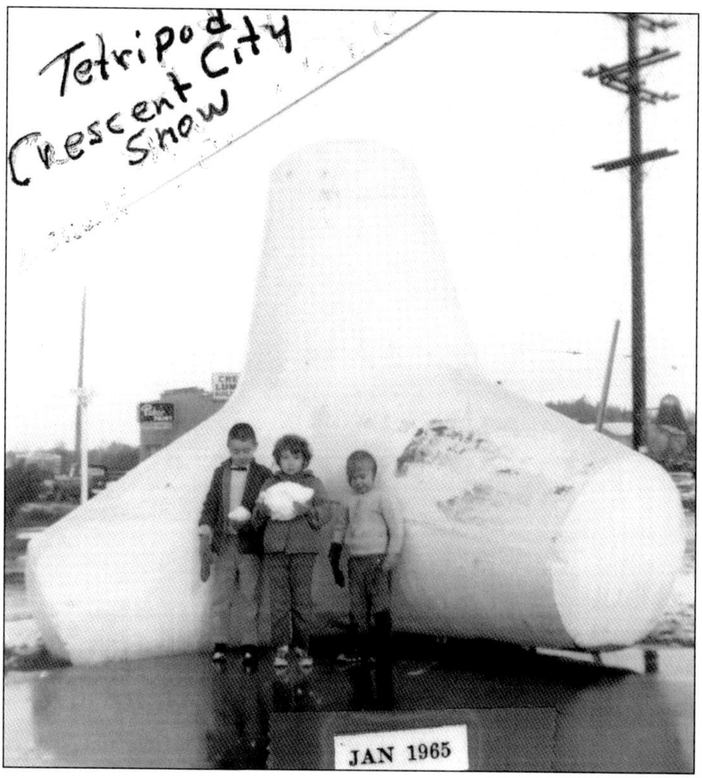

An exact replica of a tetrapod was built and placed on a monument base by William Hytinen. The 1964 tsunami knocked the tetrapod off its base and moved it. The city decided to leave it where it landed to show the power of the ocean. You can still see the tetrapod along Highway 101 at the south end of Crescent City.

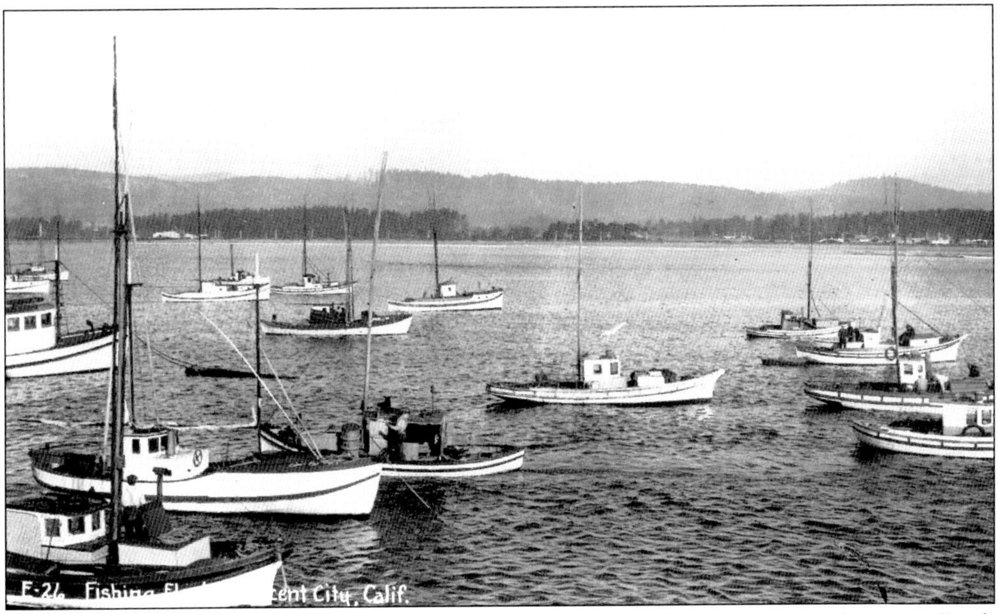

Fishing was always an important industry in Crescent City, but the completion of Citizens Dock in 1953 was a big boost for the industry. The harbor not only accommodates the fishing fleet, but private boats conduct fishing excursions for tourists as well.

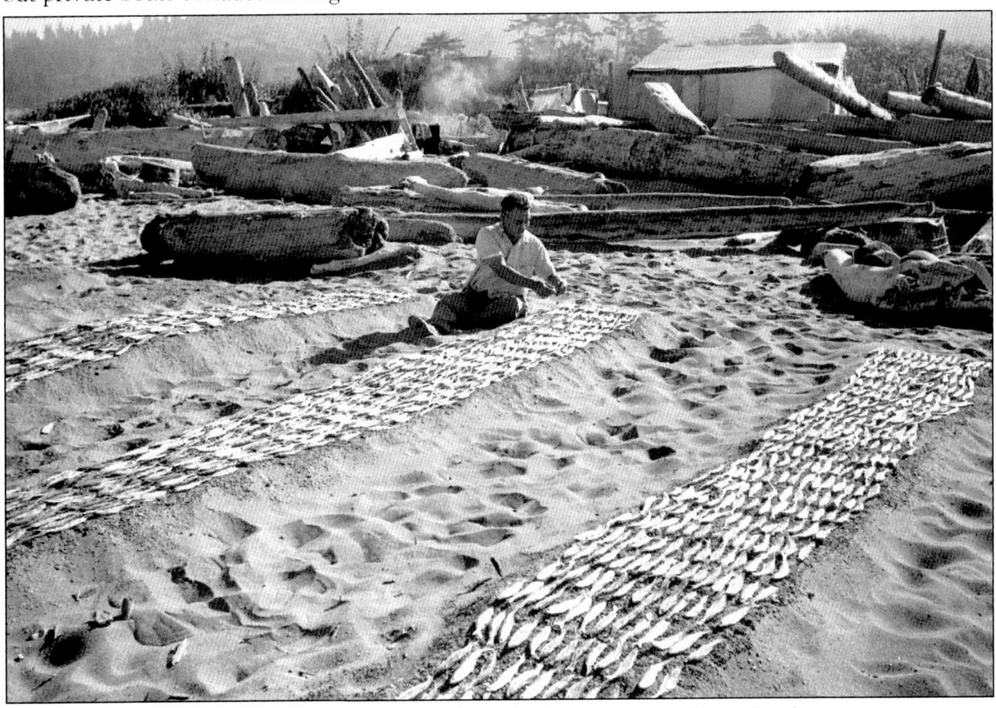

Ed Lopez works at drying smelt near Kamph Park that were caught in finely woven rope nets. The drying beds were made by mounding sand and then covering it with smooth pebbles. By tradition, the beds have to face the ocean and the fish never all face the same direction. If it were sunny and warm, the smelt can dry in a day, but it usually took two to three days with the beds being covered at night.

California state senator Randolph Collier turns the first shovel full of soil for the construction of the Oregon Mountain Tunnel while assemblyman Frank Bellotti looks on. The ceremony was held on July 8, 1960.

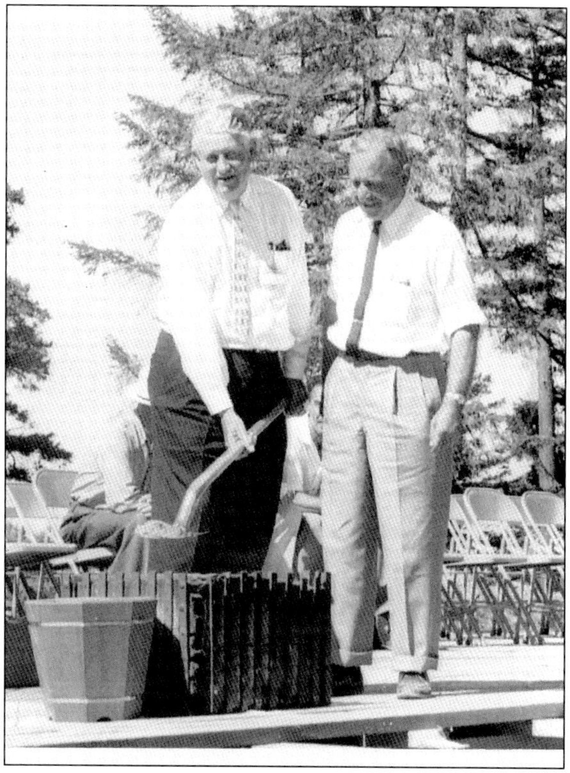

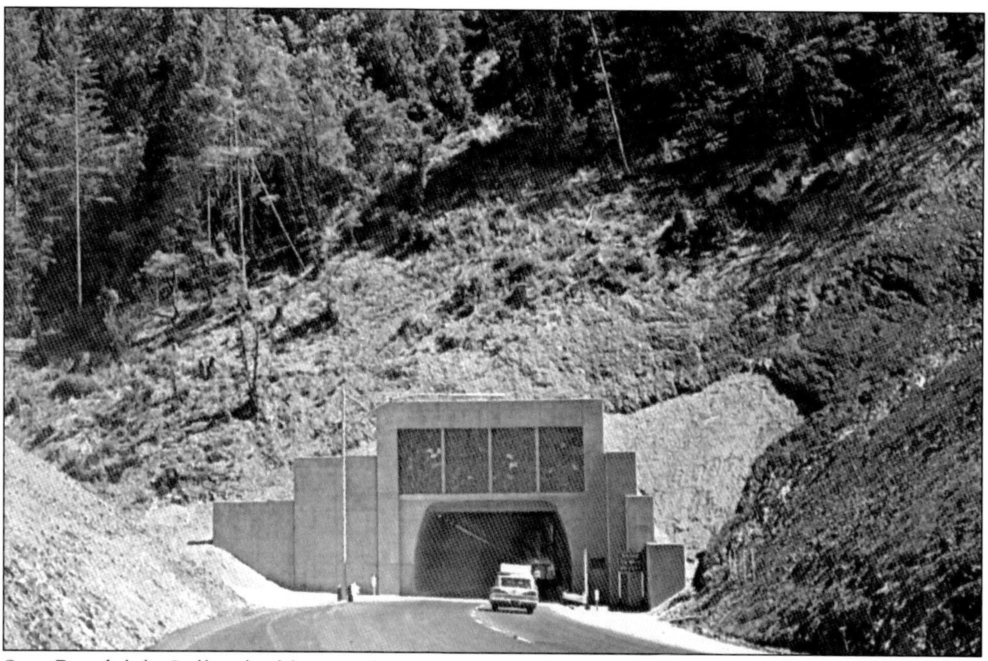

Sen. Randolph Collier had been a fervent backer of the need for a tunnel between California and Oregon. The tunnel project eliminated 128 curves and switchbacks over Oregon Mountain. The road from Crescent City to Grants Pass was often closed in the winter due to the snow on top of the mountain. The Collier Tunnel was opened to traffic on July 20, 1963.

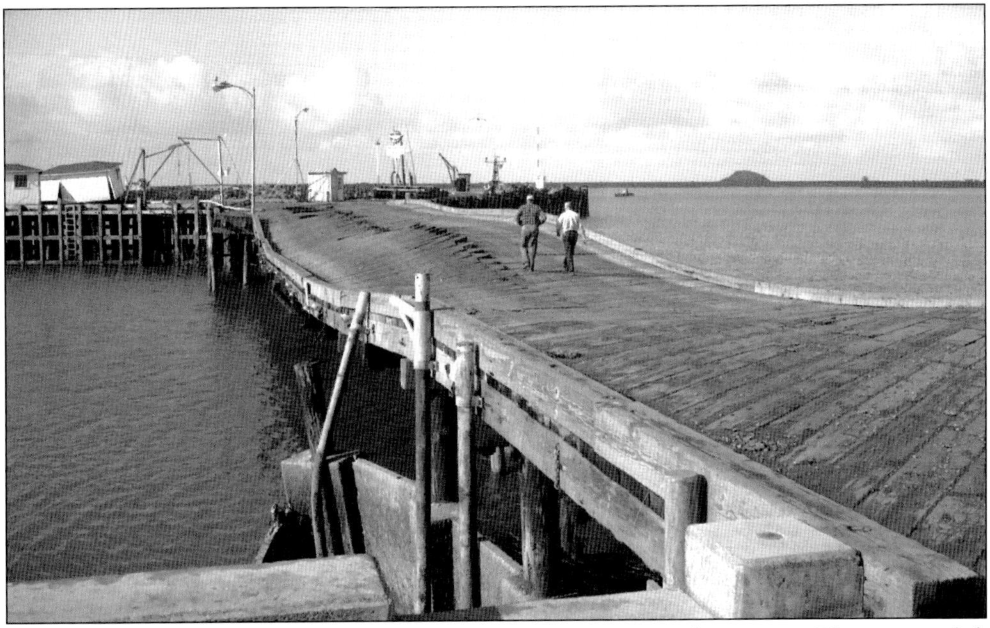

Crescent City Harbor had become the center piece of local civic achievement. The tsunami left the harbor in shambles, but did not totally destroy the docks, and it was reconstructed. The core of the inner harbor was completed in 1974 at a cost of about $3 million. The modernized facilities include space for fish buyers, restaurants, and even an art gallery.

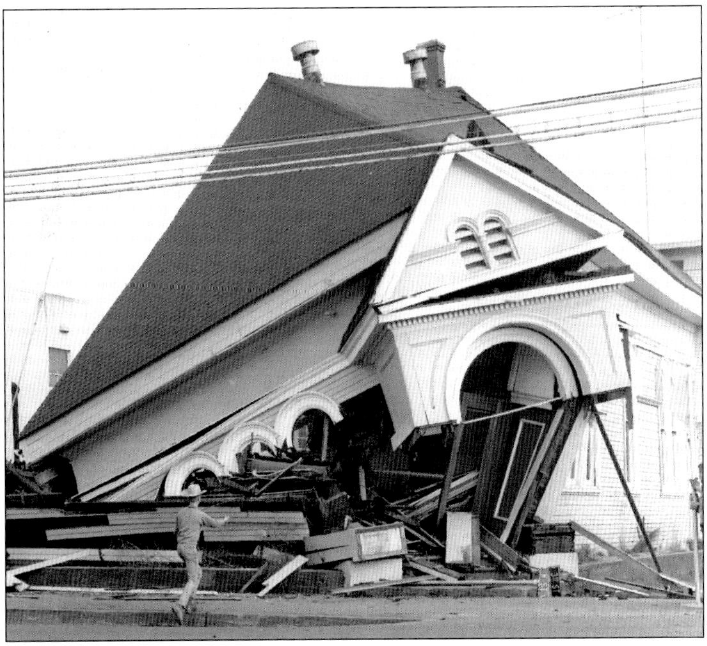

The last tsunami surged inland past Third Street, destroying most of the structures in its path. The bank located on the corner of H and Third Streets was totally destroyed. The pillars and the glass window over the door survived and are now on display at the Del Norte County Museum.

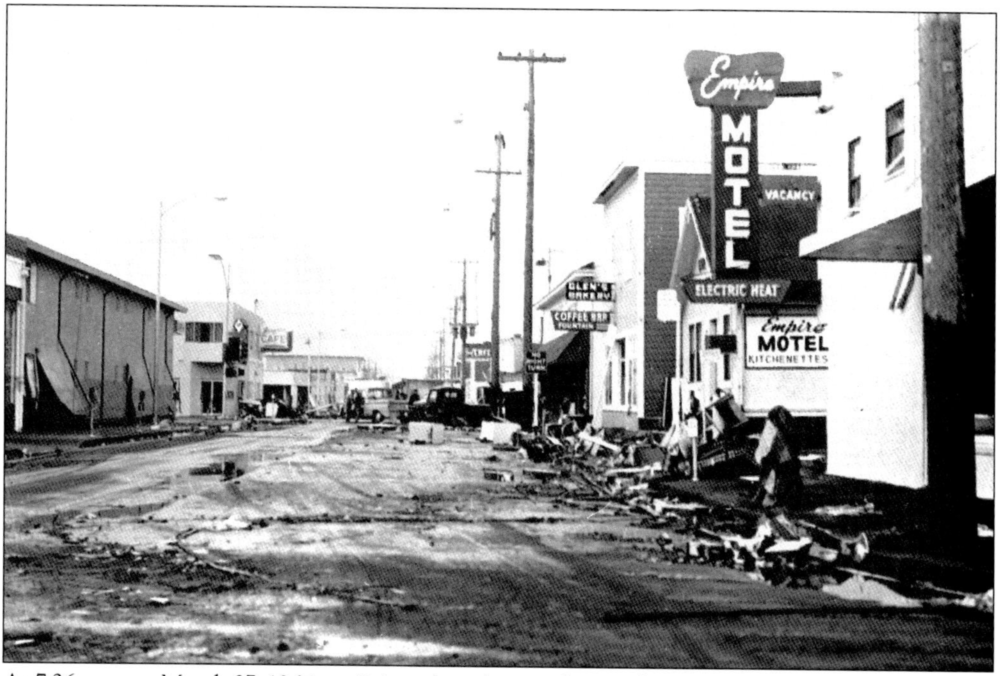

At 7:36 p.m. on March 27, 1964, an 8.4 earthquake struck near the Gulf of Alaska. This earthquake caused tsunami waves that struck Crescent City four hours later. The last wave was the largest, at a height of approximately 21 feet, and caused devastating destruction of Crescent City. This natural disaster claimed 11 lives.

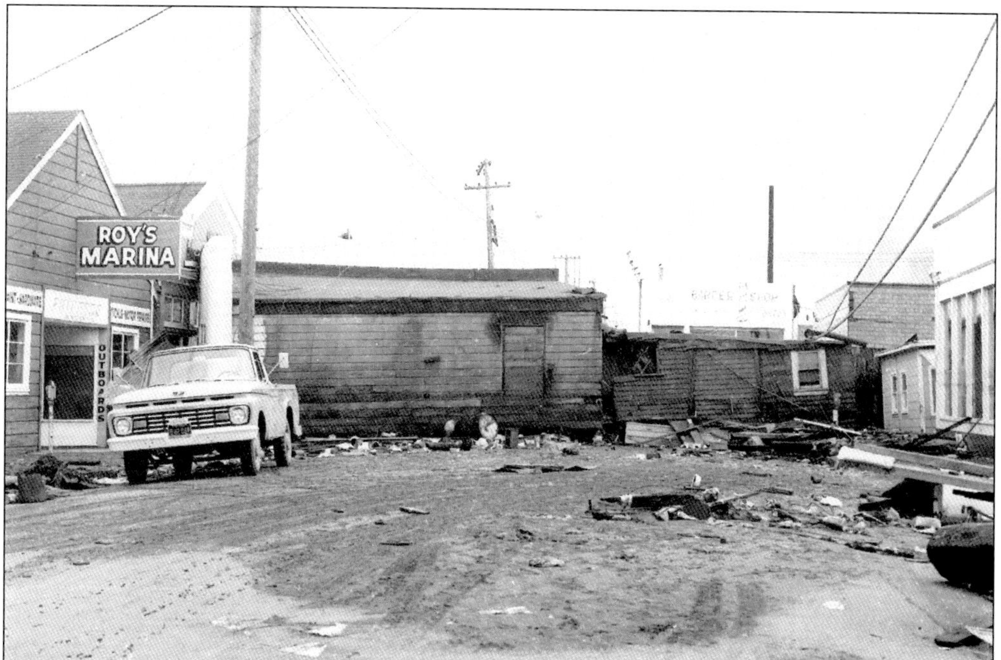

The force of the waves swept many of the buildings off their foundations, pushing them into the middle of the streets. Many of the buildings were crushed against each other. The ruined contents from inside were scattered over many blocks.

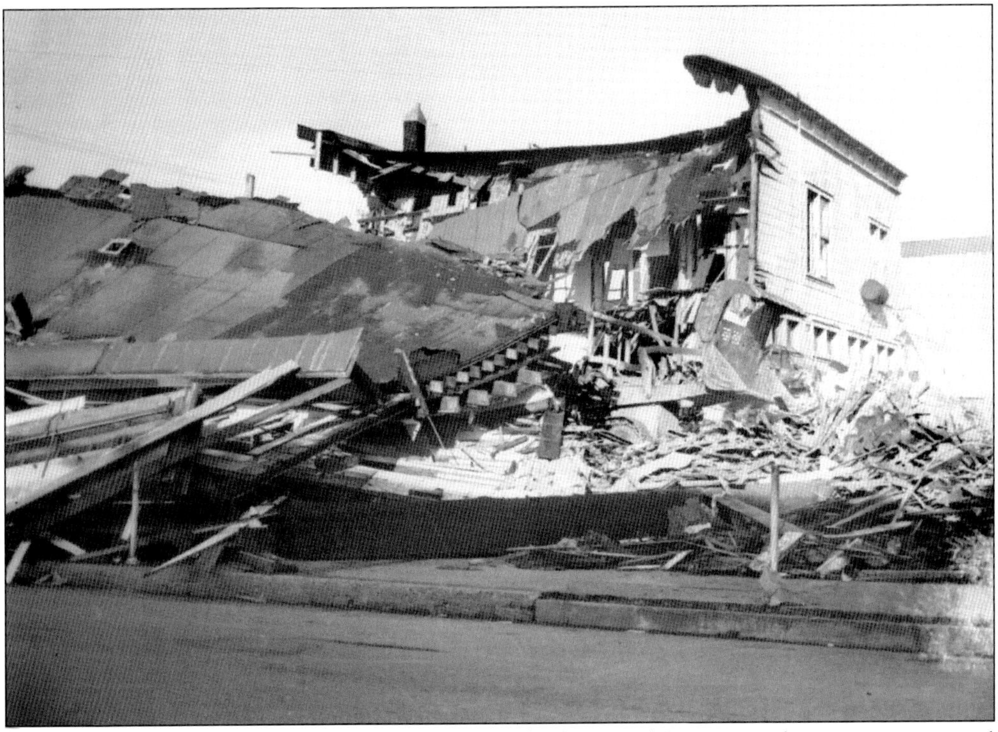

This building on Second Street was totally demolished. Second Street was the main commercial street in Crescent City at the time of the tsunamis, and none of its buildings survived. Many of the businesses never recovered.

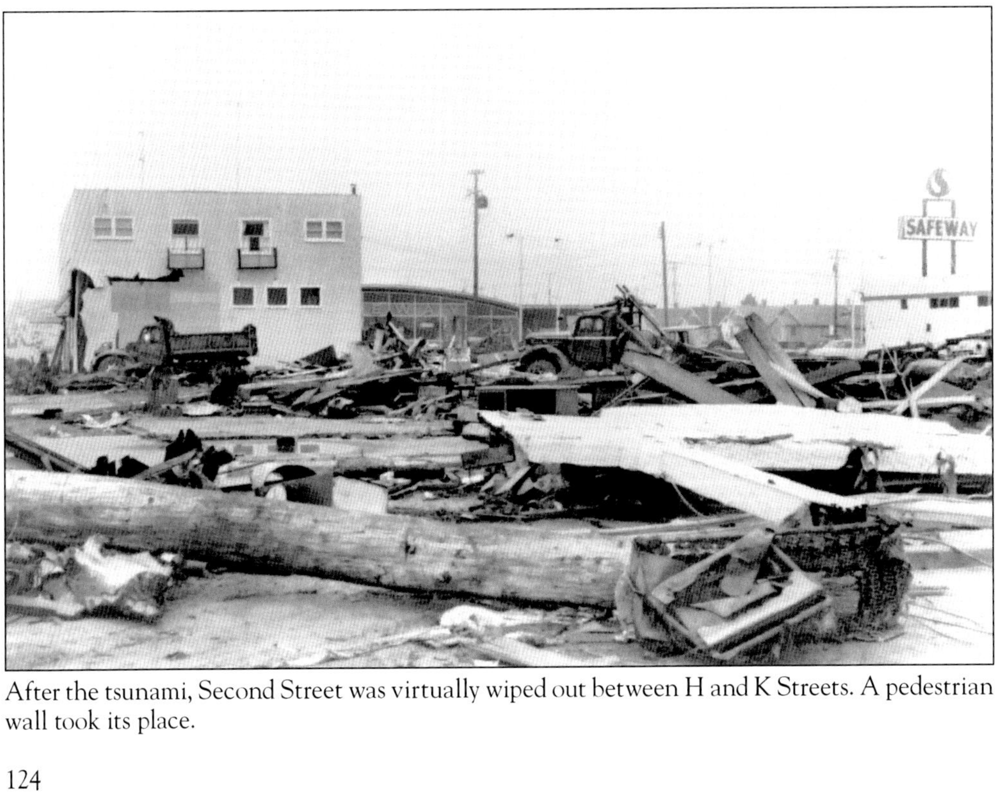

After the tsunami, Second Street was virtually wiped out between H and K Streets. A pedestrian wall took its place.

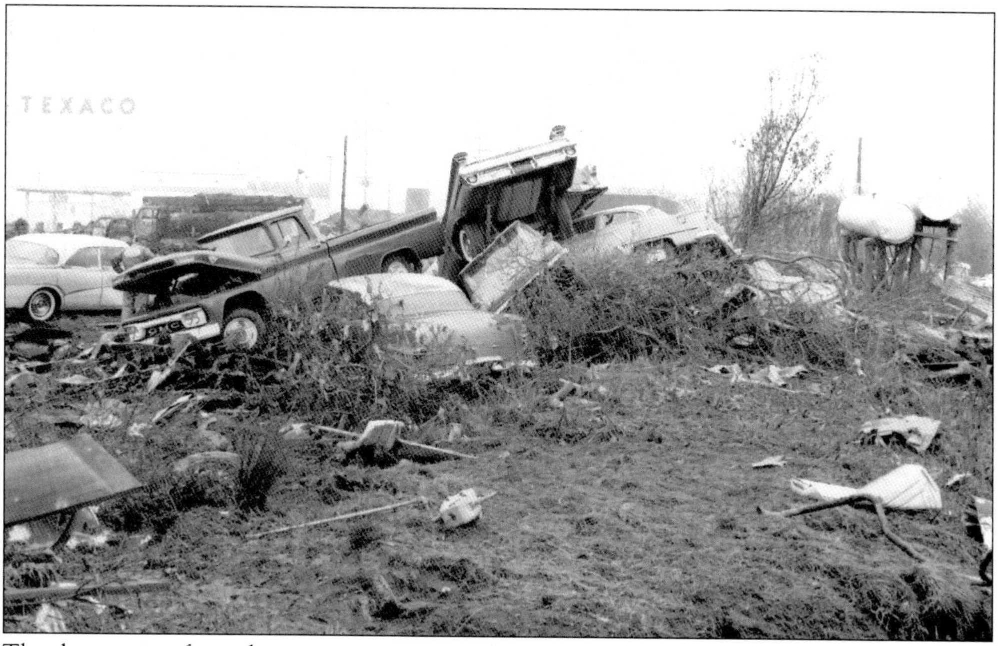

The devastation from the tsunamis was complete, and Crescent City looked like it was a war zone. More than a 1,000 vehicles had been tossed around over a five square-mile area of town, and many vehicles ended up sunk in the harbor.

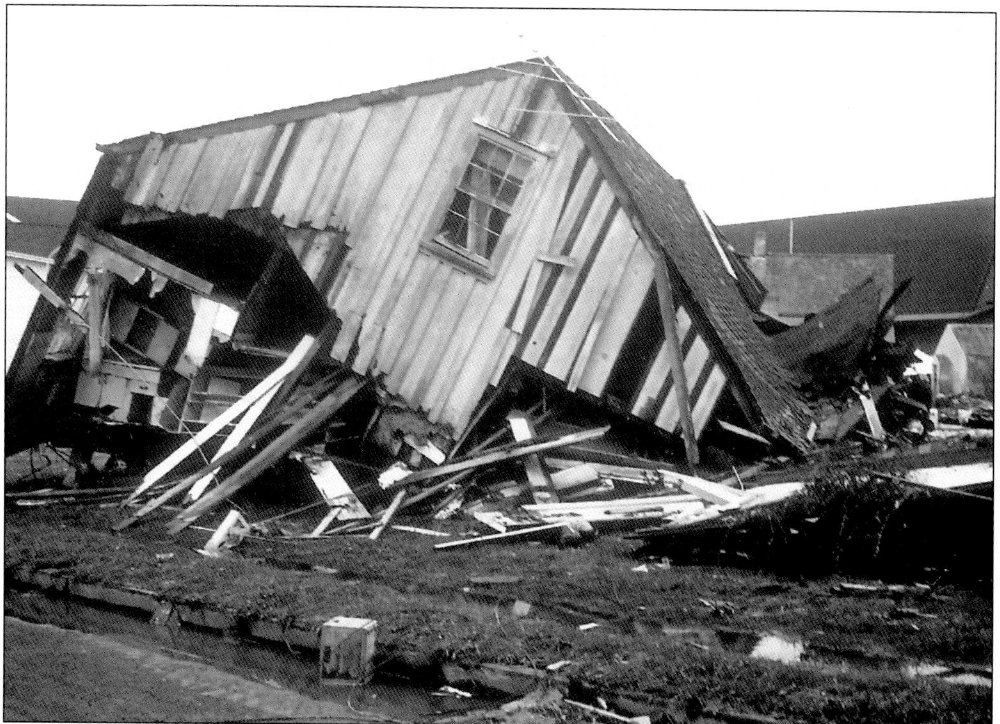

The tsunamis washed out foundations and crumpled wooden structures. The water swept inland as far as Fourth Street in some parts of town and beyond Fifth Street on M Street. Of the structures left standing, most had extensive interior damage.

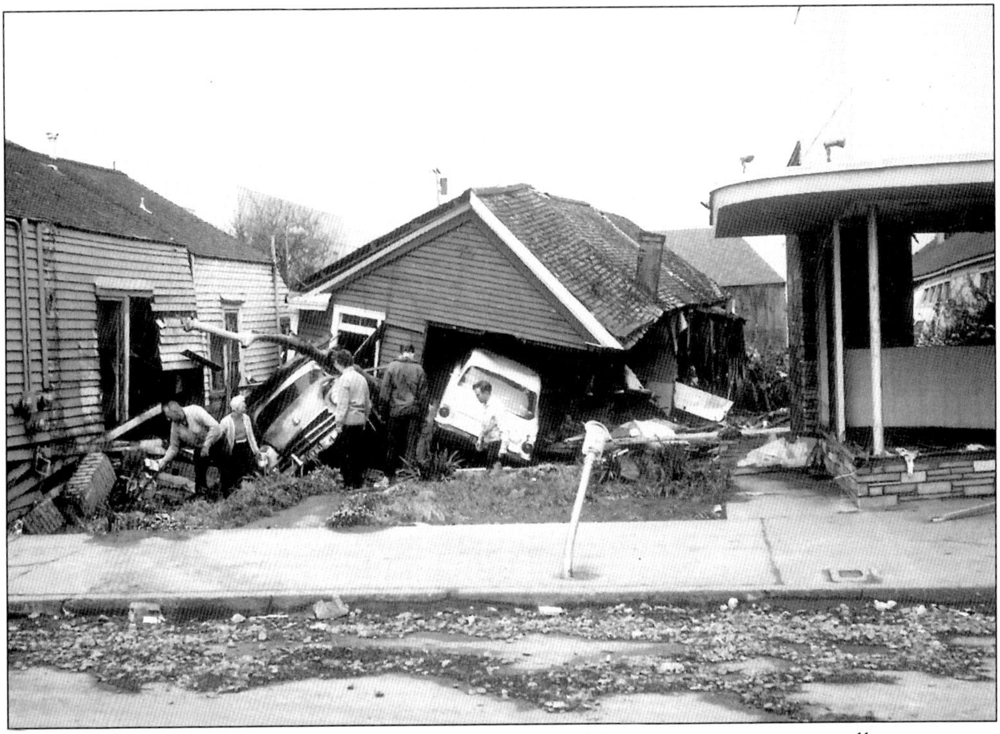

Many structures were totally demolished, yet structures standing right next to them might have received only minor damage. All of the homes hit by the tsunamis were destroyed.

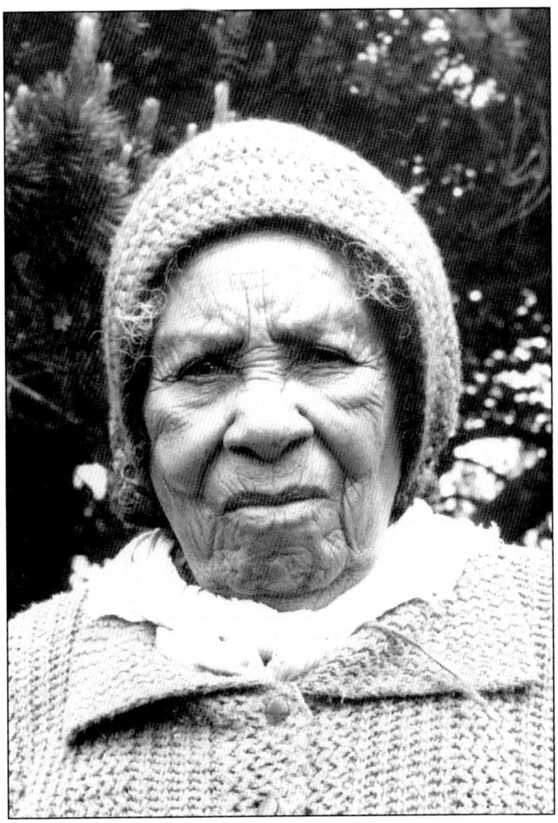

Amelia Brown, a Tolowa Indian, was honored as the Grand Marshall of the 1967 Fourth of July parade in Crescent City. She was 99 years old at the time and lived at the Smith River Rancheria.

In 1983, the Coast Guard gave the Fresnel lens from the St. George Reef Lighthouse to the Del Norte County Historical Society on permanent loan. The society built a two-story addition onto the back of the Del Norte County Museum to house the lens and it is in good working condition.

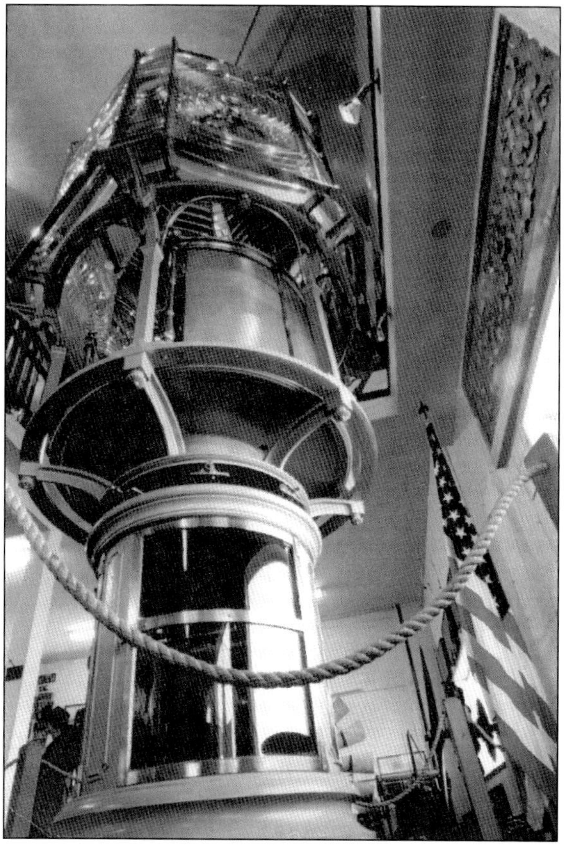

The Del Norte County Historical Society assumed operation of Battery Point Lighthouse as a museum in 1969. In 1855, the steamship *America* burned in Crescent City harbor. Three of her brass cannons were salvaged and placed on land set aside as part of the Crescent City Light Station. As three cannons were considered to be a battery, the area became known as Battery Point and the light station was subsequently called the Battery Point Lighthouse.

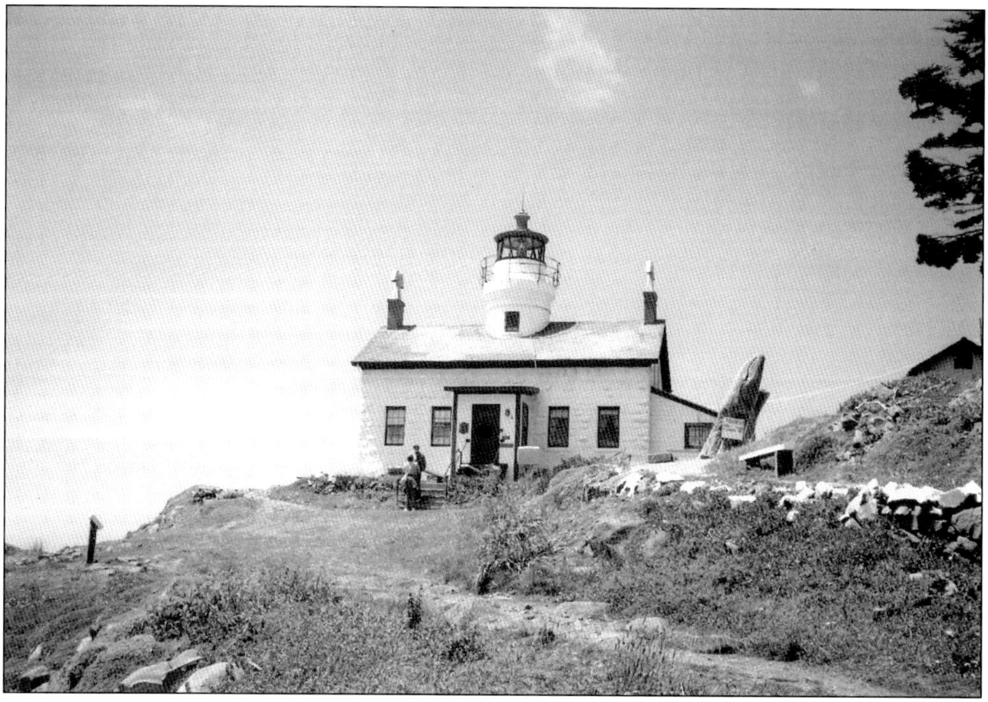

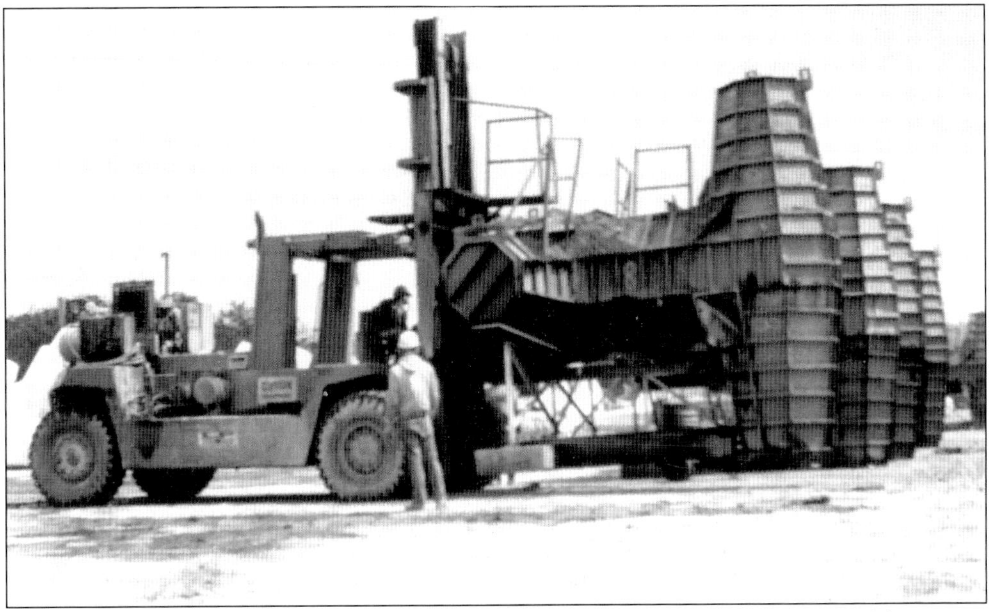

Because of the March 1964 tsunami damage to the breakwater, funds were appropriated for a major rehabilitation and expansion of the structure. The Corps of Engineers decided to experiment with *dolosse*, which are shaped like a twisted "H," weigh 40 tons each, and are 15 feet long and tall. The forms had to be moved with heavy equipment.

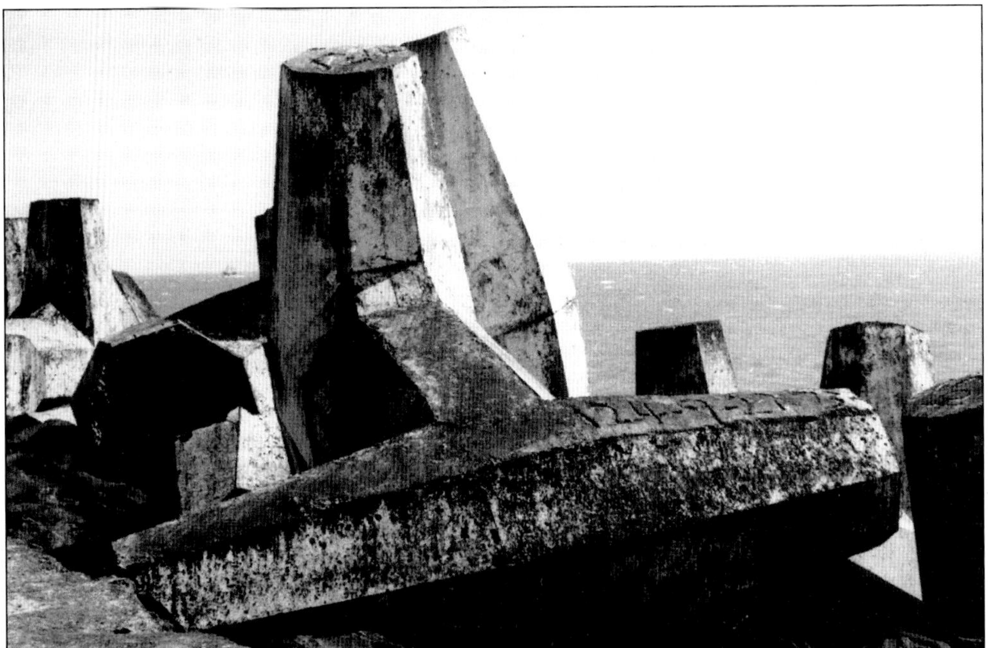

Sitting on the breakwater is this *dolos*, the Afrikaans word to describe the ankle bone of a small goat. *Dolosse* (the plural of *dolos*) were made of stainless-steel-reinforced concrete, and in 1986 the Corps of Engineers awarded a contract for $3.9 million for the placement of 769 *dolosse* on the breakwater. One *dolos* is cuurently on display at Beachfront Park, and another is at the entrance to the harbor.